IMAGES
of America

The Sisters of the Holy Spirit and Mary Immaculate

ON THE COVER: The Sisters of the Holy Spirit and Mary Immaculate pose in front of their motherhouse in 1961. This convent was built in 1922 and was located at 301 Yucca Street in San Antonio, Texas. It served as their motherhouse until 2009. (Courtesy of the Sisters of the Holy Spirit and Mary Immaculate Archives.)

IMAGES of America

THE SISTERS OF THE HOLY SPIRIT AND MARY IMMACULATE

Cecilia Gutierrez Venable and the
Sisters of the Holy Spirit and Mary Immaculate

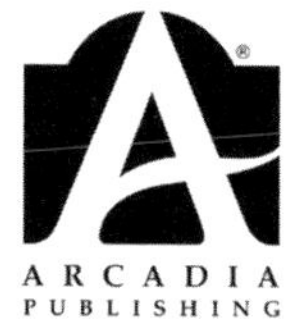

ARCADIA PUBLISHING

ISBN 978-1-4671-2924-4

Published by Arcadia Publishing
Charleston, South Carolina

Printed in the United States of America

Library of Congress Control Number: 2018930595

For all general information, please contact Arcadia Publishing:
Telephone 843-853-2070
Fax 843-853-0044
E-mail sales@arcadiapublishing.com
For customer service and orders:
Toll-Free 1-888-313-2665

Visit us on the Internet at www.arcadiapublishing.com

This book is dedicated to the legacy of our foundress, Margaret Mary Healy Murphy, and to all the Sisters of the Holy Spirit and Mary Immaculate—from the past, to the present, and in the future.

Contents

Acknowledgments 6

Introduction 7

1. Building a Legacy: 1833–1892 9
2. Building a Community and Mission: 1893–1918 15
3. Expanding the Ministry: 1919–1943 25
4. Diversifying the Ministry: 1944–1968 35
5. Imprinting a New Continent: 1969–1993 61
6. Looking Back and Celebrating 125 Years: 1994–2018 85

Sisters of the Holy Spirit and Mary Immaculate (2018) 126

Bibliography 127

ACKNOWLEDGMENTS

The Sisters of the Holy Spirit and Mary Immaculate have more than a century's worth of history. They left their imprint throughout the world, and this book seeks to reveal some of their exploits, accomplishments, and innovations in education, health, and improving the welfare of others. Their devotion to the teachings of the Catholic Church under the guidance of the Holy Spirit also enabled them to introduce and strengthen the Catholic faith for many people.

This book is a product of the support by all the Sisters of the Holy Spirit and Mary Immaculate. Their guidance and input in sharing their stories and pictures made this work possible. I would also like to thank archivist Sr. Louise Smith with the Sisters of St. Mary of Namur for the use of their photographs, Brother Ed Loche from the Archdiocese of San Antonio, Andrea Estes (the owner of Mount Echo Ranch), and especially Srs. Marguerite Connors, Mary Fagan, and Geraldine Klein, who read this manuscript.

Images for this book, unless otherwise noted, are courtesy of the Sisters of the Holy Spirit and Mary Immaculate Archives.

—Cecilia Gutierrez Venable
Historian and Archivist
Sisters of the Holy Spirit and Mary Immaculate

INTRODUCTION

The Sisters of the Holy Spirit and Mary Immaculate celebrate their 125th year of service in 2018. They have a long and diverse history of working with the poor and aiding people of color. The founding of this order is an interesting and unique story that begins with Margaret Mary Healy Murphy, a widow who in 1884 envisioned this order of sisters and placed them on a path to improve the lives of all those they touched.

Margaret Mary Healy was born in Cahirciveen, County Kerry, Ireland, on May 4, 1833, to Jane Murphy Healy and Richard Healy. At the age of six, Margaret lost her mother after the birth of her sister, Jeannie. Since her father was the town doctor, it was difficult for him to care for an infant daughter, so Jeannie went to live with her aunt. Margaret's two brothers moved to the United States with relatives, and Margaret remained with her father.

In 1845, economic conditions in Ireland became increasingly grave due to oppression by the British government, as well as the potato blight, which had destroyed the dietary staple of the country. Consequently, Richard Healy followed his sons and relatives to America. Applying as ship's doctor, he sailed to the United States with Margaret. The family reunited in West Virginia, but the trip weighed heavily on Richard's health, and he died on the way to New Orleans.

Arriving in the bustling city of New Orleans, the Healys decided to follow Zachary Taylor's army to Brownsville. Taylor, recruiting men in New Orleans, received orders from Pres. James K. Polk to march to Brownsville and squelch any resistance by the Mexican government over the annexation of Texas. The Mexican army crossed the border but was easily defeated. The US Army pushed forward and stationed men in Matamoros. The Healys decided to open a boardinghouse, the Healy Hotel, for these soldiers. While working there, Margaret met John Bernard Murphy. When she turned 16, they married in 1849.

After the Mexican-American War ended in 1848, the Army dispersed and the hotel closed. The young couple moved north and ultimately settled in Corpus Christi, where Murphy studied law and partnered with future Texas governor Edmund J. Davis. Murphy became a judge, worked on the Texas constitution, and finally became mayor of Corpus Christi. Margaret helped her husband with his work and continued aiding the sick. When the yellow fever epidemic hit Corpus Christi in the mid-1860s, she aided the helpless victims. Later, Margaret opened three separate hospitals to serve African Americans, Mexicans, and Anglos. The couple never had children, but they adopted three and were instrumental in bringing the Sisters of St. Mary of Namur to Texas. This congregation opened the first Catholic boarding school in the Lone Star State, with one of the Murphy children enrolled in its first class.

In 1884, John Bernard Murphy died. The following year, Margaret bought her brother-in-law's ranch, Mount Echo, located halfway between Corpus Christi and San Antonio. San Antonio at this time was booming, and people flocked to its center. The Galveston, Harrisburg & San Antonio Railway carried people to the Alamo City in 1877, as did the International–Great Northern in 1881. By the 1900s, the population doubled. Margaret decided to move to San Antonio, too.

Upon her arrival, Margaret noticed the disparity between the races. She was keenly aware of prejudice because of her relation to Daniel O'Connell, the first Catholic to sit in the British Parliament, who spoke out against slavery in America as early as 1829. It was O'Connell's influence that most likely inspired her to open the three separate race-based hospitals in Corpus Christi. Margaret also felt the pangs of prejudice because she moved into the United States when the short-lived Know Nothing Party ideology infiltrated Texas. This nativist party spoke out against Catholics and immigrants. Margaret's sensitivity to bias and bigotry were stoked by the homily of Fr. John Maloney, OMI, while she attended Mass on Pentecost Sunday in 1887. He expressed the need for schools and churches for African Americans in San Antonio. He raised the issue because the American bishops voiced their concerns during the Third Plenary Council meeting in Baltimore in 1884.

After consulting with the bishop, Margaret sold part of her ranch to build a school and church for African Americans. The buildings were completed in 1888 and opened tuition-free. This Catholic school and church were the second in the state and the first in San Antonio to be built for African American children.

St. Peter Claver School flourished, but Margaret could not find enough teachers to support the students. She appealed to various orders, but they were unable to help. Consequently, Margaret decided to start her own congregation of sisters. She studied with the Sisters of St. Mary of Namur, where her sister Jeannie was the local superior. Margaret became mother superior of the first order of sisters in Texas to have the specific ministry for working with the poor and people of color, the Sisters of the Holy Spirit (Ghost) and Mary Immaculate. Since she struggled with finding women to enter this new order, Margaret turned to her native home in Ireland. She subsequently made four trips, in 1896, 1899, 1902, and 1906, to recruit women interested in dedicating their lives to the mission of the Sisters of the Holy Spirit and Mary Immaculate.

This fledgling community began to take root; however, they experienced a setback when Mother Margaret died in 1907. At the time of her death, Mother Margaret left behind 15 professed sisters and two postulants (women who are candidates to join the order). The mission at St. Peter Claver School in San Antonio thrived with an ever-increasing population. The sisters also staffed Our Lady of Guadalupe School in Laredo, Texas, and ventured beyond the Lone Star State's border to Oaxaca, Mexico, where they operated the Casa de Cuna orphanage. All of these sisters and their mission added to the great accomplishments of Mother Margaret. She spent her life healing people with the knowledge she gained from her father, and in her later years her ministry allowed the poor and people of color an exemplary education and provided them the tools for social uplift. Her attitudes transcended the social norms of the era, and her legacy lives on in the Sisters of the Holy Spirit and Mary Immaculate and all the lives they have touched in the world.

One

Building a Legacy 1833–1892

In 1833, the British Parliament abolished slavery throughout its empire, excluding the East India Company. That same year, Daniel O'Connell, one of the proponents of this law, welcomed a new relative, Margaret Mary Healy. Margaret was born on May 4, 1833, to Jane and Richard Healy. Margaret's mother died when she was six, and she immigrated with her father to the United States. When she was 16, she met and married John Bernard Murphy. He became mayor of Corpus Christi but died before the end of his term in 1884.

Margaret purchased a ranch, Mount Echo, from her brother-in-law in 1885 and then moved to San Antonio, where she was troubled by the lack of a Catholic school and church for African Americans. With the bishop's blessing, she decided to sell part of her ranch to construct the school and church. She bought land on the city's East Side for the building, but the city's elite hampered the process. She persevered, and St. Peter Claver Church and School opened in 1888. This school was the first Catholic African American school in San Antonio and the second in the state of Texas. Staffing the school proved difficult because of prejudice and the lack of religious women to staff this institution. Margaret's solution was to form a new congregation to teach at the school.

Margaret Mary Healy posed for this Louis De Planque image. De Planque, a famous itinerant photographer in South Texas and Mexico, took many photographs of important people in the area. He was most noted for his urban landscapes. Margaret was born in County Kerry, Ireland, on May 4, 1833, and was in her late teens at the time of this photograph.

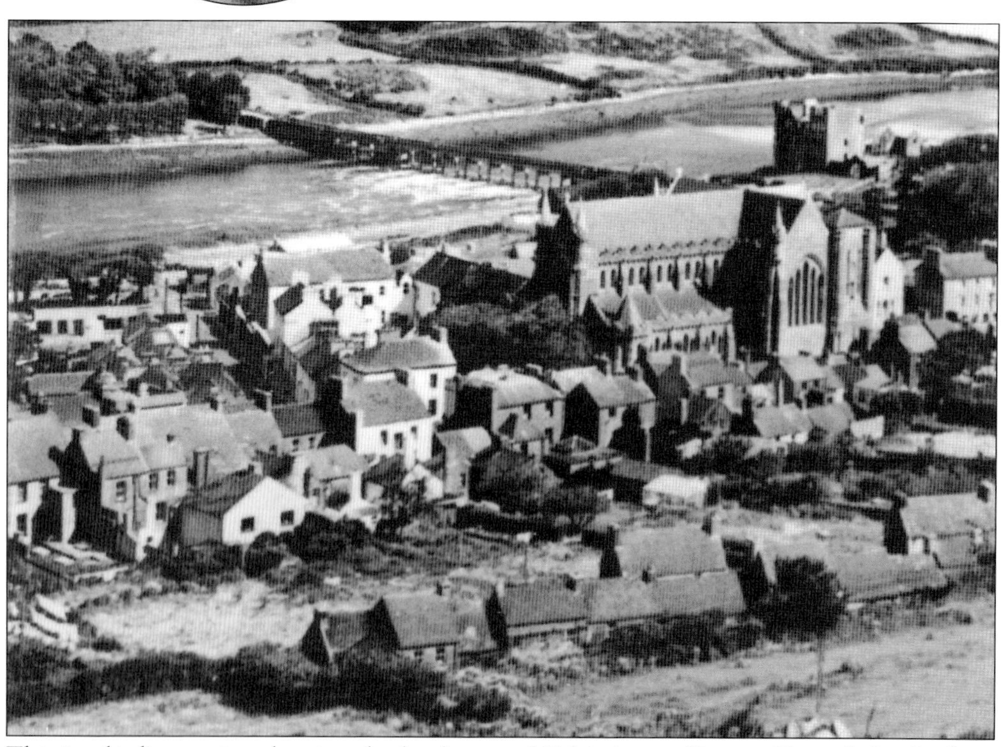

This is a bird's-eye view showing the landscape of Cahirciveen, County Kerry, Ireland, where Margaret Healy Murphy was born. Her father was a physician there and operated a small hospital in the area before he immigrated to America in 1845.

John Bernard Murphy sat for this photograph as a young man. He had an illustrious career as a soldier for Zachary Taylor's army during the annexation of Texas, edited and owned the newspaper *Gazette*, fought in the Civil War, worked with Edmund J. Davis (future governor of Texas), and became the district attorney, judge, and finally mayor of Corpus Christi. Murphy was born in County Cork, Ireland, and died in Corpus Christi in 1884.

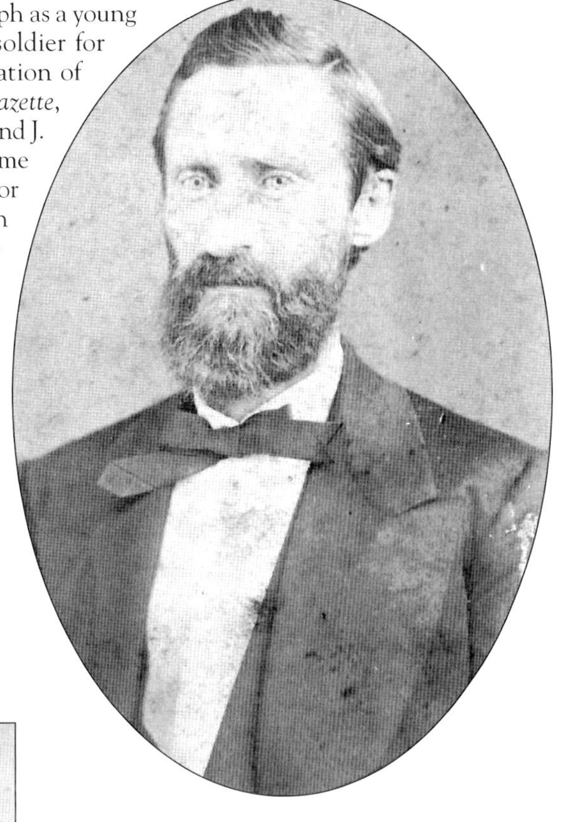

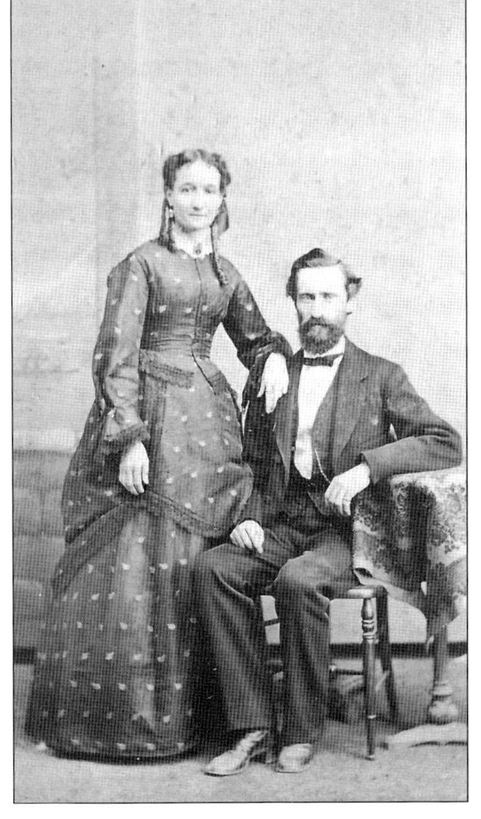

Margaret Mary Healy Murphy and John Bernard Murphy posed in De Planque's studio for this image. Margaret Mary Healy operated the Healy Hotel in Matamoros, Mexico. While there, she met Murphy and after courting for a year the couple married on May 7, 1849, at the cathedral in Brownsville.

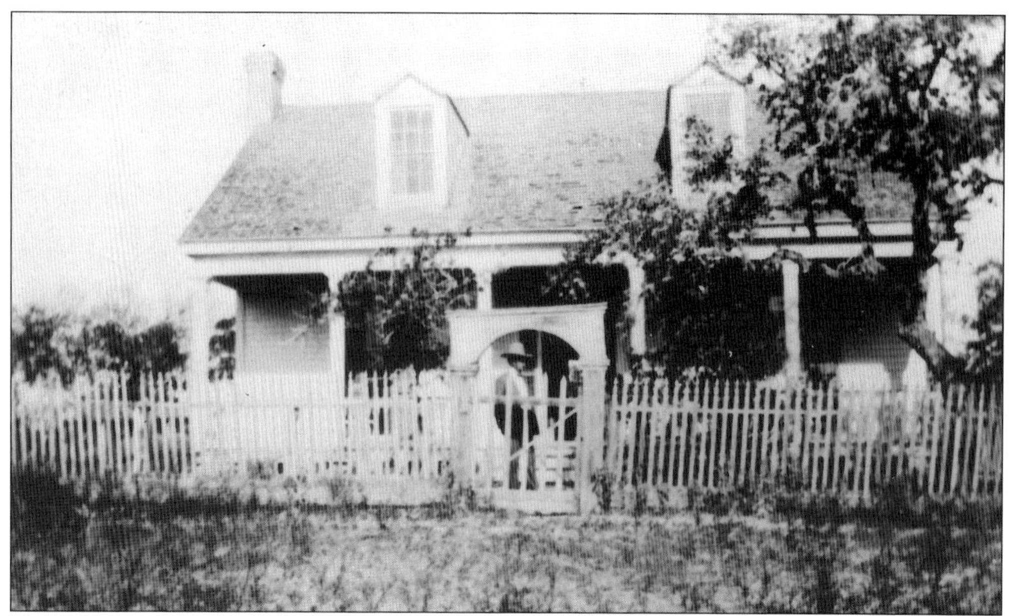

Pictured here is Margaret Mary's home at Mount Echo, where she lived before she moved to San Antonio. After John Bernard died, she bought this ranch in 1885. In 1888, she sold part of the land to build St. Peter Claver Catholic Church and School. After founding the Sisters of the Holy Spirit and Mary Immaculate, she used the house as a retreat and also brought postulants and novices from Ireland to acclimate to Texas and their new spiritual calling.

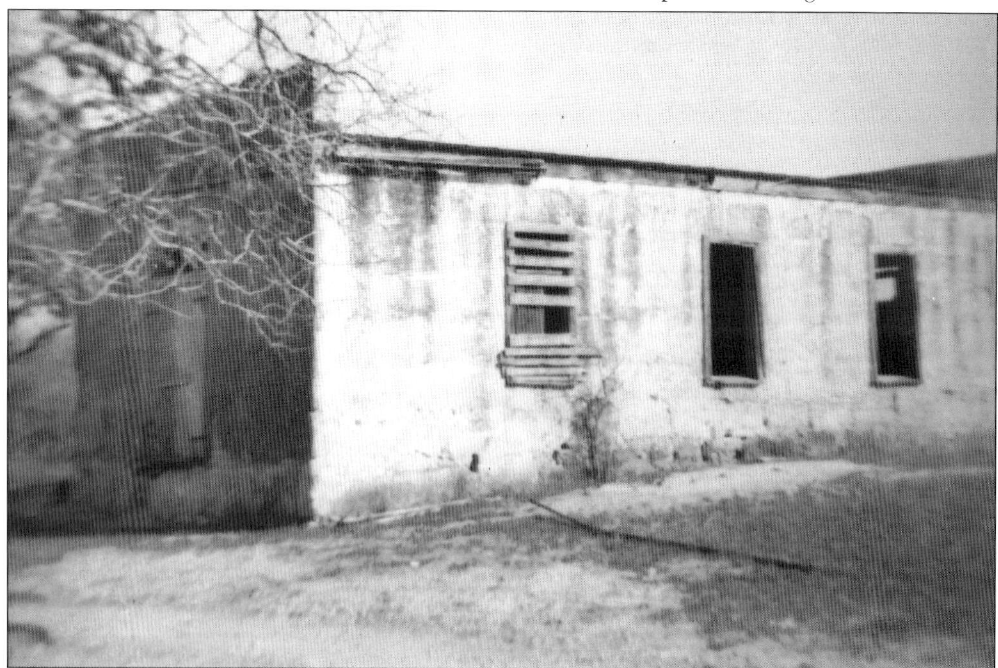

This stone building at Mount Echo was converted to St. Stephen's Chapel and blessed by the Right Reverend Peter Verdaguer, vicar apostolic of Brownsville, on October 18, 1893. The chapel was used by the people in the area and the sisters when they were on retreat. The building was destroyed during a hurricane, and only a stone outline remains.

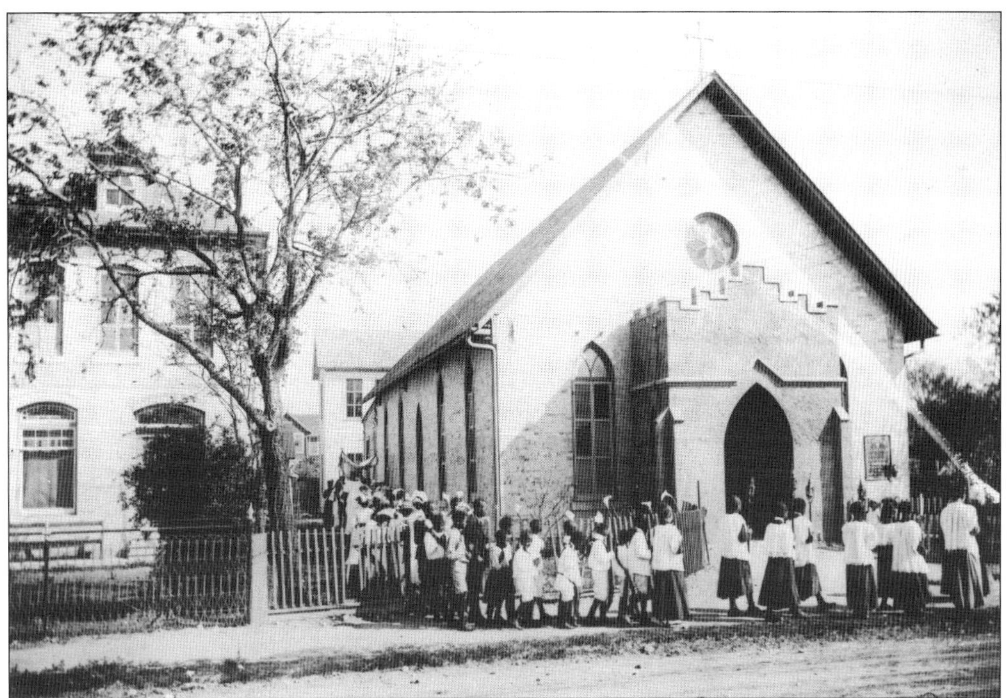

Students are pictured in procession around St. Peter Claver Church in 1903. Margaret Mary Healy Murphy had the church built in 1888. The first Catholic church and school for African Americans in San Antonio quickly grew, and soon other buildings were added. This school provided many children with the tools needed for continuing their education and becoming community leaders.

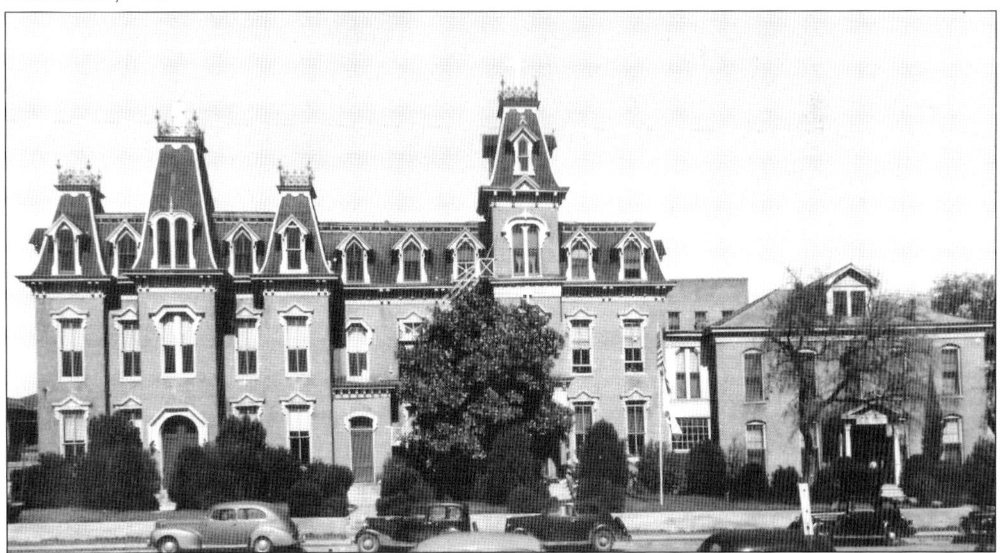

The Sisters of St. Mary of Namur arrived in Texas on September 23, 1873, and built this structure, Sacred Heart Academy, the following year. John and Margaret Mary Healy Murphy helped the sisters start a boarding school in Waco, Texas, and enrolled their adopted daughter in its first class. Margaret studied at the Waco facility before becoming a sister. (Courtesy of Sisters of St. Mary of Namur Archives.)

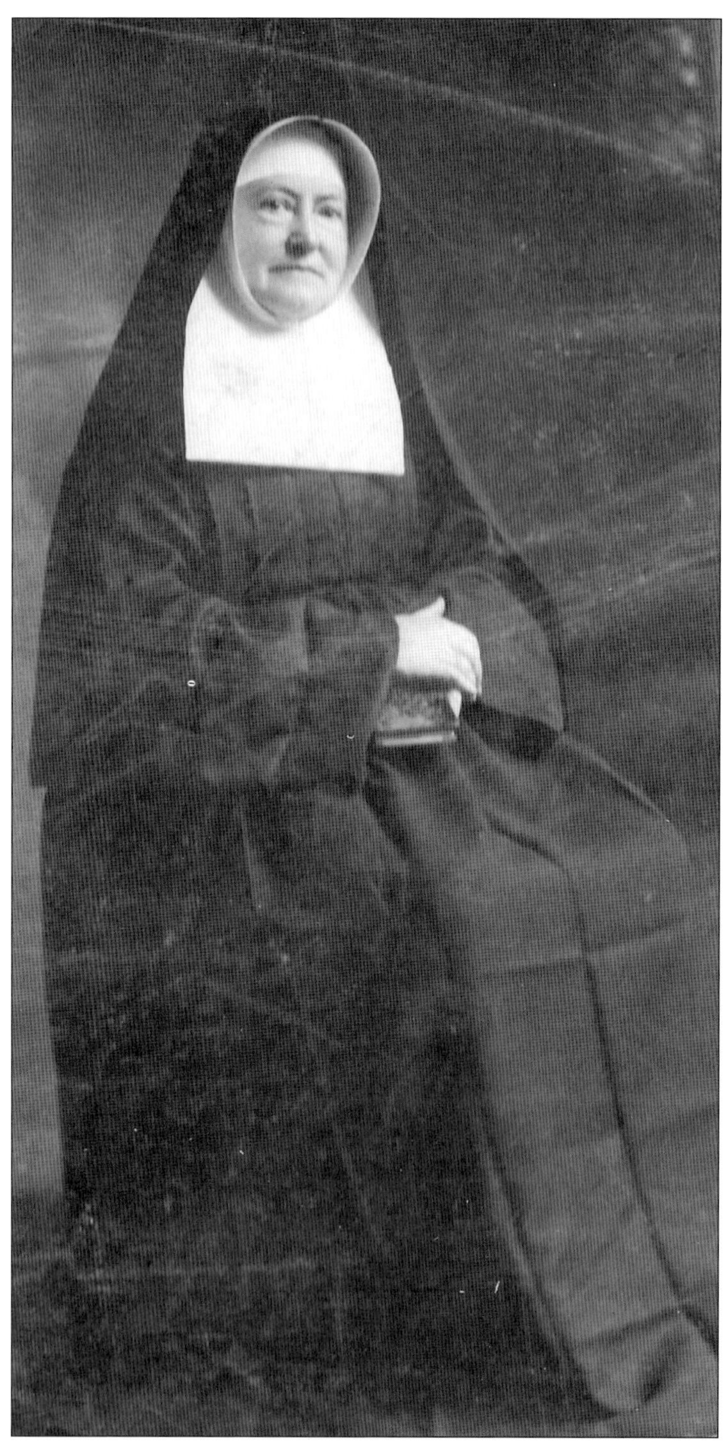

Mother Angela Healy was a sister of St. Mary of Namur and the younger biological sister of Margaret Mary Healy Murphy. Sister Angela grew up with her cousins and joined the sisters in Belgium. She then traveled to New York and later to Waco, Texas, to begin the boarding school. (Courtesy of Sisters of St. Mary of Namur Archives.)

Two

Building a Community and Mission 1893–1918

St. Peter Claver School opened in 1888. Enrollment continued to increase, but it became difficult to find teachers. Margaret decided to form a new congregation that would minister to the poor and people of color. She went to study with the order that her sister Jeannie had joined, the Sisters of St. Mary of Namur. A year later, in 1893, she became Mother Margaret Mary Healy Murphy of the Sisters of the Holy Spirit and Mary Immaculate, the first congregation founded in the state of Texas for the express purpose of ministering to the poor and people of color. Margaret now needed to find young women to join them.

In order to increase her congregation, Margaret returned to Ireland in 1896, 1899, 1902, and 1906 to recruit women for this new order of sisters. However, the last trip left her weakened, and she died in 1907. Margaret left behind 15 professed sisters and two postulants. At the time of her death, they had three missions: St. Peter Claver in San Antonio, Casa de Cuna in Oaxaca, and Our Lady of Guadalupe in Laredo.

The bishop appointed Sr. Mary Aloysius McMullen to assume the position of general superior until the community voted for a replacement. During her tenure, the community did not recruit or expand its missions, but Sister Mary prepared the sisters to vote for their first elected general superior in 1909.

The sisters chose wisely when they named Sr. Evangelist Jennings to be their first elected general superior. A spiritually dedicated, hardworking, and ambitious leader, Sister Evangelist spurred the community into action. She actively recruited women to join the sisters and almost doubled the number of nuns by the time her tenure expired in 1923. She also widened the sisters' footprint in the United States to include 17 more schools in the South. Sister Evangelist generated a lot of construction around the school when she added an additional wing to St. Peter Claver School in 1914. The fledgling congregation soared in its first 25 years.

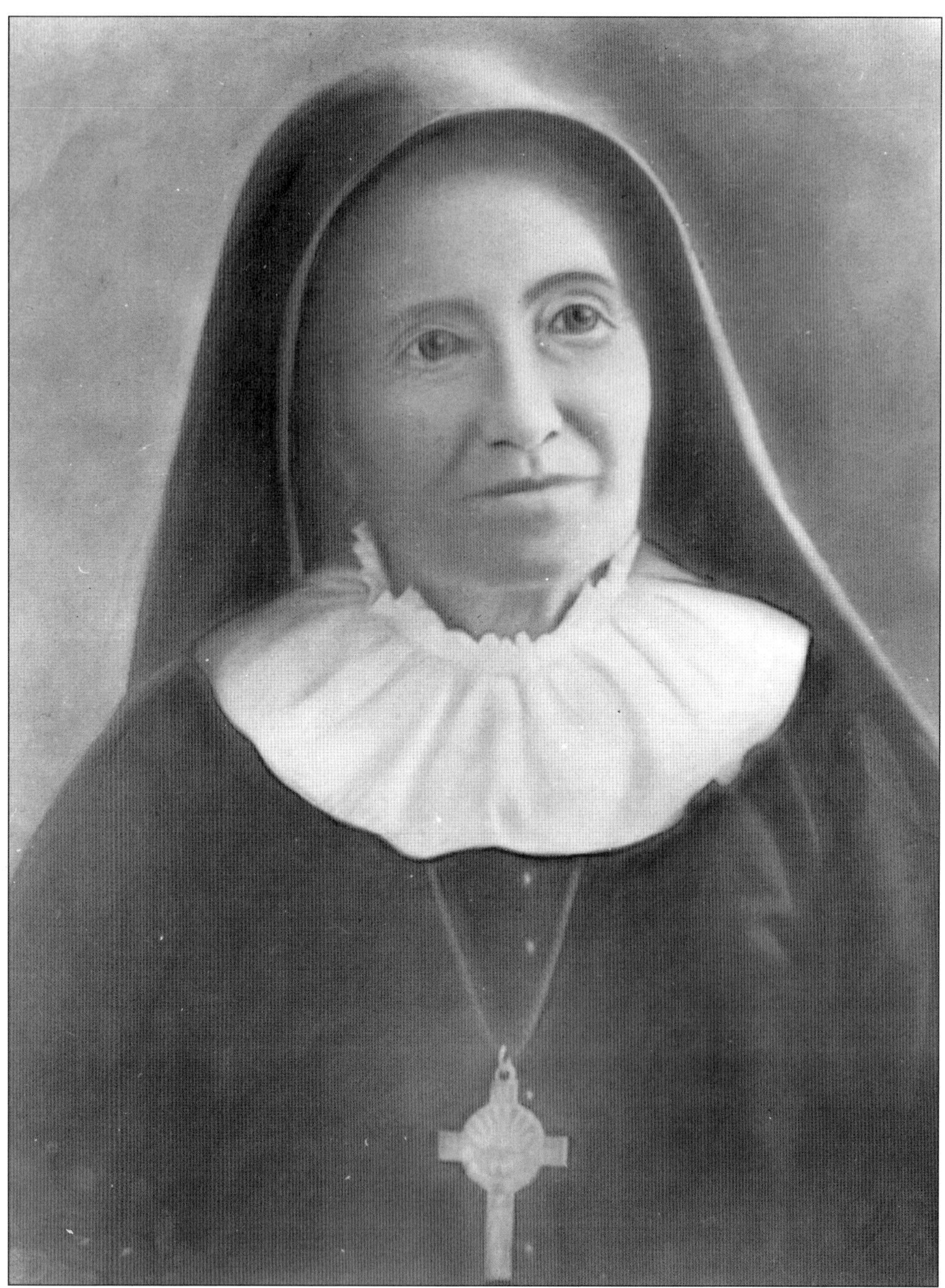

Pictured here is Mother Margaret Mary Healy Murphy, healer, businesswoman, and entrepreneur. She built the first Catholic church and school for African Americans in San Antonio in 1888, and created a new order of sisters, the Sisters of the Holy Spirit and Mary Immaculate, in 1893. She served the congregation as the first general superior until her death in 1907.

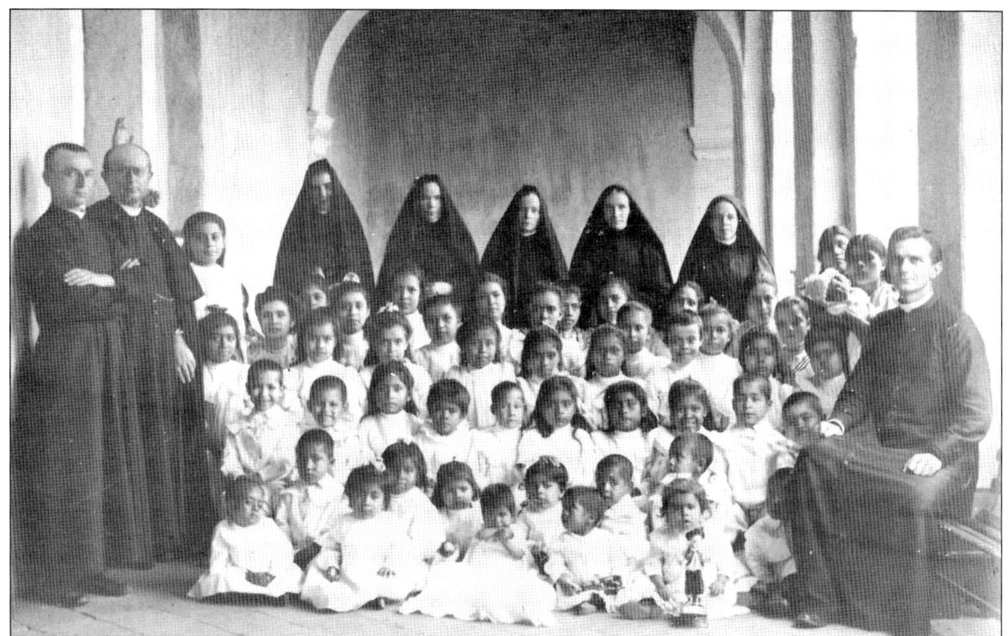

The children and staff of Casa de Cuna in Oaxaca, Mexico, pose in 1901. Bishop Gillow of Oaxaca asked for sisters to work in the orphanage and boarding school. Five sisters cared for the young children and taught those of school age. Four years later, however, the sisters were forced to return to San Antonio because of the upheaval associated with the Mexican Revolution. Pictured from left to right in the back are Srs. Teresa, Gertrude, Evangelist, Cecilia, and Agnes.

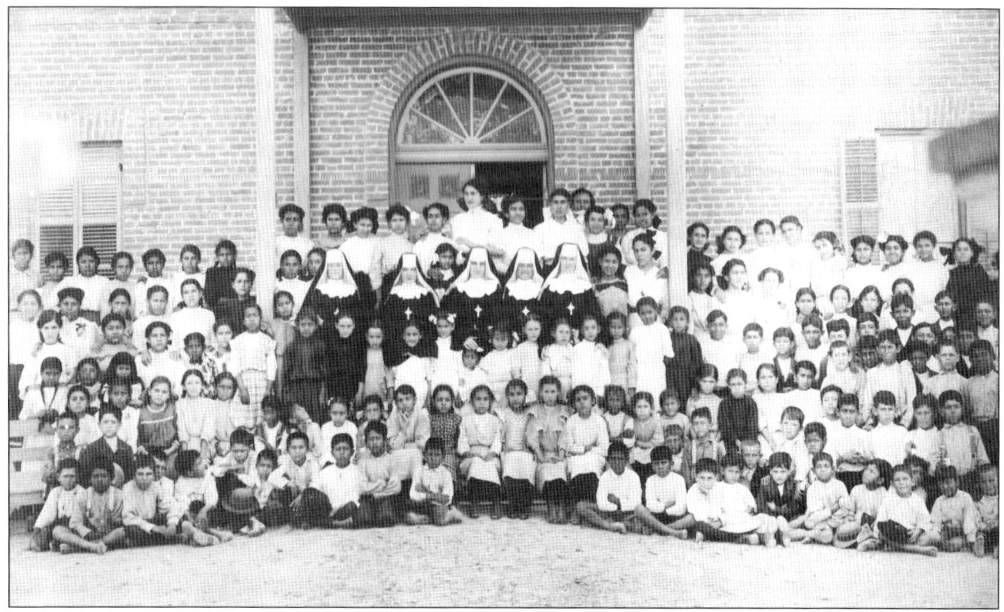

Members of the 1905 class of Our Lady of Guadalupe in Laredo, Texas, stand in front of their school. The Sisters of the Holy Spirit and Mary Immaculate were asked to staff the school, and Srs. Mary Francis, Mary Michael, and Mary Genevieve were its first teachers. Sr. Mary Francis served as the superior at the convent. To the delight of Mother Margaret, the children performed a program for her when she visited.

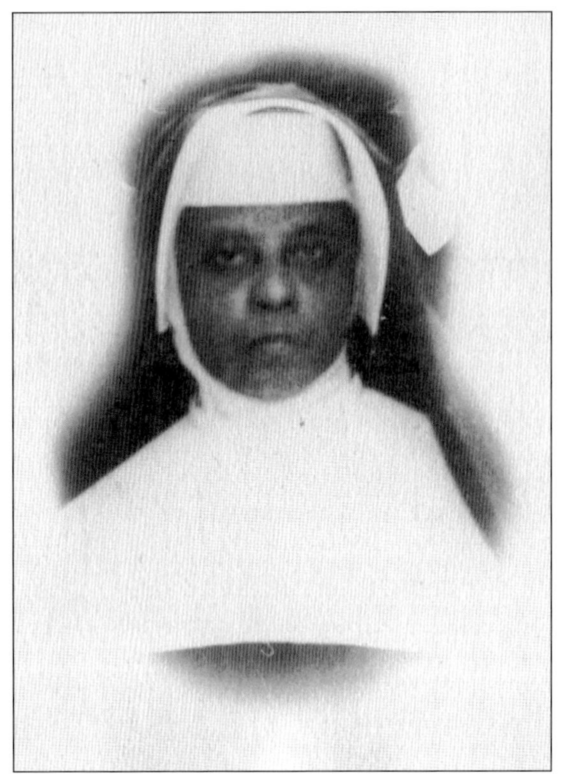

Mary Louise Glenn, who attended St. Peter Claver School in San Antonio, informed Mother Margaret that she was going to become a sister. She entered the community of the Oblate Sisters of Providence in Baltimore. She was the first student taught by the Sisters of the Holy Spirit who decided to become a sister.

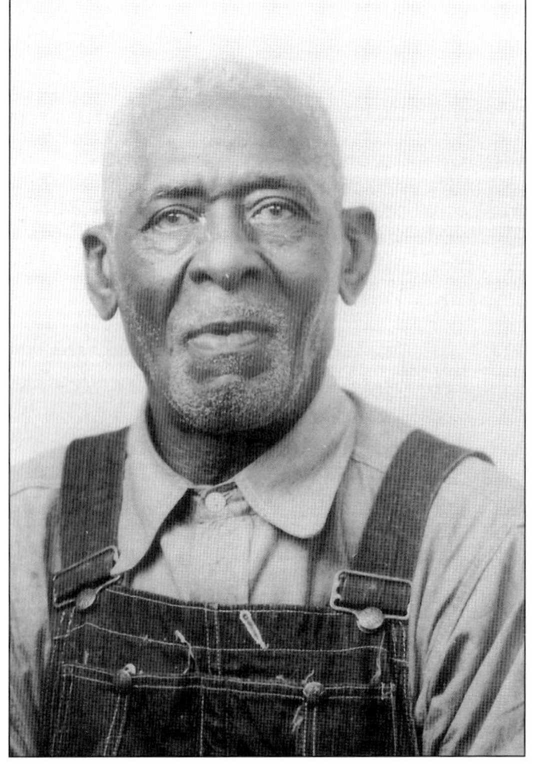

Stanley Howard posed for this photograph in his later years. He was one of the first students the sisters taught in Victoria, Texas, at St. John the Baptist Academy. In 1898, Mother Margaret purchased the land and refurbished a building to be used as this school. Howard had fond memories of the sisters who gave him music lessons, and he used his talent to play for his church.

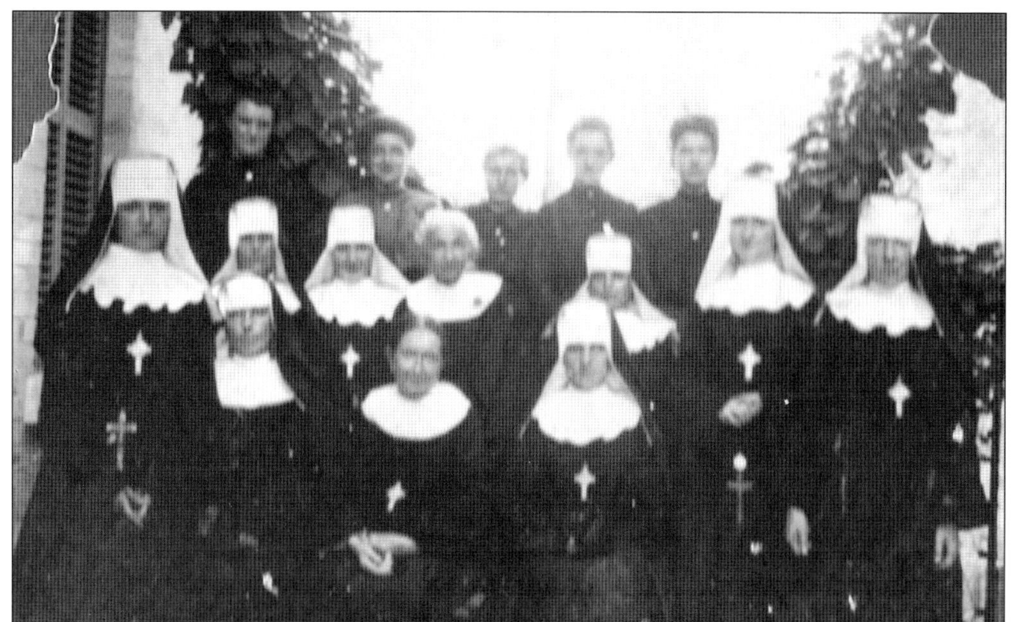

In this early 20th century photograph, Mother Margaret is sitting left of Sister Aloysius (front) with the congregation of the Sisters of the Holy Spirit and Mary Immaculate in San Antonio, Texas.

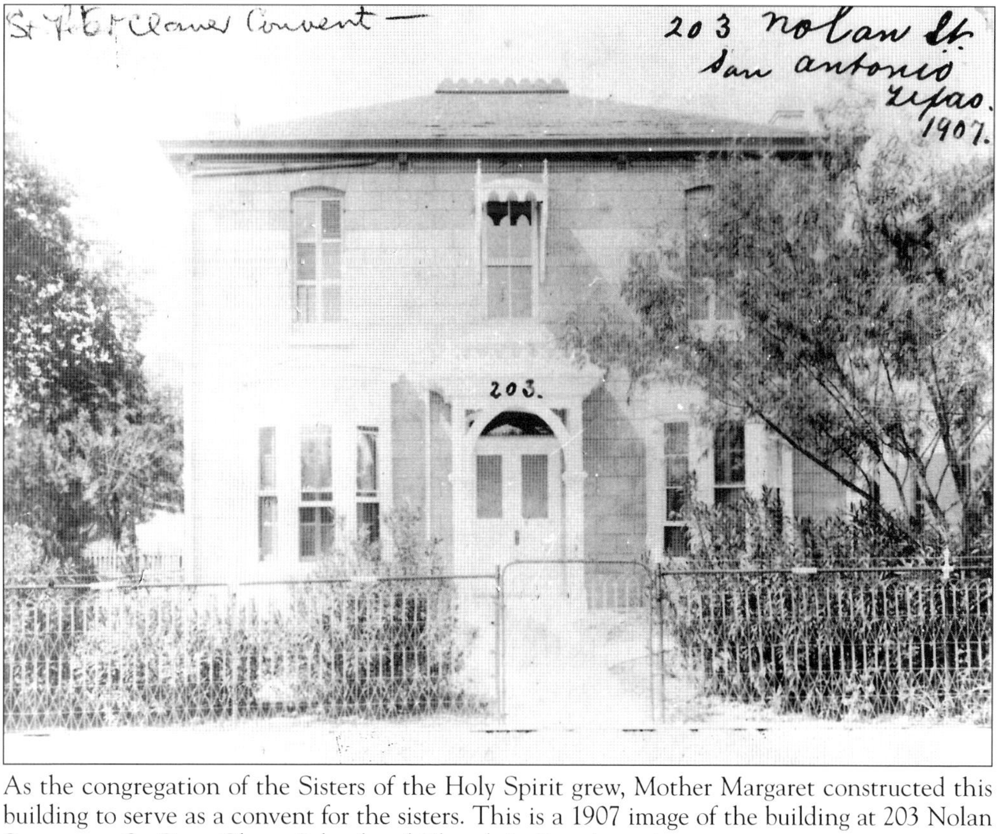

As the congregation of the Sisters of the Holy Spirit grew, Mother Margaret constructed this building to serve as a convent for the sisters. This is a 1907 image of the building at 203 Nolan Street near St. Peter Claver School and Church in San Antonio.

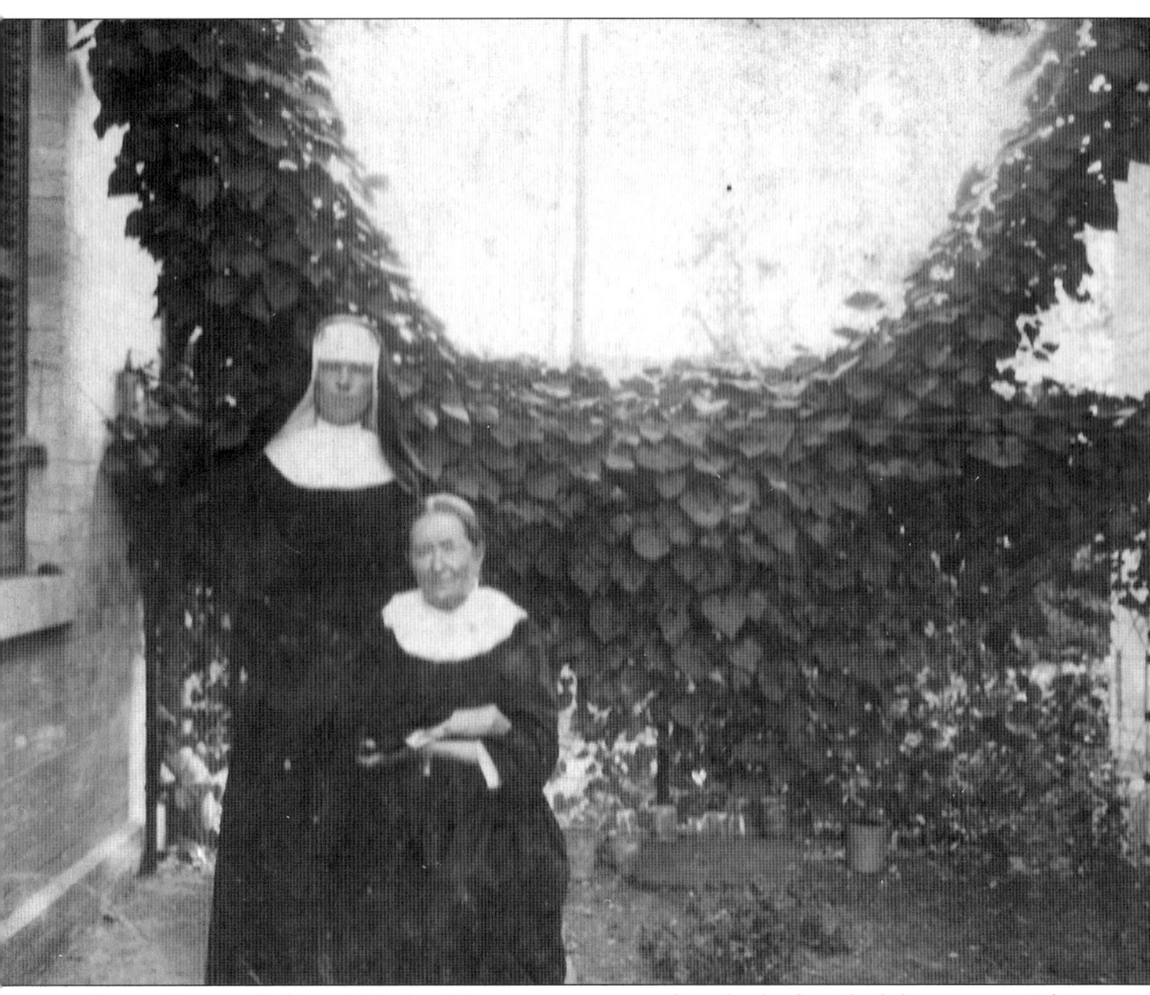

Sister Aloysius (left) and Mother Margaret are pictured in the backyard of the convent. This is the last known image of Mother Margaret before her death. After returning from Ireland in search of young women to join the congregation, Margaret fell ill. She still traveled down to Oaxaca and Laredo to visit these missions, but when she returned she became increasingly sick, and on August 25, 1907, she died. She was buried next to her husband in Holy Cross Cemetery in Corpus Christi.

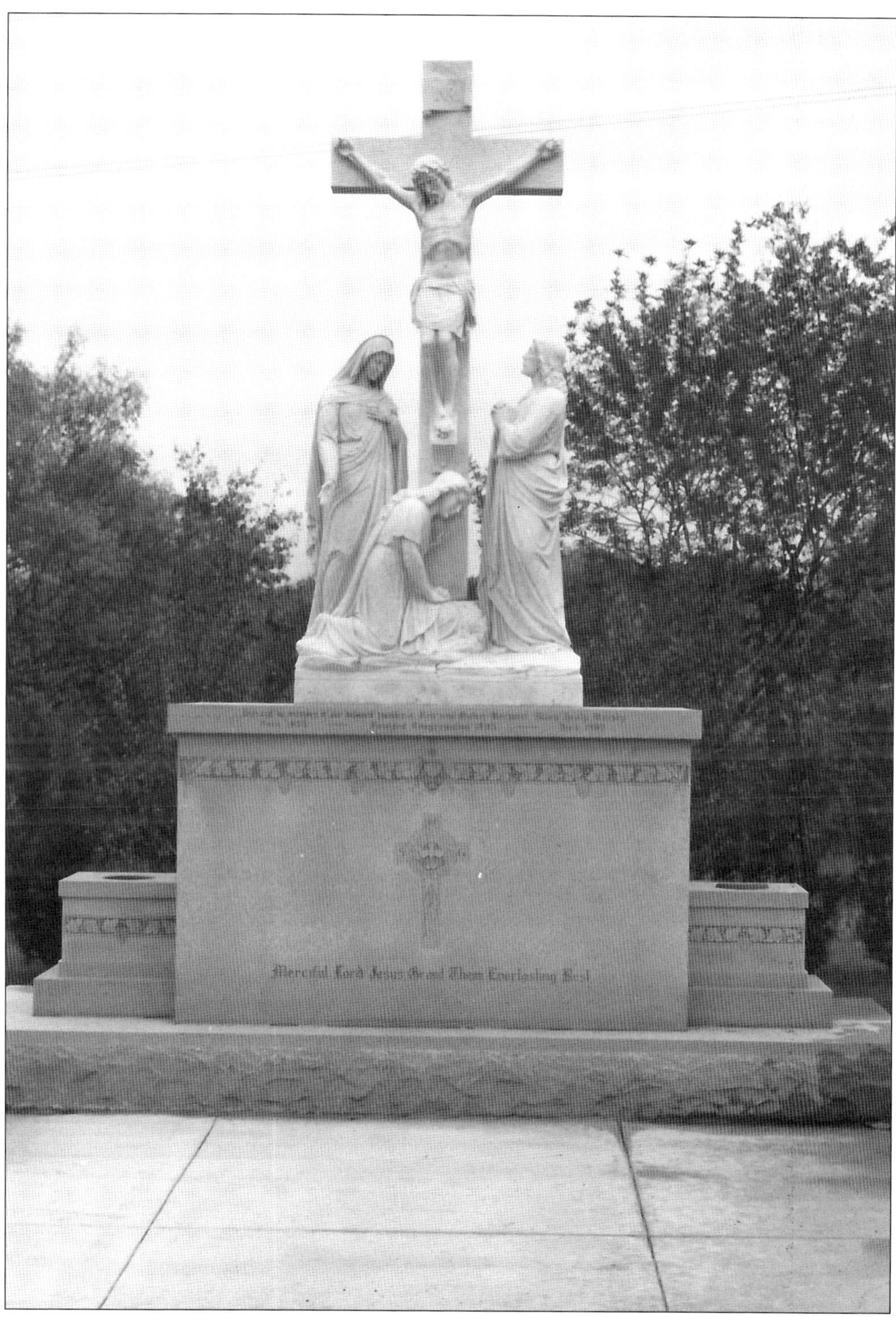

This monument stands in the cemetery of the Sisters of the Holy Spirit and Mary Immaculate next to the Yucca Street convent. The statue is dedicated to the memory of Mother Margaret Mary Healy Murphy, who died in 1907 at the age of 74.

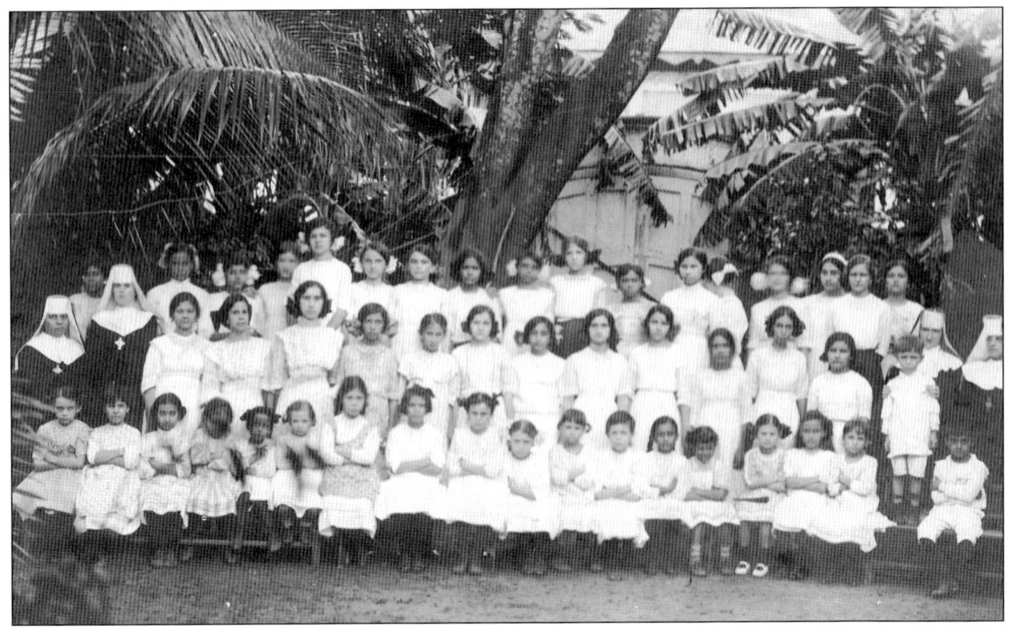

The students of San Juan Bautista in Tabasco, Mexico, pose under a huge tree in front of their school. Bishop Leonardo Castellanos asked for the Sisters of the Holy Spirit, so five sisters—Evangelist Jennings, Genevieve McSweeney, Vincent Murray, Soledad Crespo, and Michael Ballesteros—sailed from Galveston to San Juan to open this school in 1911. Unfortunately, the sisters returned to San Antonio the following year because of a yellow fever outbreak and political upheaval in Mexico.

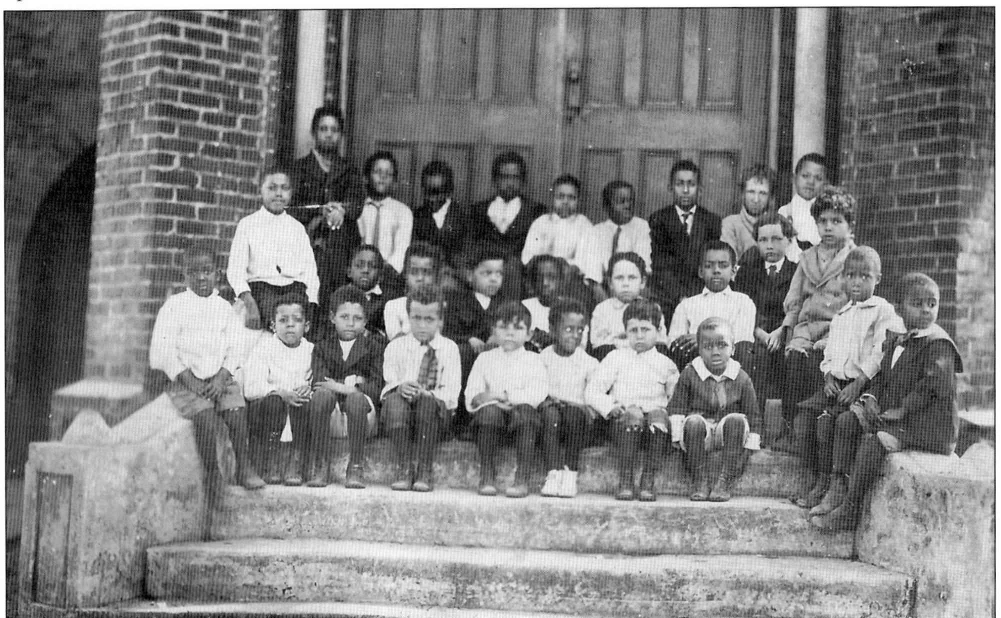

The children of St. Peter Claver School in Mobile, Alabama, pose in 1911. The school had formerly served a Baptist congregation and was purchased and repurposed as a Catholic church in 1911. The basement of this building was converted into five classrooms for the students. The Sisters of the Holy Spirit and Mary Immaculate taught in this school until 1943.

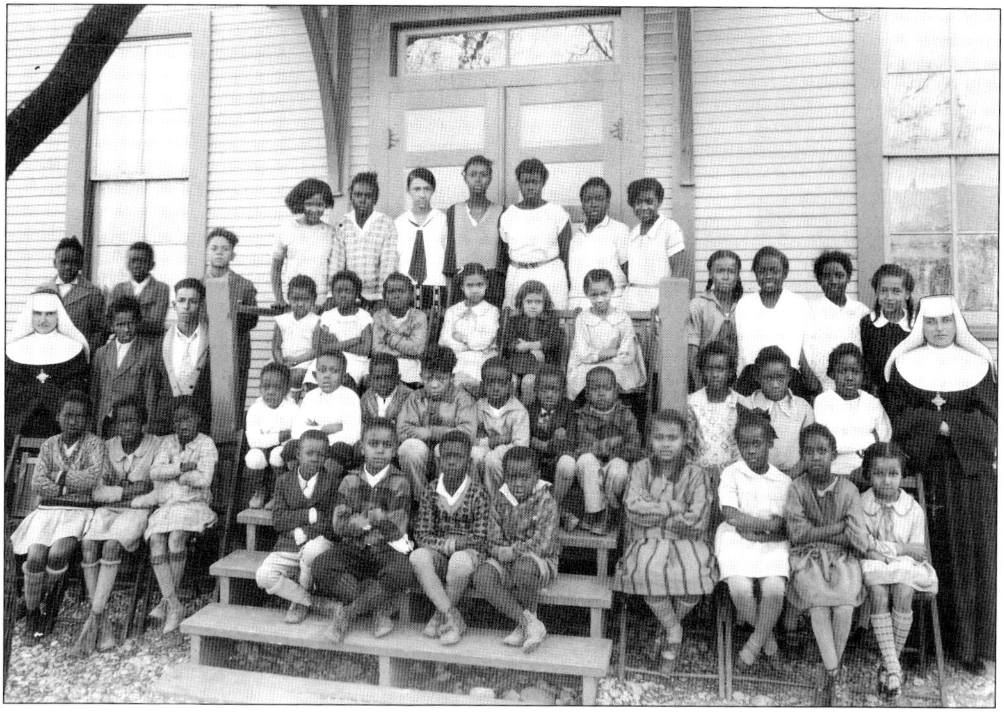

Students sit in front of St. Catherine's School in 1914. St. Katharine Drexel provided funds for Rev. H. Kane to repurpose the old Methodist church into a Catholic parish to serve the African American community on the West Side of San Antonio. The Sisters of the Holy Spirit and Mary Immaculate taught at the school until it closed in 1955.

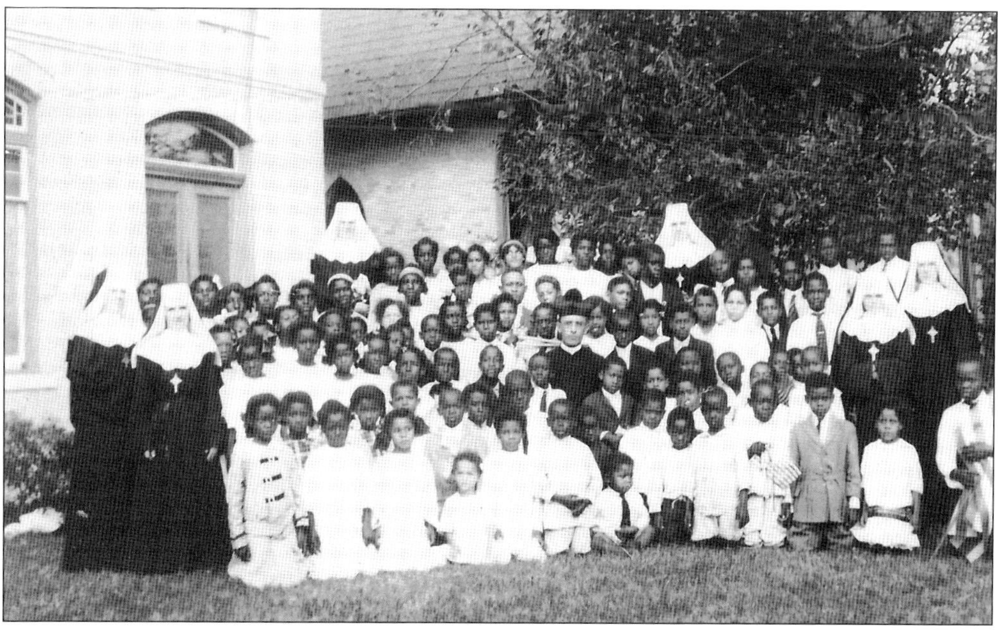

Sisters of the Holy Spirit and Mary Immaculate pose with their students from St. Peter Claver in 1915. The school was built in 1888, but with the increasing number of children, a two-story addition was built in 1913.

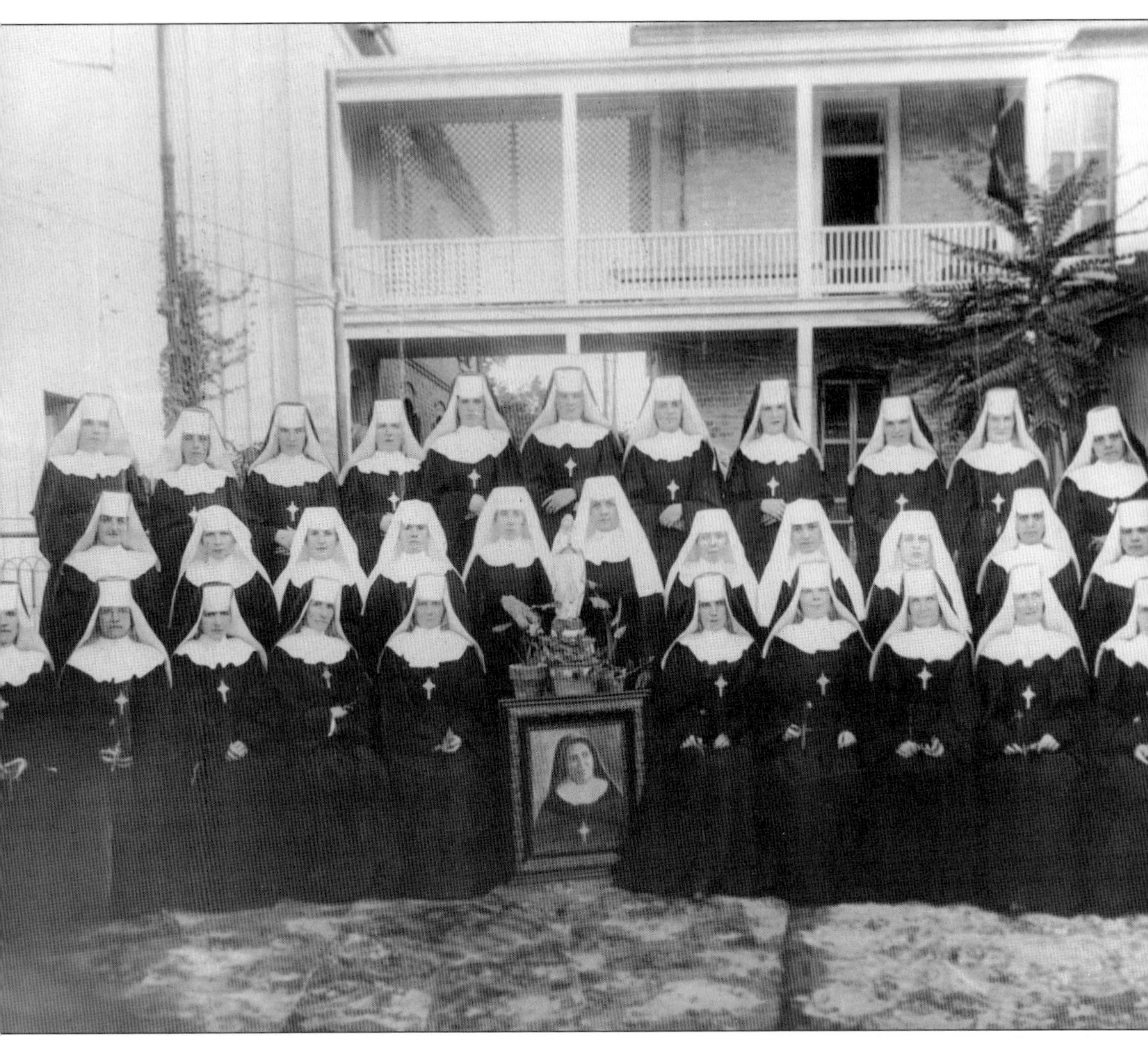

The 1912 Congregation of the Sisters of the Holy Spirit and Mary Immaculate poses in front of the Nolan Street convent. From left to right are (first row) Srs. Celestine, Michael, Stanislaus, Cecilia, Evangelist, Francis, Gertrude, Joseph, Genevieve, and Veronica; (second row) Srs. Dominic, Bernadette, Barbara, Ursula, Brendan, Agatha, Monica, Raphael, Kevin, Mechtilde, and Rose; (third row) Srs. Columba, Gerard, Patrick, Ignatius, Vincent, Benedict, Magdalen, Paul, Imelda, Alphonsus, and Soledad.

Three

Expanding the Ministry 1919–1943

The sisters began the next 25 years of their community with a growing need for space to house the new sisters. Sister Evangelist bought land on the East Side of San Antonio and started construction of a new motherhouse in 1922.

By 1923, the momentum started by Sister Evangelist continued with the election of Sr. Francis Hughes in 1923. This general superior faced new obstacles that stifled the country but may have spurred growth within the community. The coming of the Depression encouraged women to join communities in the quest for a secure future. However, the real increase of sisters occurred with the opening of St. Philip's Convent in County Galway, Ireland. Sister Francis also had the daunting task of seeking canonical approval for their order in compliance with the new Code of Canon Law in 1917. As in Sister Evangelist's administration, the number of missions increased by 24 and the sisters also branched out from teaching to health care, with the opening of a Brownsville nursing home.

The administration of Sr. Agatha Ryan, beginning in 1935, realized Sister Francis's efforts, because the congregation received the final approbation of its constitution from Rome in 1938. Sister Agatha's mission was to continue the growth of the congregation, so when World War II made it difficult to communicate and travel to Ireland, the sisters received permission to start a novitiate (where novices could profess their first vows) at St. Philip's. Under her watch, the number of missions where the sisters taught increased by 16, and in San Antonio, St. Peter Claver added a new high school.

Mother Margaret's dream for this congregation came to fruition in the celebration of the 50th anniversary of the Sisters of the Holy Spirit and Mary Immaculate. The number of sisters increased, and their missions now covered most of the South.

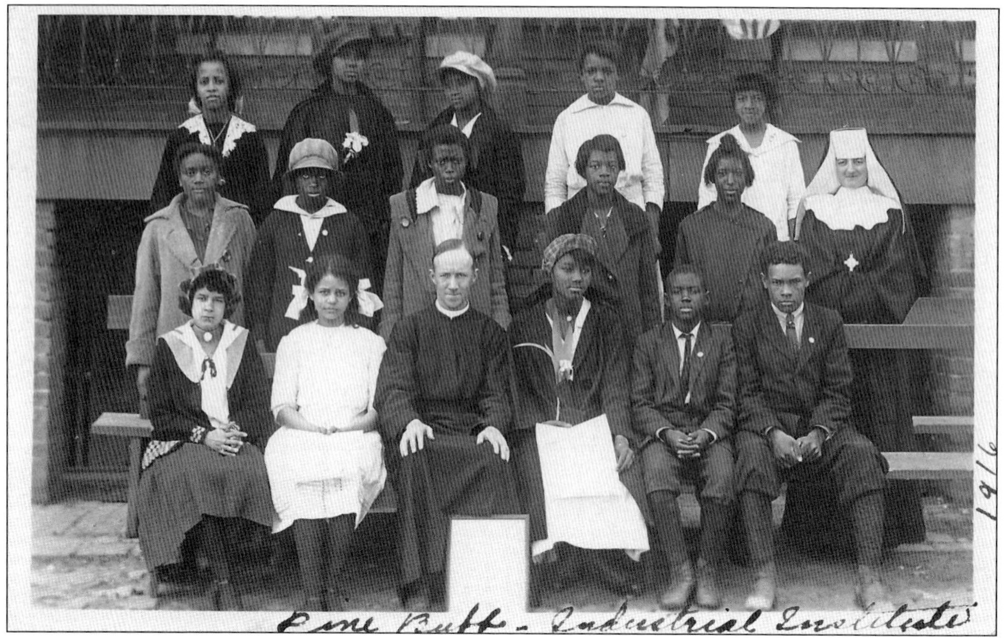

The class of 1913 of the Colored Industrial Institute in Pine Bluff, Arkansas, poses with their pastor and Sister Stanislaus. This school opened in 1889 and was the first Catholic school for African Americans in Arkansas. Five sisters from the Sisters of the Holy Spirit and Mary Immaculate arrived in 1913 to teach at the school. The sisters left in 1927.

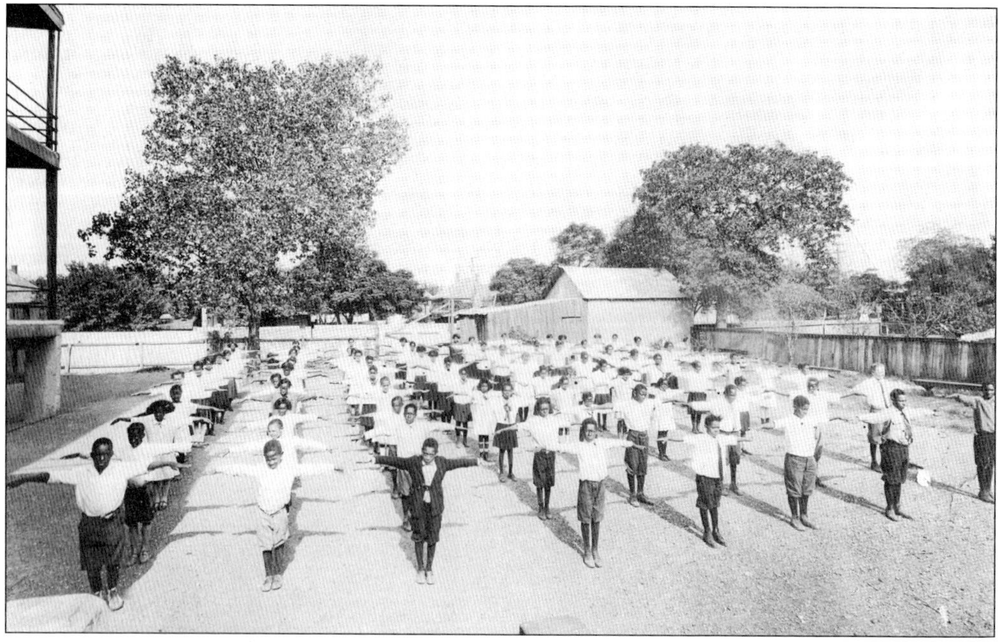

It is exercise time for the students of the Sisters' Institute in Dallas, Texas, in 1922. Rev. J.J. Ferdinand, SSJ, built this school, the first African American school in the Diocese of Dallas in 1908. The Sisters of the Holy Spirit and Mary Immaculate arrived in 1910 to staff the school and taught there until the school closed in 1987. In 1930, the school's name changed to St. Peter Parochial School.

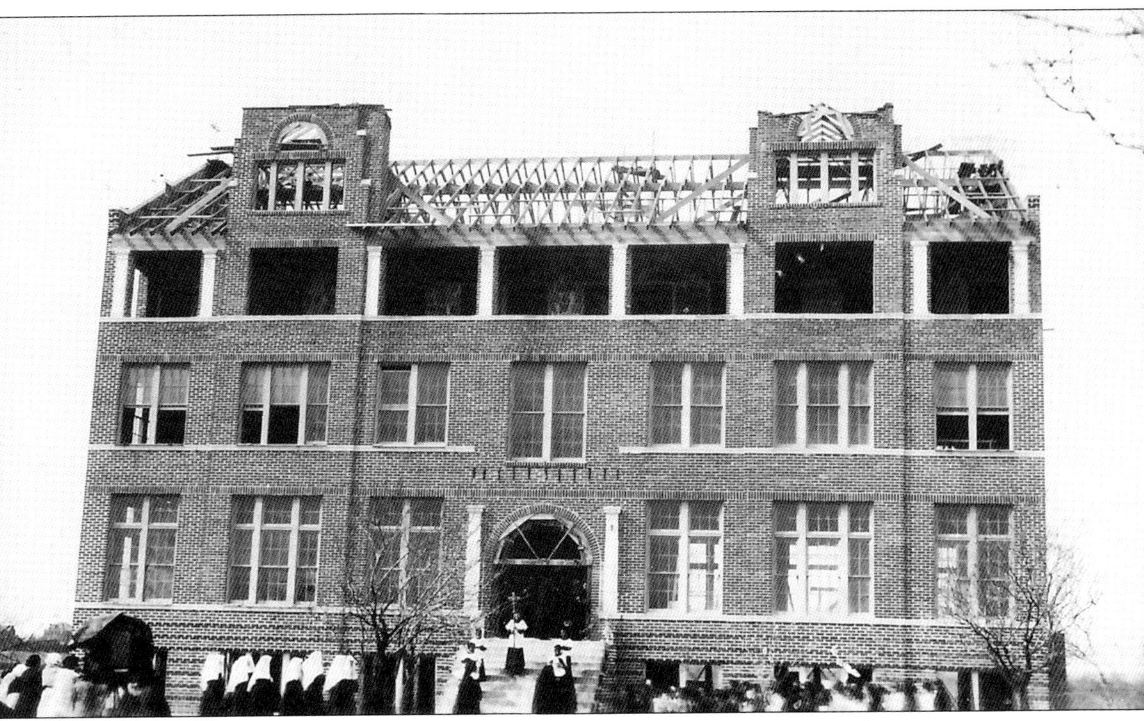

The convent for the Sisters of the Holy Spirit and Mary Immaculate was under construction in this 1922 photograph. The convent, located at 301 Yucca Street in the Grandview subdivision of San Antonio, received several extensions through the years, first in 1928 and again in 1962. The motherhouse served the congregation until 2009, when the sisters constructed a new building across the street.

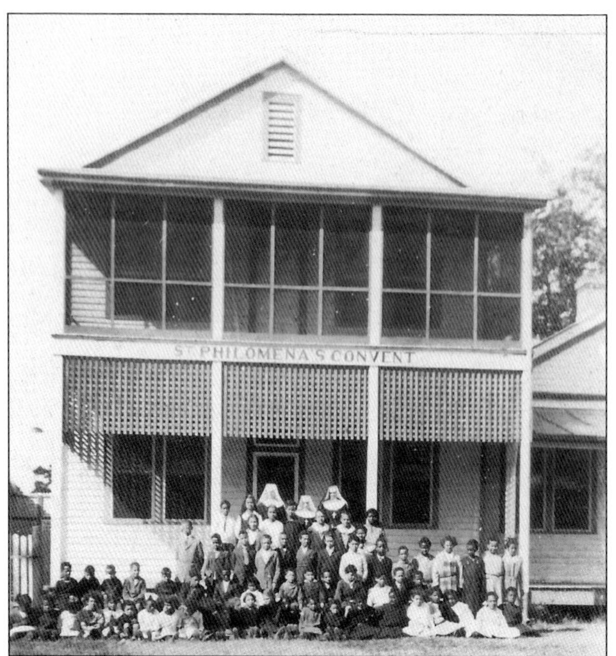

The children of St. Philomena pose in front of the school and convent in Pass Christian, Mississippi, in the 1920s. The Sisters of the Holy Spirit and Mary Immaculate taught in this school from 1921 until 1966. Enrollment declined at this school, but the sisters would return in 1984, working in religious education and pastoral ministry.

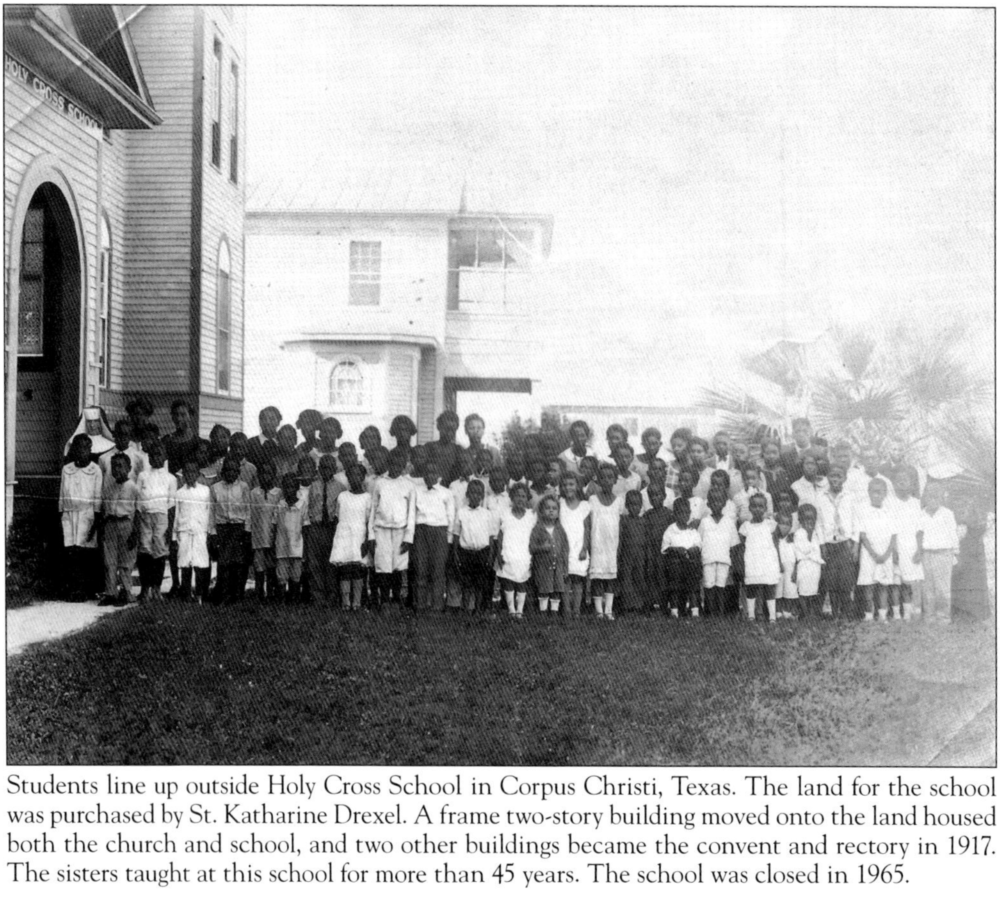

Students line up outside Holy Cross School in Corpus Christi, Texas. The land for the school was purchased by St. Katharine Drexel. A frame two-story building moved onto the land housed both the church and school, and two other buildings became the convent and rectory in 1917. The sisters taught at this school for more than 45 years. The school was closed in 1965.

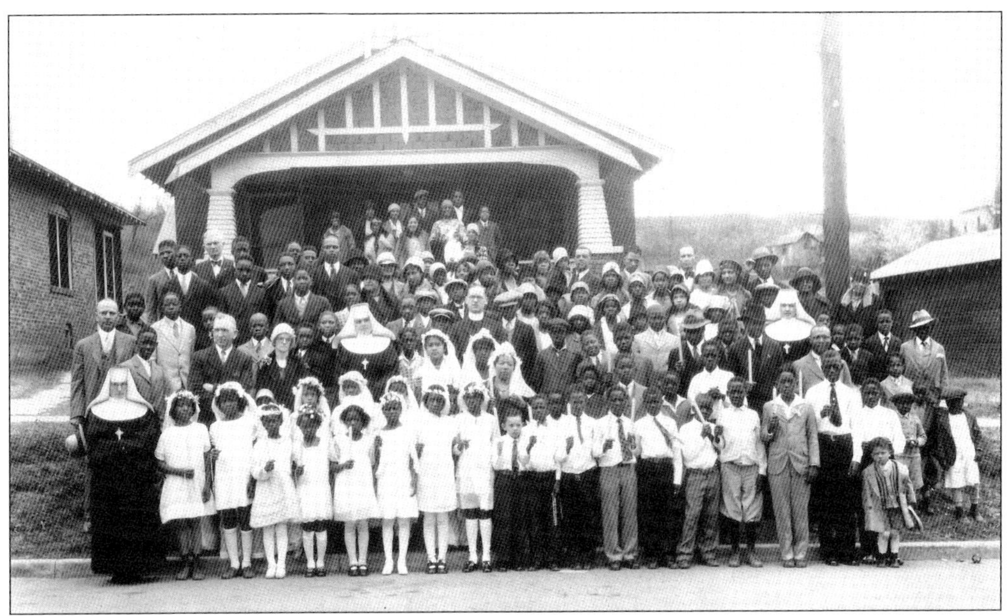

In 1926, children who received their Holy Communion pose with their families in front of St. Monica's School at 401 East Haskell in Tulsa, Oklahoma. This building was donated by the Goodwin family and served as the school and convent. On Sunday, the desks were removed for Mass. As the school grew, a parish formed and a church was constructed in 1930. The sisters taught in this school until 1939.

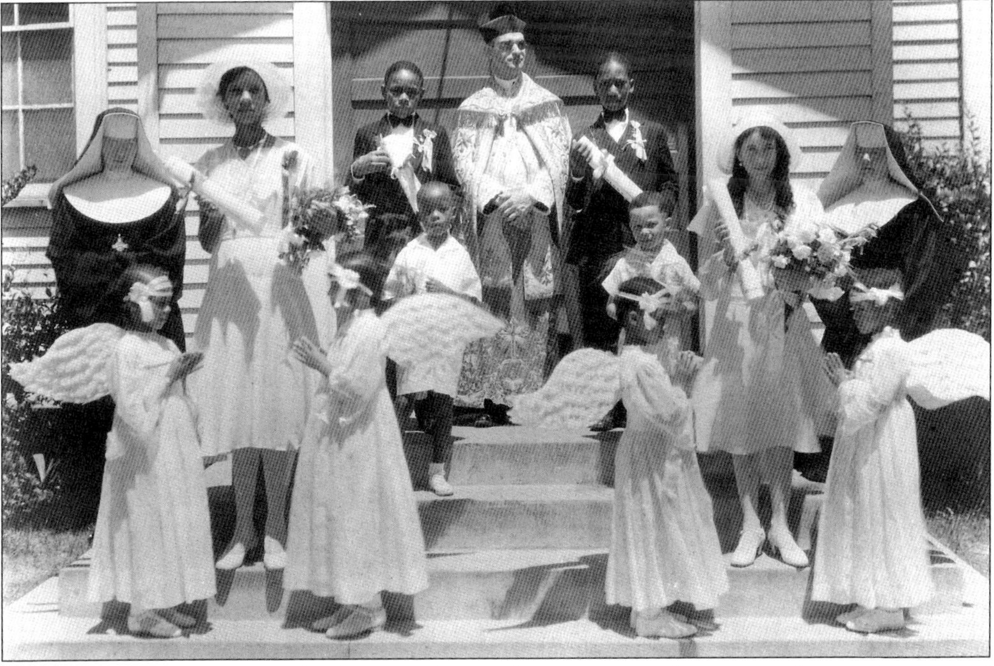

The children of St. James School in Pritchard, Alabama, dressed up as angels, stand in front of Srs. Mary Ursula and Mary Andrew. Father Schmitz (back center) was the pastor. The Sisters of the Holy Spirit and Mary Immaculate assumed the running of the school in 1928 and remained at this institution until 1943.

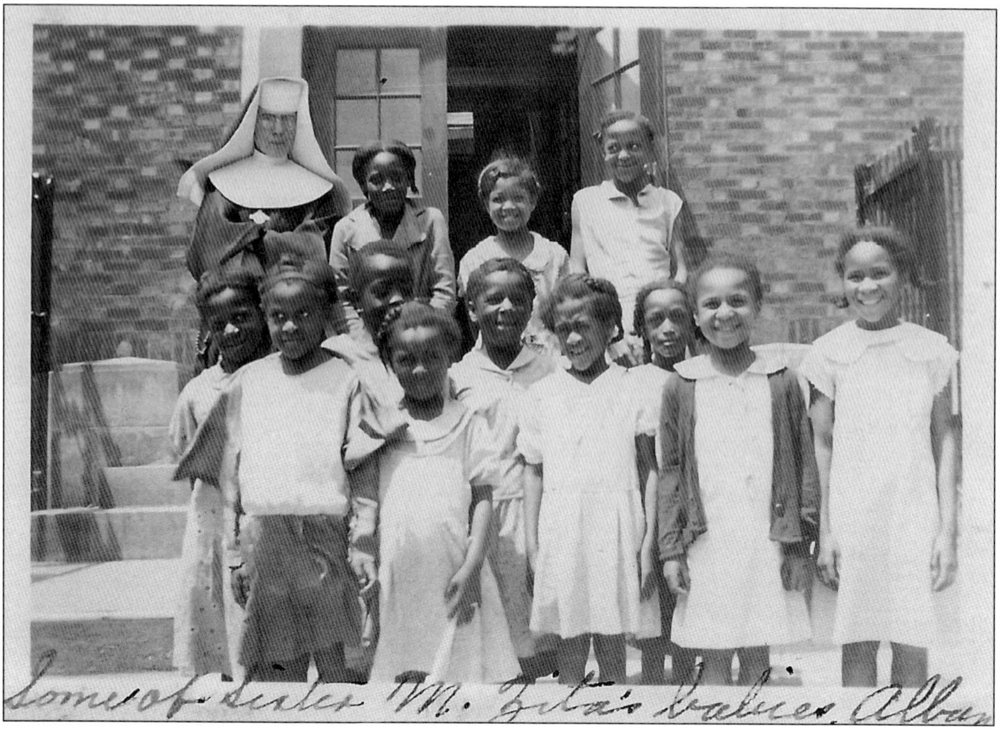

Sr. Mary Zita poses with some of her students in front of St. Philip the Apostle School in Albany, New York. The Sisters of the Holy Spirit and Mary Immaculate opened the converted parish center, which by then contained classrooms, in 1931. They remained there until 1960 when the school closed.

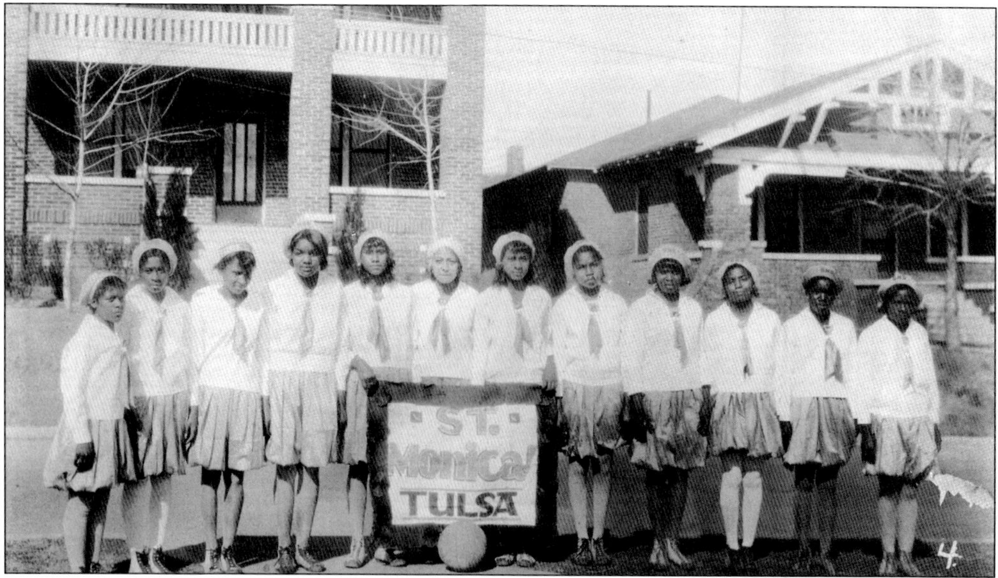

The girls' basketball team of St. Monica's in Tulsa, Oklahoma, stands in front of their school in their uniforms. The Sisters of the Holy Spirit and Mary Immaculate encouraged sports and taught in this school until 1939. They received no payment for their educational services other than the salary donated by choir director Leo Freeman.

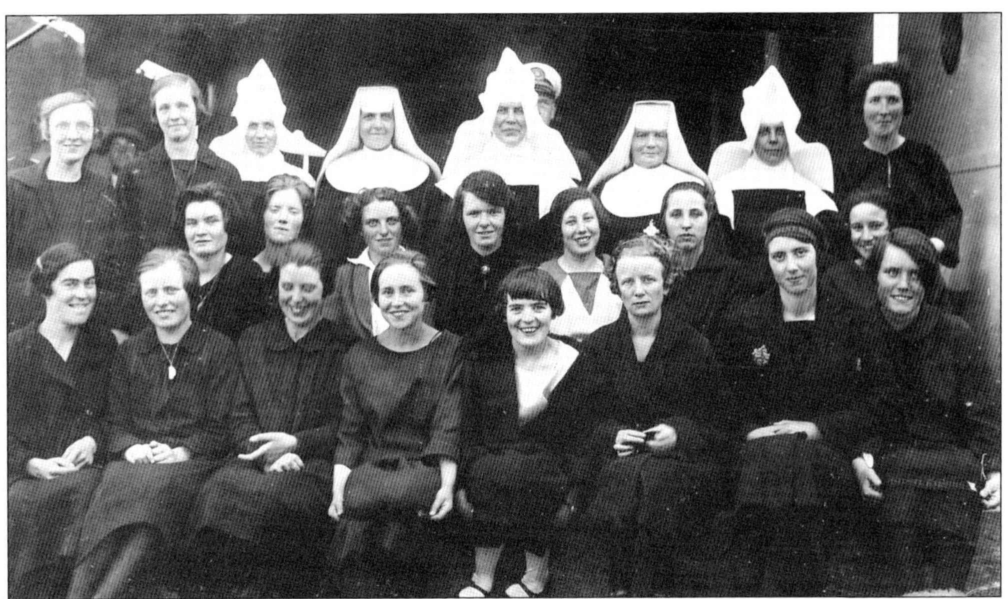

This group of postulants from Ireland arrived in San Antonio, Texas, on August 27, 1927. Three of the sisters with the white veils were from a congregation in Yugoslavia. From left to right are (first row) Catherine Fitzmaurice, Christina Whelahan, Mary Agnes Cahill, Elizabeth Baxter, Alice O'Brien (sister of Sister Aquinas), Sarah Mulcahy, Helen O'Neill, and Annie Delahunty; (second row) Johanna Hanley, Annie Reid, Annie Ruane, Annie O'Connor, Mary Helena Byrne, Josephine Newton, and Mary Anne Kelly; (third row) Mary Hendrick, Cecilia Hannon, unidentified, Sr. Magdalen Egan, unidentified, Sr. Evangelist Jennings, unidentified, and Catherine Carolan.

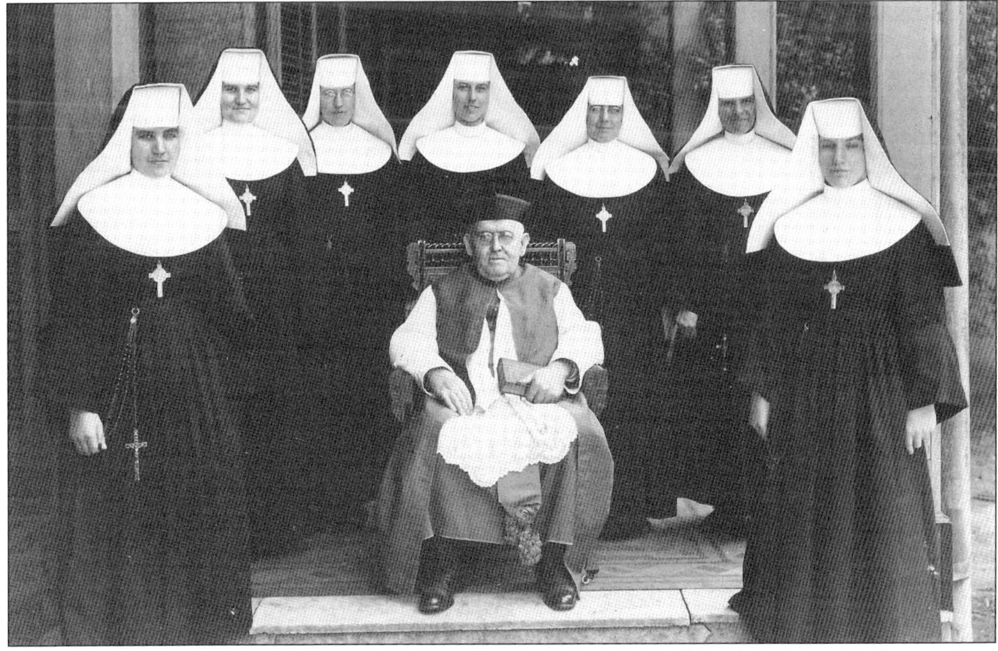

The Sisters of St. Teresa's School in New Orleans, Louisiana, posed for this picture with Very Rev. Canon Leander Roth, pastor of the church. From left to right are Srs. M. Aidan, M. Infant Jesus, M. Aloysius, M. Lucy Walsh, M. Christopher, M. Jarlath Finnerty, and M. Stephen Walsh.

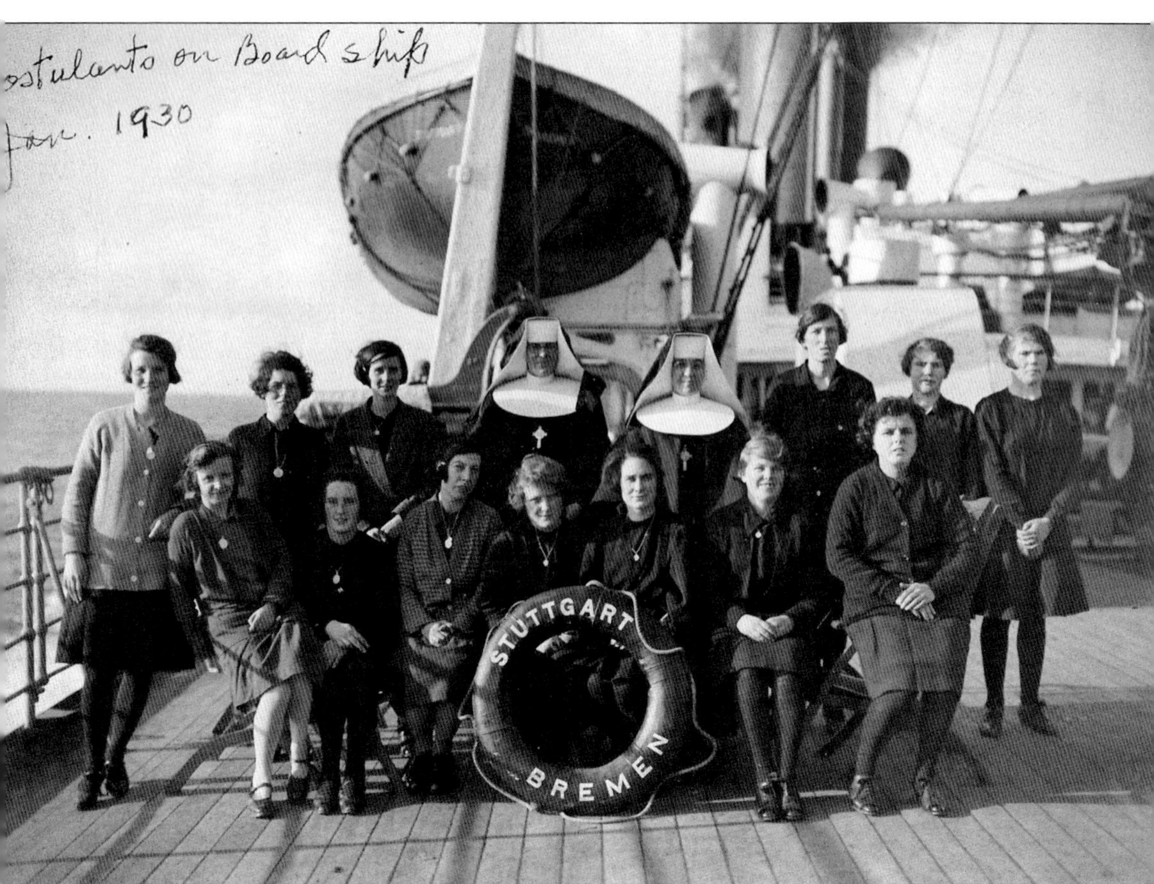

These postulants are pictured aboard the passenger ship *Stuttgart* en route from Cobh, Ireland, to New York in 1930. From left to right are (seated) Srs. Eulalia Hefferman, Celsus Hanrahan, Celia Brennan, Declan McMahon, Assumpta O'Dwyer, Reparata Murphy, and Presentation Murphy; (standing) Srs. Infant Jesus McIntagert, Margaret Mary Murray, and Mercy Carey, Srs. Benedict and Francis (who accompanied the postulants), Emiliana Jennings, Sebastian Lynch, and Roch Lynch.

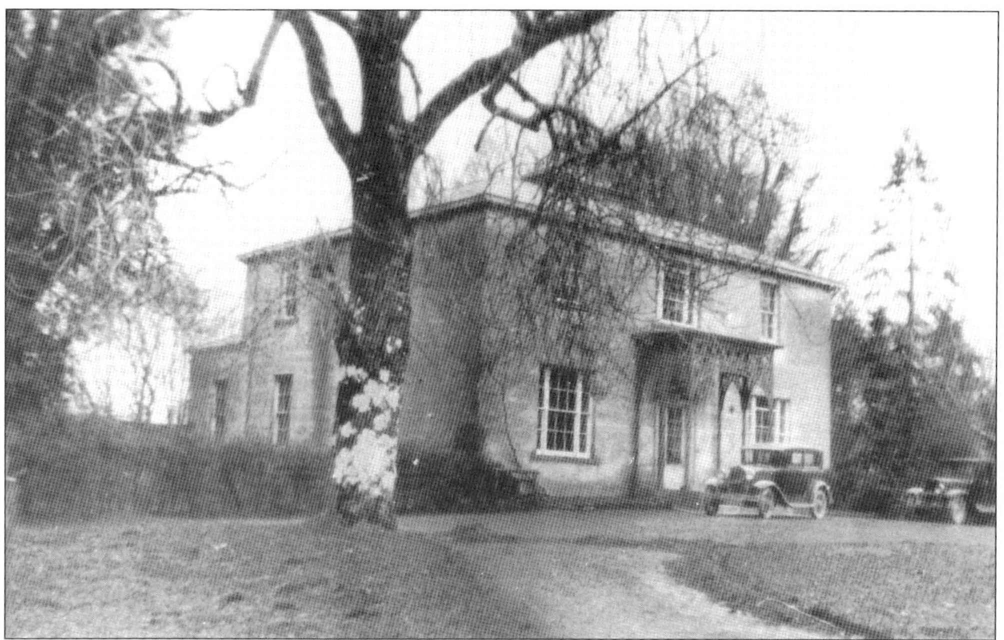

In 1933, the Sisters of the Holy Spirit and Mary Immaculate purchased the Dower House of the Grattan Bellew estate in Mount Bellew, Ireland, to be repurposed as St. Philip's Convent. The sisters opened a school and recruited several young women to join the congregation. The sisters closed the facility in 1965.

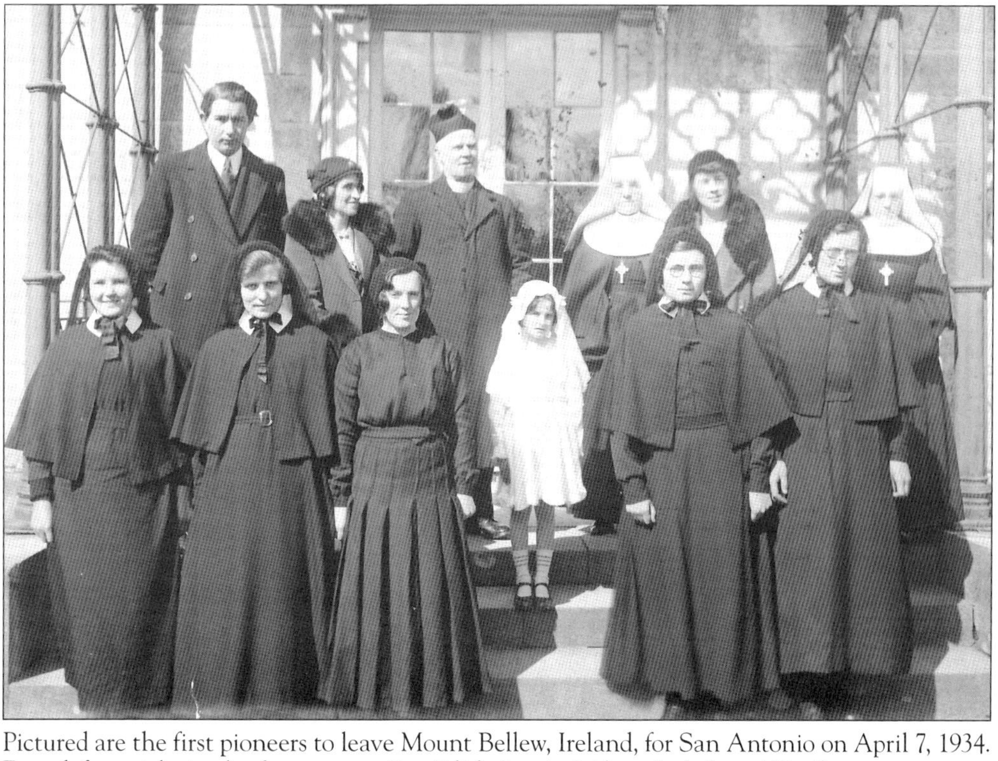

Pictured are the first pioneers to leave Mount Bellew, Ireland, for San Antonio on April 7, 1934. From left to right in the first row are Srs. Edith, Louis, Isidore, Isabel, and Sheila.

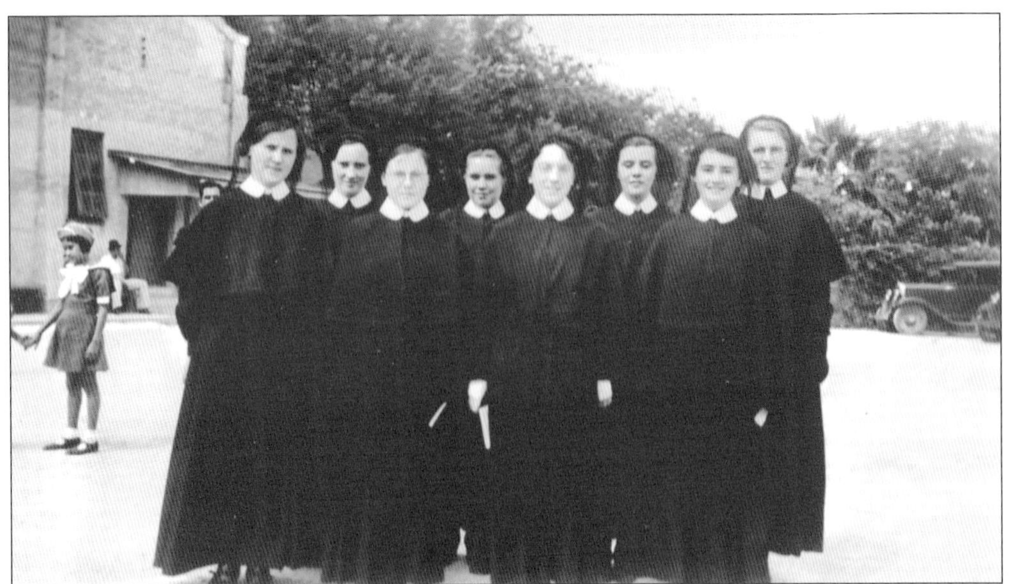

A group of postulants gather for this photograph in 1938. From left to right are Srs. Placidus (Catherine) Devilly, Marcellus (Mary) Walsh, Donatus (Patsy) Devlin, Bartholomew (Mary) Garrehy, Winifred (Claire) Connellon, Luke (Josephine) McGarry, Adrian (Esther) Robinson, and Euphrasia (Mary) Mockler.

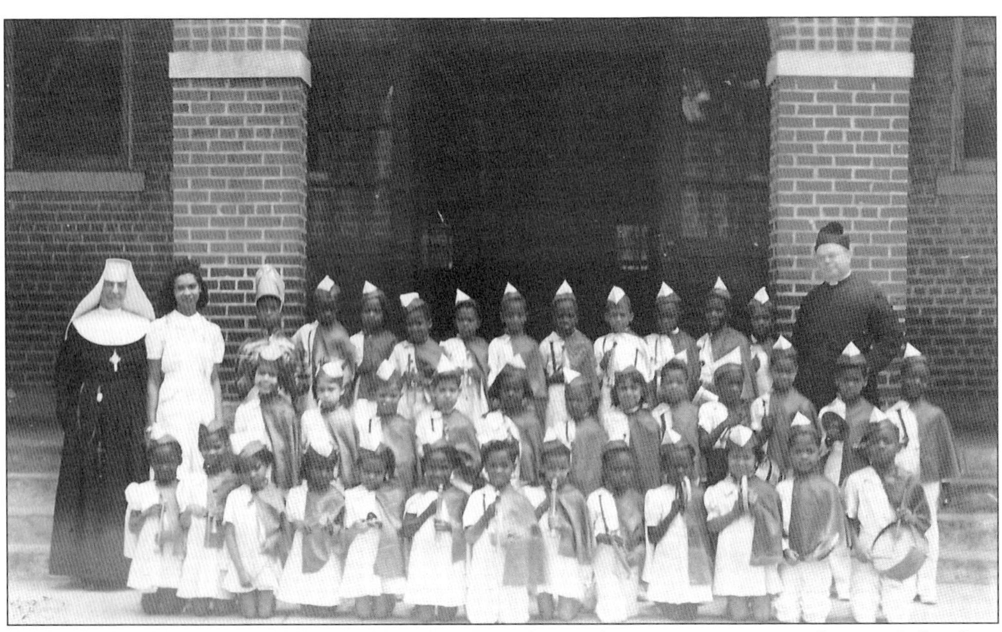

Sr. Crescentia O'Brien stands with her band students of Most Pure Heart of Mary School in Mobile, Alabama. The Sisters of the Holy Spirit and Mary Immaculate arrived in 1911 and taught in the school until 1943.

Four

Diversifying the Ministry 1944–1968

After World War II, the United States rebuilt its infrastructure. Veterans returned home, and some attended school to increase their families' wages. The Catholic schools prospered, but by the end of the 1960s things began to change.

The next two administrations of the Sisters of the Holy Spirit and Mary Immaculate led by Sr. Imelda Brannelly in 1947–1959 and Sr. Ambrose Griffin in 1959–1965 experienced social and political turmoil, along with changes in the church. At the beginning of the 1950s, the congregation continued with the Sisters of the Holy Spirit and Mary Immaculate increasing their numbers as well as their missions. However, by the last half of the 1960s, the numbers began to decline. One event that led to this decrease was the closing of the convent in Ireland in 1965. The number of sisters emerging from the area diminished, and the sisters were forced to close their school. During this same time, the Second Vatican Council (Vatican II) sought to reorganize the church to appeal to a more modern world. The Sisters of the Holy Spirit accommodated these changes in their governmental structure, spiritual life, and dress, but while most of the congregation adapted, a number of sisters left the community. Also during this time in the United States, the case of *Brown v. Board of Education of Topeka* in 1954 desegregated the schools, although much of the South did not desegregate for another 10 years—and in some areas it took even longer. (The NAACP's tactic to litigate first for higher education was effective, and it started to tear down the walls of segregation.) However, this affected the mission of the Sisters of the Holy Spirit because they were no longer working exclusively with people of color. The local Catholic dioceses often combined schools and raised tuition, so many students left the Catholic school system.

While the community celebrated 75 years as a congregation, they also experienced many changes that would propel them to diversify their ministries and expand their reach in the future.

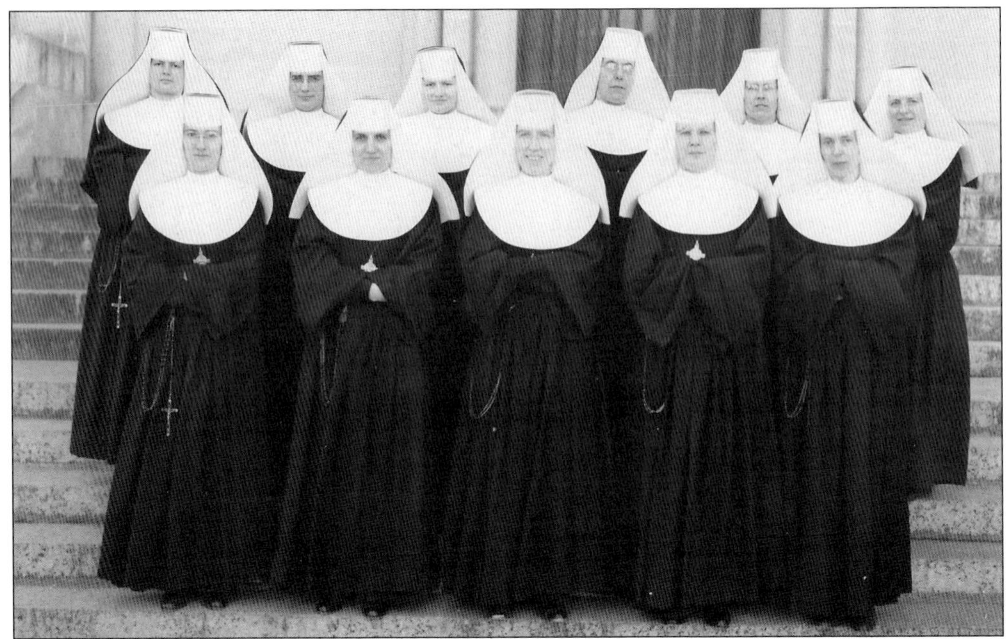

In 1947, the Sisters of the Holy Spirit and Mary Immaculate stand in front of Little Flower School in San Antonio. The sisters began teaching there in 1926. From left to right are (first row) Srs. Marcellus, Augustine, Emmanuel, Ambrose, and Perpetua; (second row) Srs. Josephine, Assumpta, David, Cresentia, Chryostom, and Mary of the Angels.

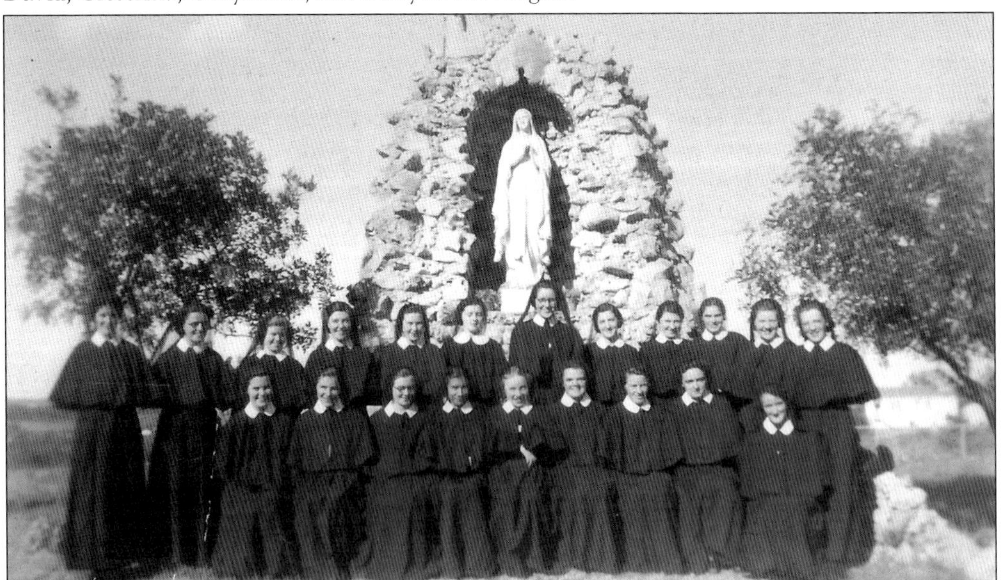

By the summer of 1950, the number of postulants entering the community was 21, with 14 entering the novitiate in August 1950 and the other postulants entering the novitiate in 1951. Pictured from left to right are (first row) Marguerite Connors, Mona Gavin, Patricia Tierney, Joan Rivers, Betty Gordon, Philomena Murphy, Marie Leonard, Ita O'Connell, and Sarah Anne Kenny; (second row) Eileen Mannion, Rosaleen Carey, Kathleen Kilbride, Imelda Coyne, Bernadette McNamara, Margaret Ward, Theresa O'Toole, Teresa Queally, Mary Hayes, Teresa Healy, Nancy Finnerty, and Bridget Donnellan.

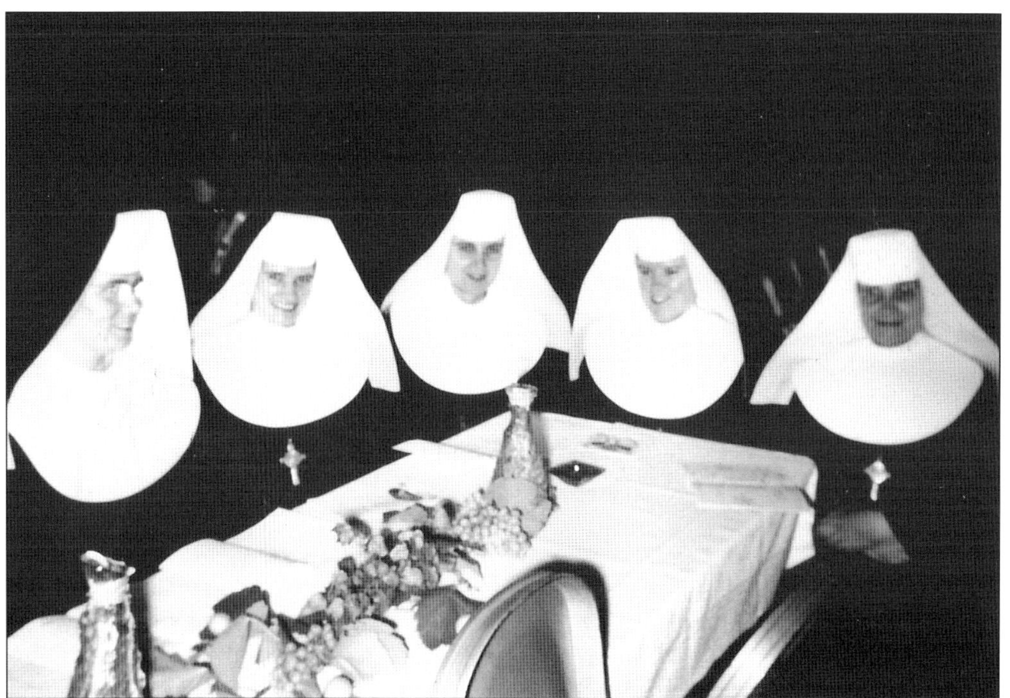

From left to right, Srs. Martha Pohl, Rosetta Leonard, Rose McHugh, Aidan Downey, and Eugene Newton await a delicious dinner prepared by Sister Rose in 1959 in Brownsville, Texas.

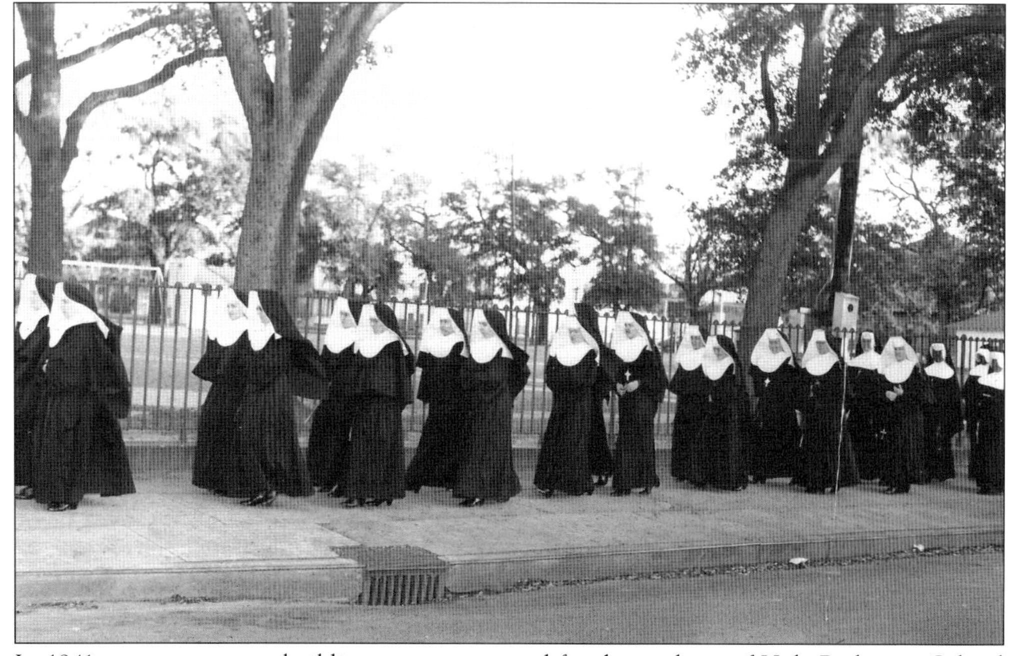

In 1941, a new two-story building was constructed for the students of Holy Redeemer School in New Orleans, Louisiana. The Sisters of the Holy Spirit and Mary Immaculate attended the blessing of the new school and are seen here leaving the school for the church.

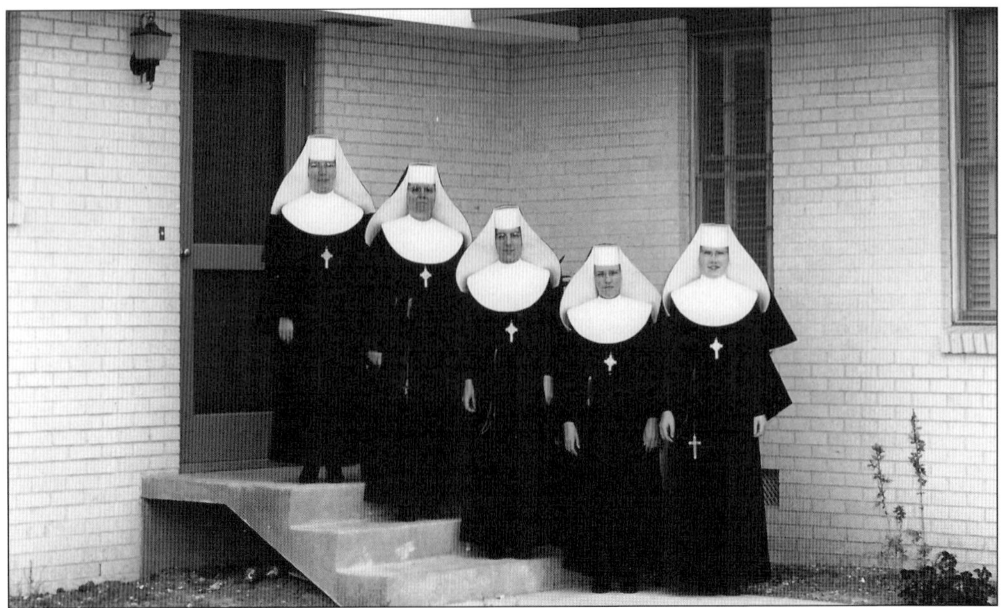

Srs. Zita Lyons, Germaine DeMar, Veronica Connellon, Antoinette Connaughton, and Henrietta Scarry pose here in front of St. Bernard's Convent in Dallas, Texas. The Sisters of the Holy Spirit opened the school in 1948 and taught there until they withdrew from the school in 1983.

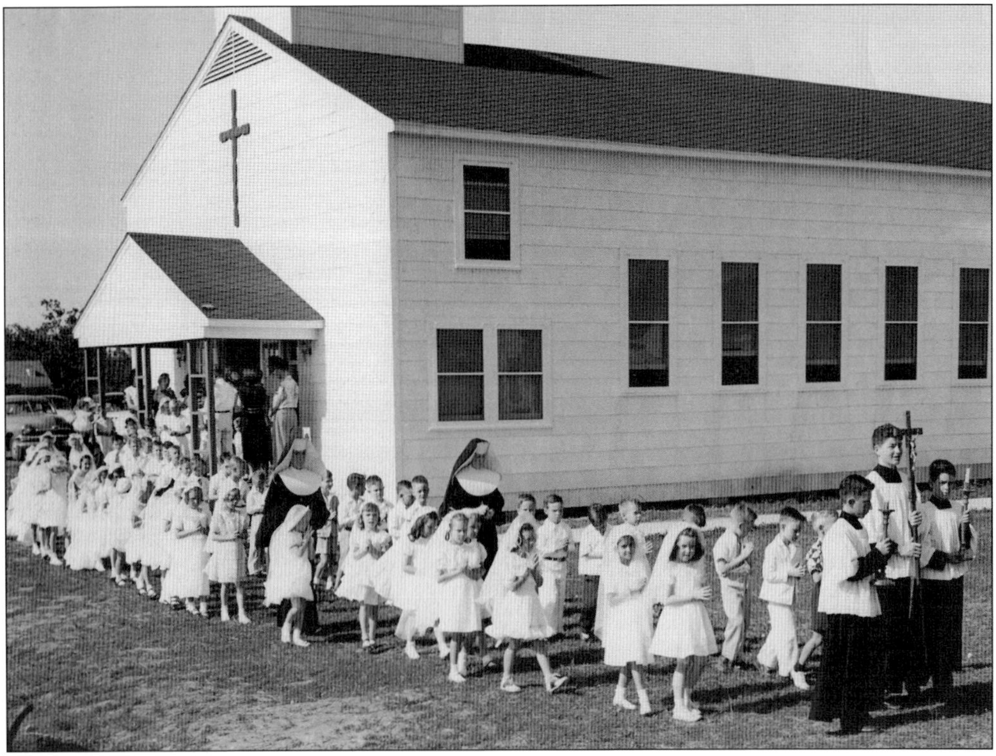

In the 1950s, the Sisters of the Holy Spirit and Mary Immaculate taught at the Holy Ghost School in Bellaire, Texas. Srs. Patricia Walsh and Gabriel Hession are pictured leading the first graders to church to receive their first communion.

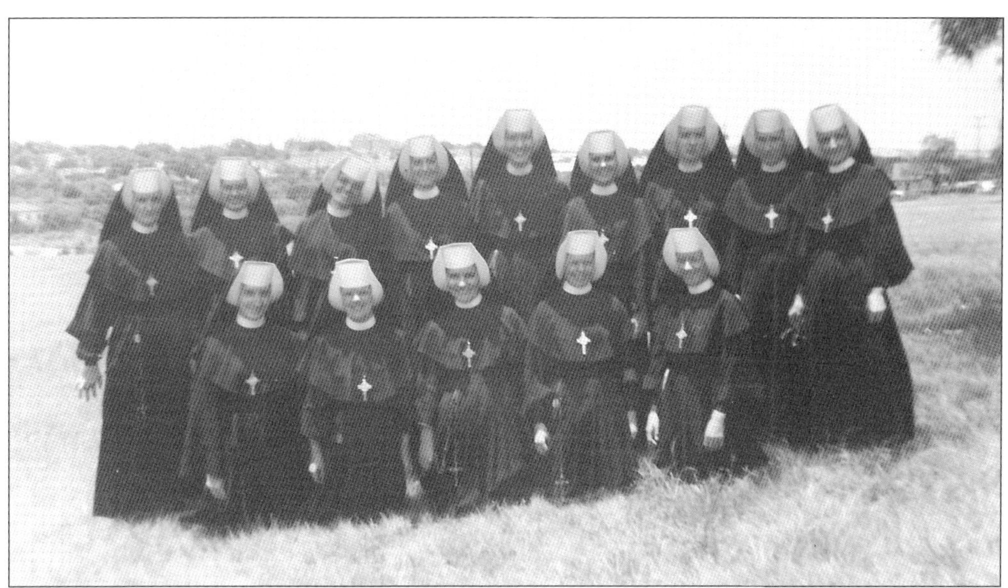

These 14 sisters received into the novitiate in August 1950 were known as the Holy Year Novices. They are pictured in August 1951 on the day they took their temporary vows. From left to right are (first row) Srs. Mary Rumold Queally, Mary Goretti Murphy, Mary Celestine Gavin, Mary Cyprian McBride, and Mary Victory Leonard; (second row) Srs. Sarah Ann Kenny, Mary Clotilda Healy, Mary Sennan Carey, Mary Silverius Mannion, Mary Visitation O'Toole, Mary Laurentia Connors, Mary Petronilla Ward, Mary Roberta Hayes, and Mary Rosario O'Connell.

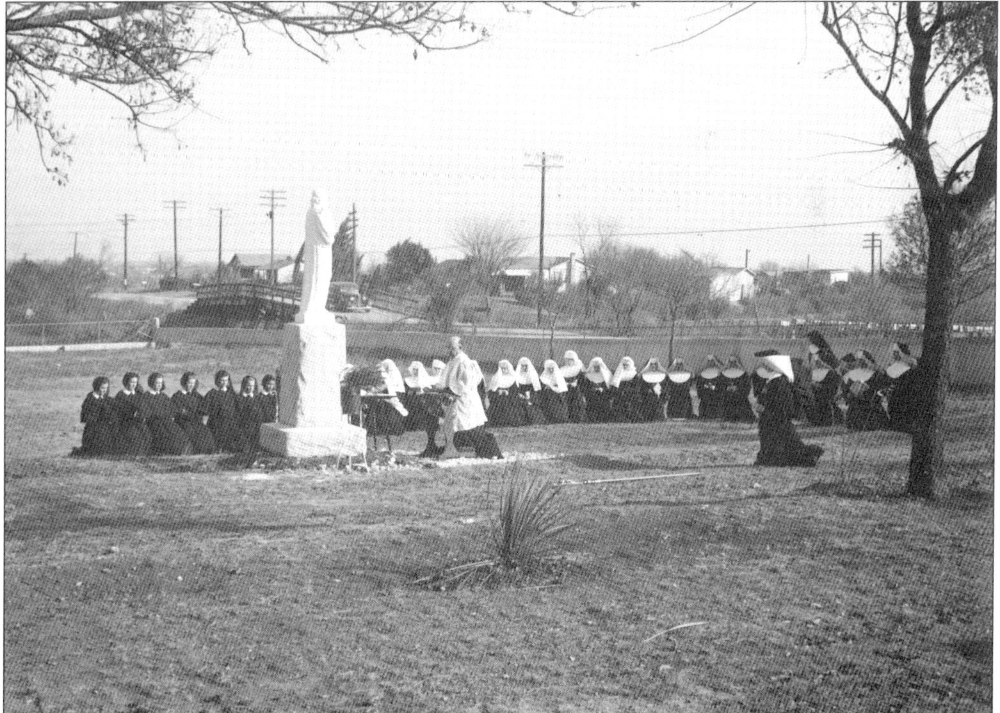

These sisters kneel for the blessing of the statue of St. Joseph in January 1951, in San Antonio behind the motherhouse at 301 Yucca Street.

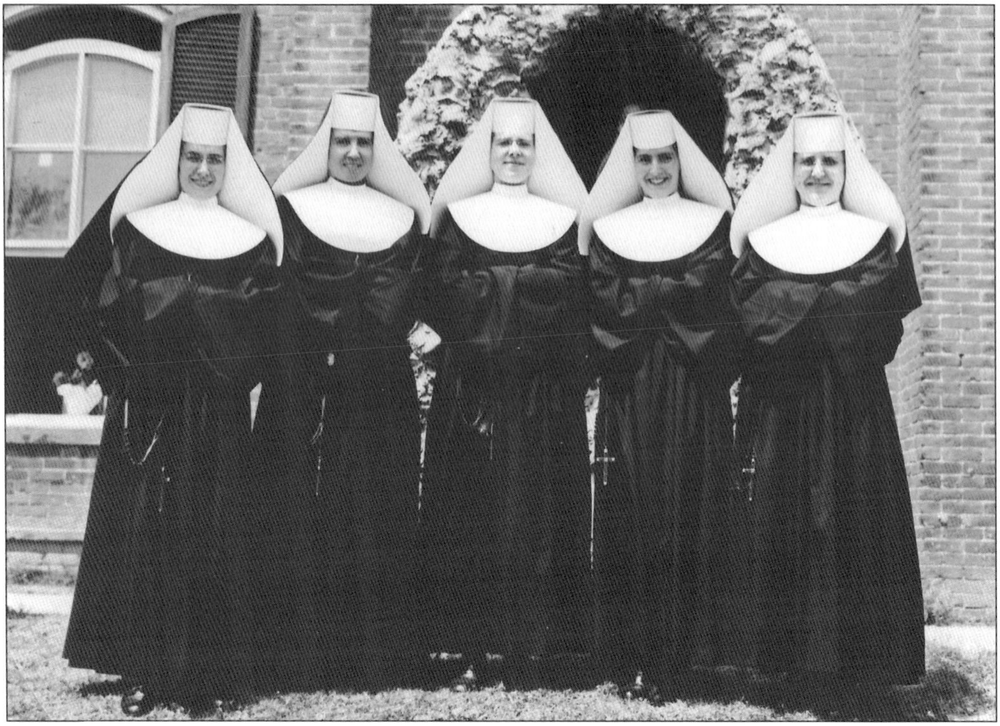

Srs. Mary Casmir, Mary Perpetual Help, Mary Cletus, Mary Silverius, and Mary Placidus pose in front of St. Francis School in Natchez, Mississippi. The Sisters of the Holy Spirit and Mary Immaculate began teaching at this school in 1921. The last Holy Spirit principal administered during the 1990–1991 school year. The sisters are still in ministry with the Early Childhood Program at Holy Family Parish.

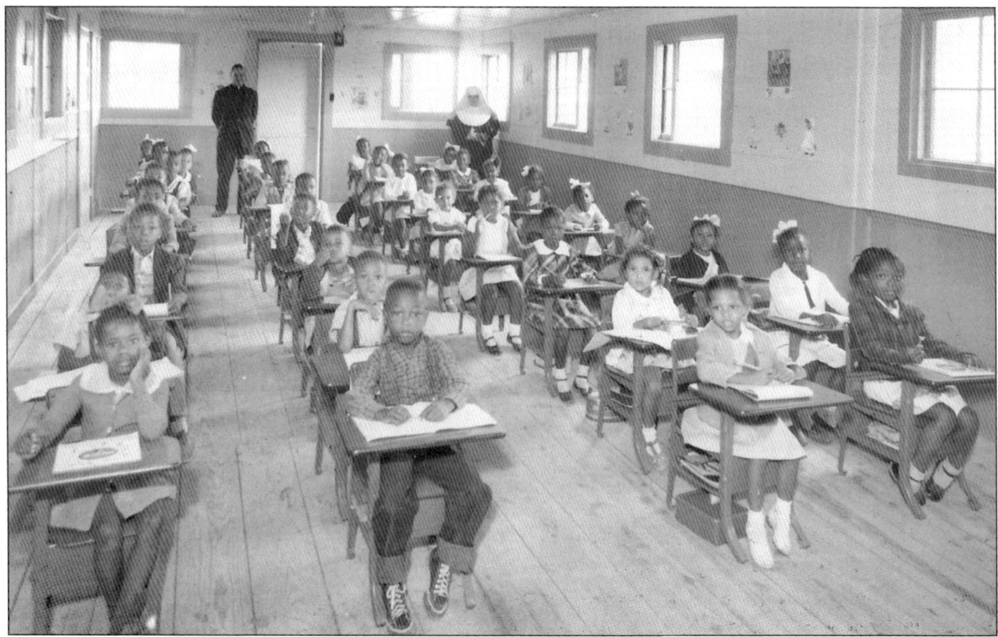

Sr. Mercedes Kiely surveys her class at Immaculate Heart of Mary School in Dallas, Texas.

These sisters rolled up their sleeves, pinned their veils up, and kicked off their shoes to go fishing. Their efforts yielded this little fish.

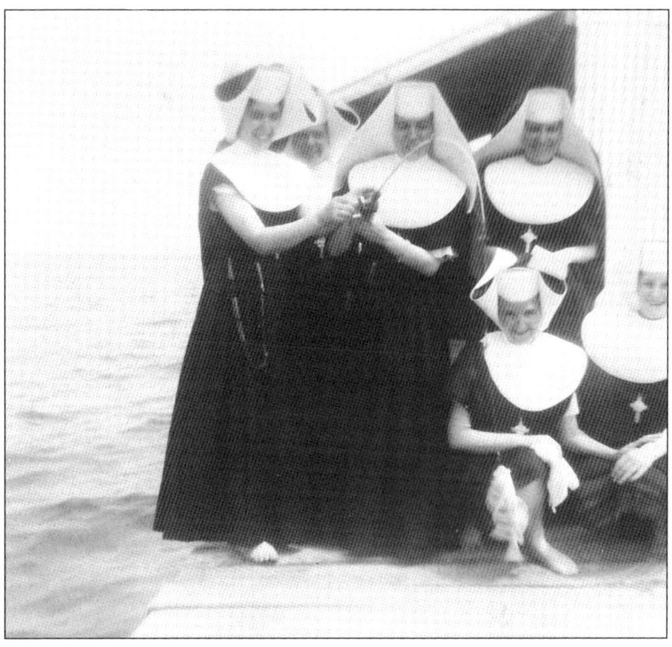

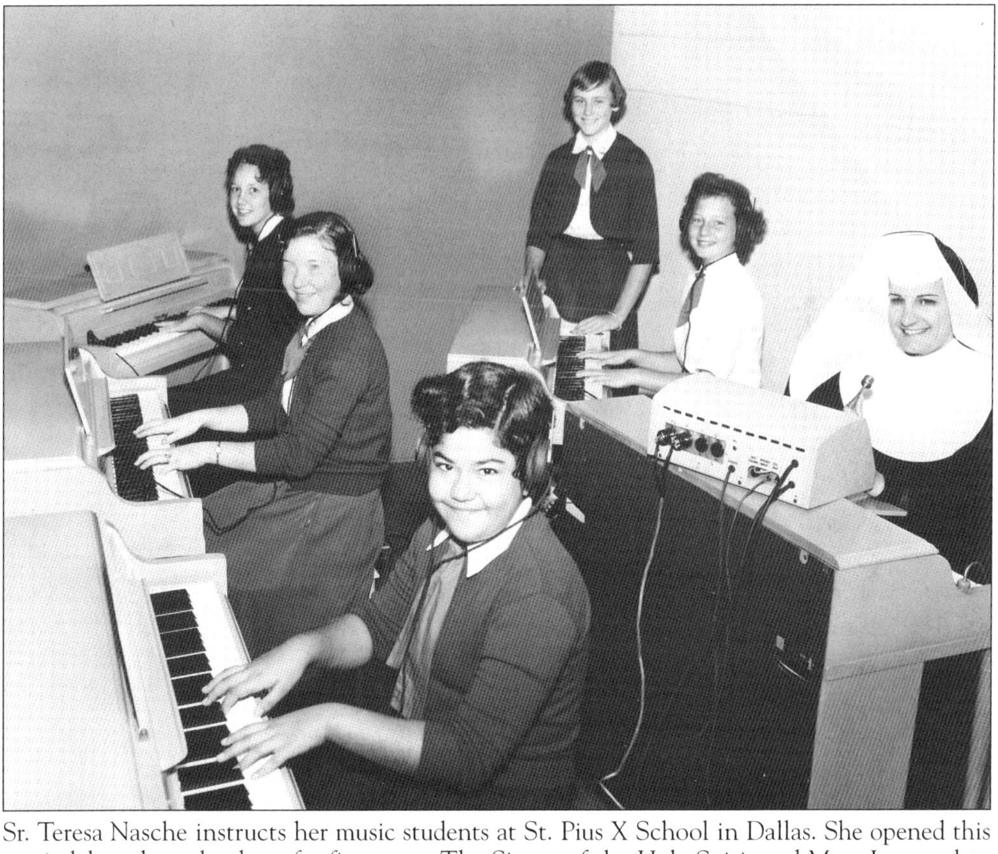

Sr. Teresa Nasche instructs her music students at St. Pius X School in Dallas. She opened this music lab and taught there for five years. The Sisters of the Holy Spirit and Mary Immaculate opened St. Pius X in 1955 and remained there until 1985.

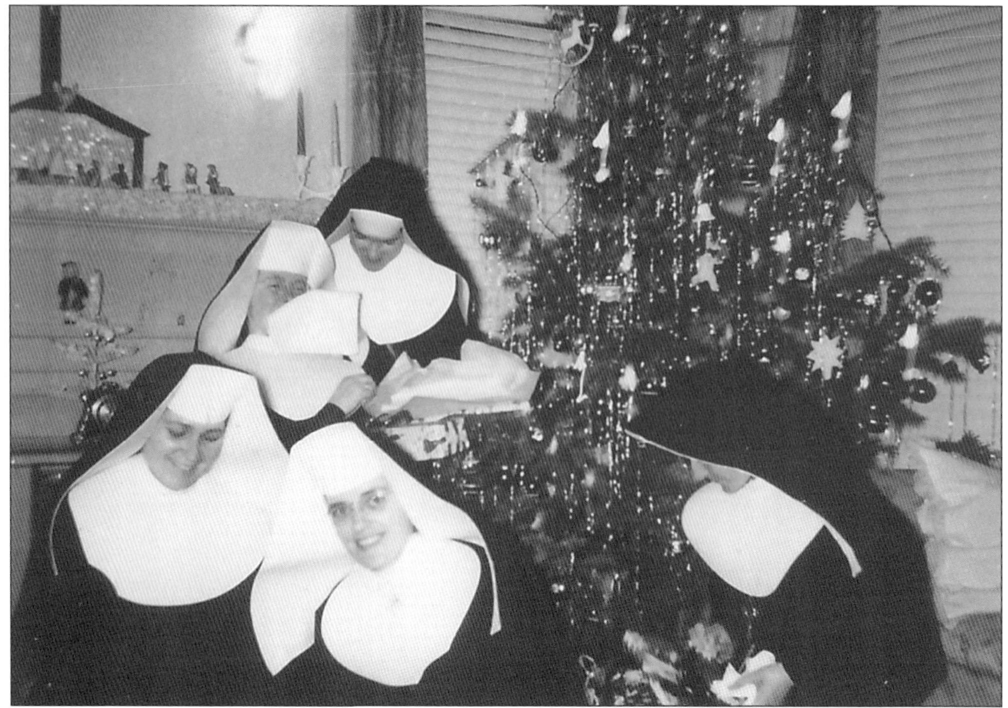

Srs. Annette, Anita, Leslie, Eugenius, and Dorothy open Christmas presents under the tree at St. Philip's Convent in Dallas. St. Philip's School was formed to relieve overcrowding from St. Augustine Parish. The sisters opened the school in 1955, and the small house shown here, located on Nelson Drive, served as the convent.

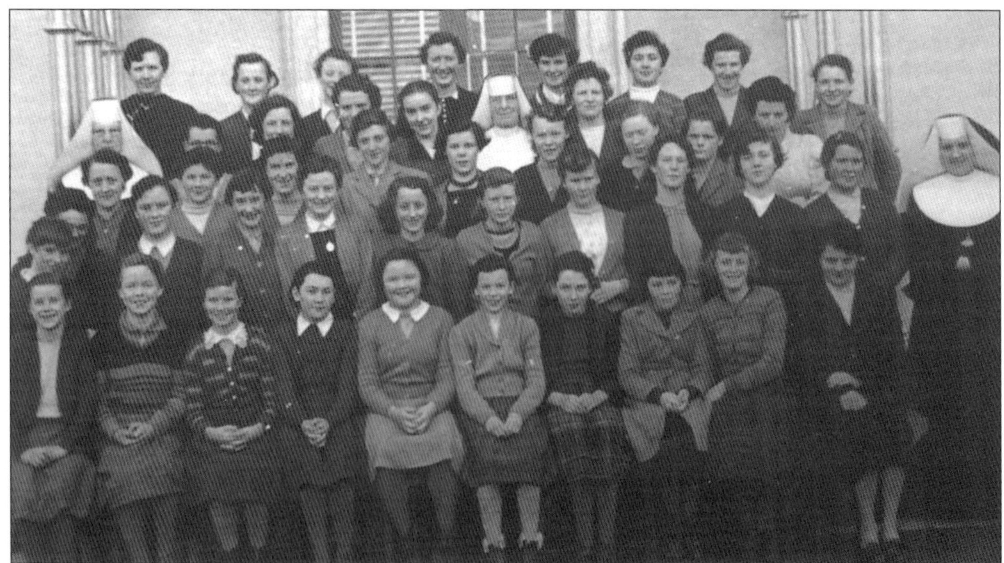

Pictured in 1960 are the students and teachers of the first foundation *Scoll n Coroine Muire* in Mount Bellew, Ireland. Eleven of these students became Sisters of the Holy Spirit: Peggy Kenny, Breda Mitchell, Dympna Clarke, Kathleen Cunningham, Brid Gavin, Mary Crehan, Maureen Leonard, Esther Dempsey, Brid Ruane, Mary Theresa Gordon, and Anne Reynolds. (Courtesy of Dr. Gabriel O'Connor.)

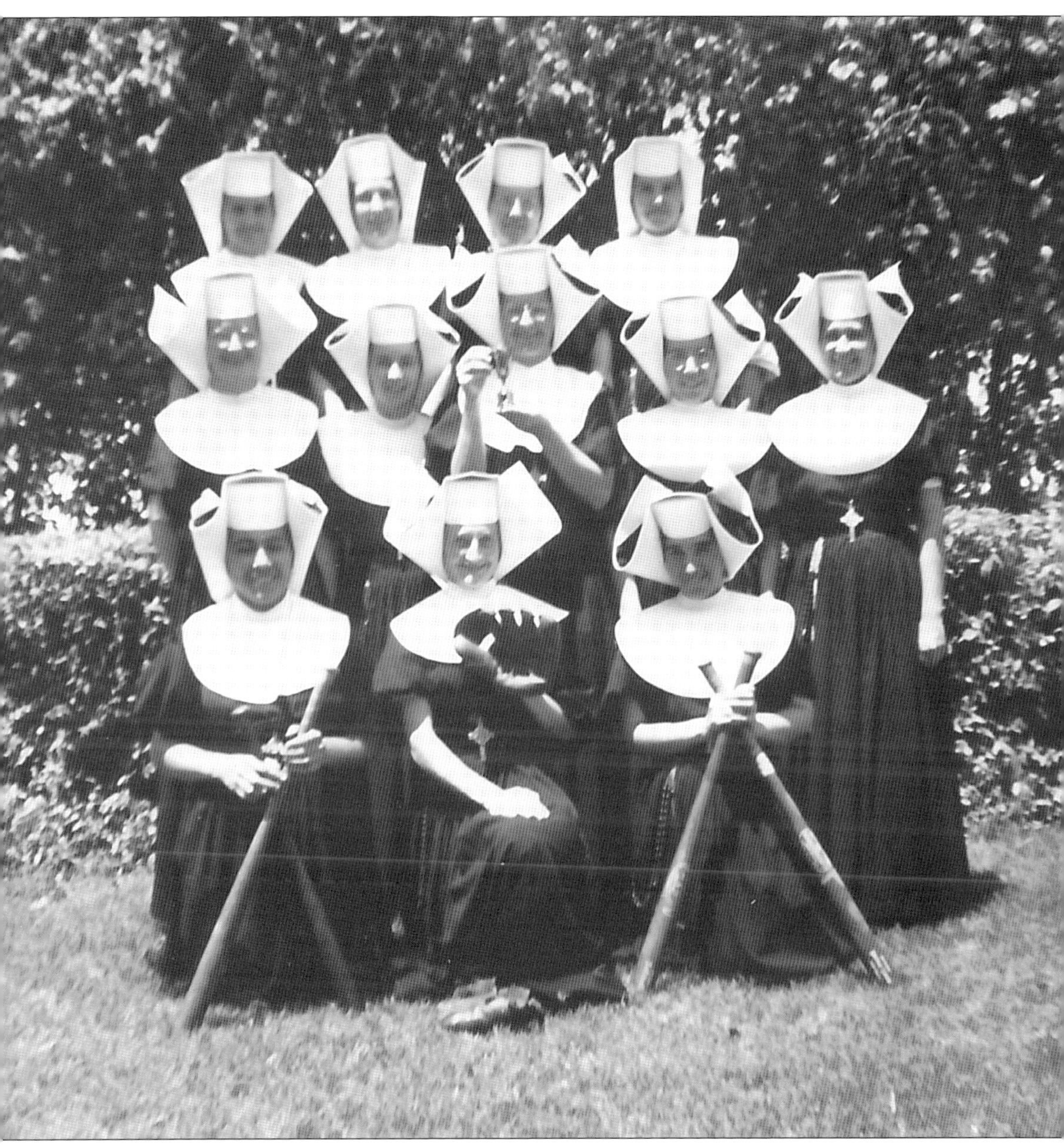

During the 1950s and 1960s, most of the sisters were involved in education ministry. At the close of the school year, all of the sisters returned to the motherhouse for some "R&R." All participated in an annual retreat, days of spiritual renewal, classes at one of the local universities, family home visits, and other activities. In the evening, the sisters enjoyed movies outdoors on the side of the garage wall at the convent—similar to a drive-in. Nuns picked up their stools from the dining room and had a choice of sitting anywhere in the yard. Another activity in which the sisters participated was softball. Their habit skirts were pinned up, sleeves rolled up past the elbows, and veils pinned back with a clothespin. Competition was stiff. This picture features the happy championship team. From left to right are (first row) Srs. Irene, Jarleth, and Lucia; (second row) Srs. Anthony, Rosaleen, Gerald, Martinette, and Leslie; (third row) Srs. Laurentia, Oliver, Georgina, and Evelyn.

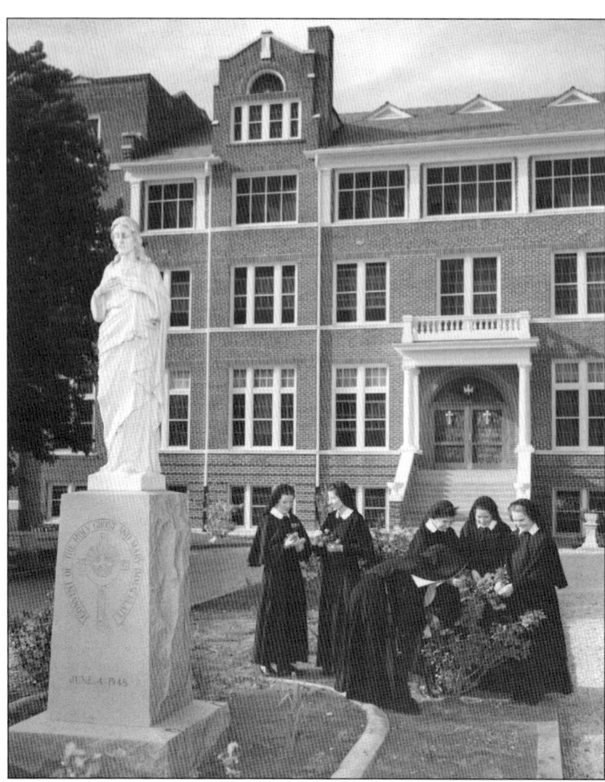

Postulants gather around the beautiful flowers outside the 1922 motherhouse on Yucca Street in San Antonio.

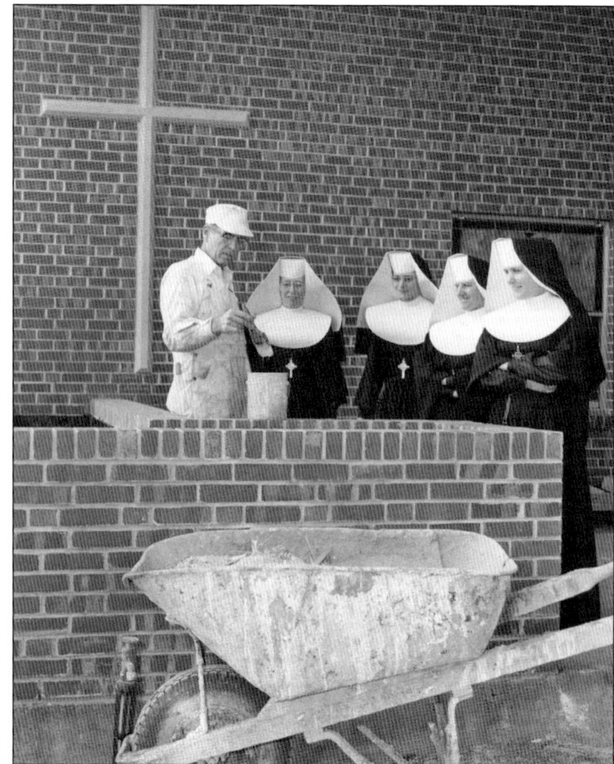

Srs. Monica, Nora, Fintan, and Juliana observe the construction of St. Pius X Convent in Dallas.

Srs. Teresa Reynolds, Carmelita Mulry, Monica Carroll, Doloretta Madigan, Teresa Nasche, and Helena Hayden take a ride on the glass-bottom boats in San Marcos, Texas.

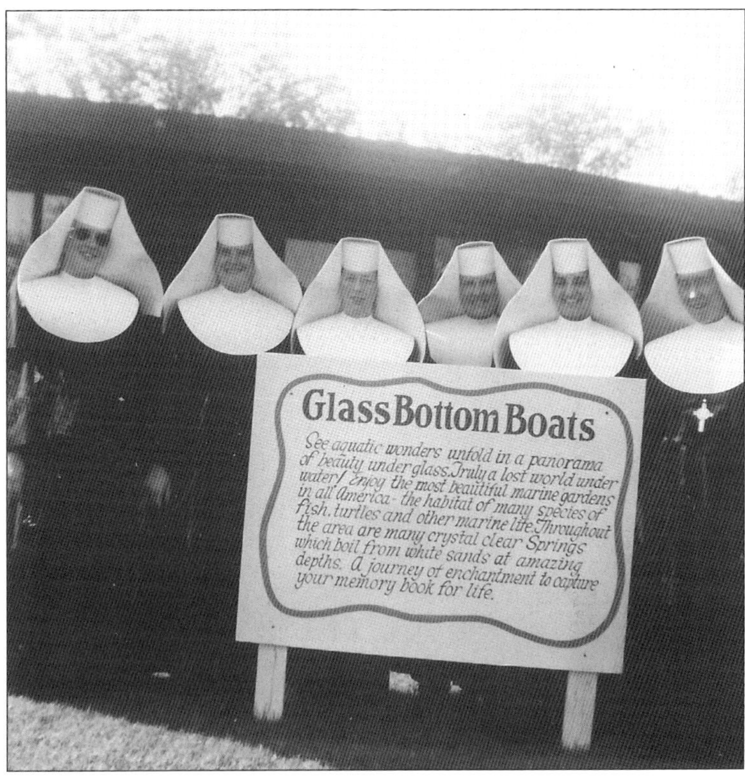

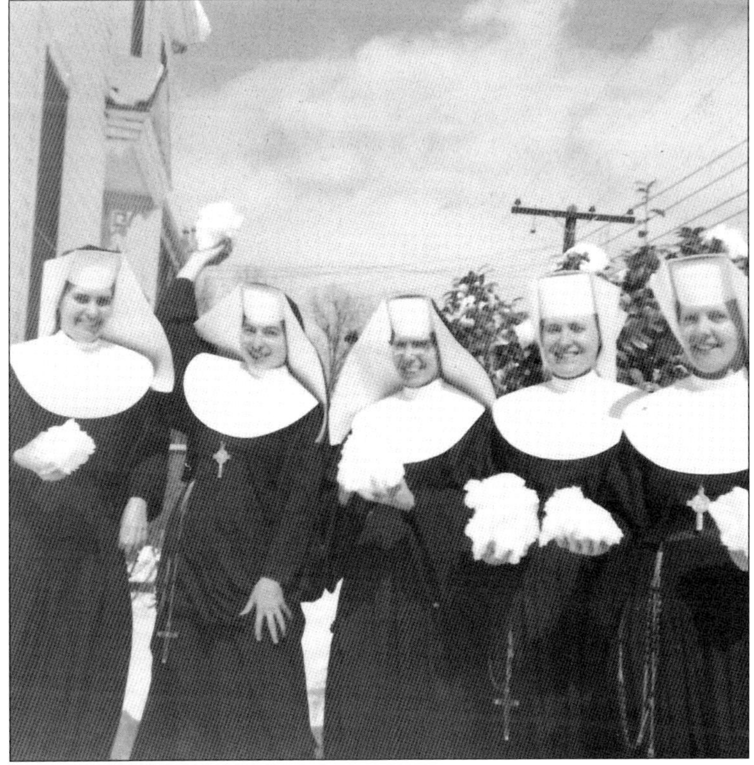

The sisters in Natchez, Mississippi, experienced an unusual snowfall and decided to run outside and make snowballs. From left to right are Srs. Marguerite Connors, Glenice Rivers, Regina McGee, Magdelan Kilbane, and Agnes Glynn.

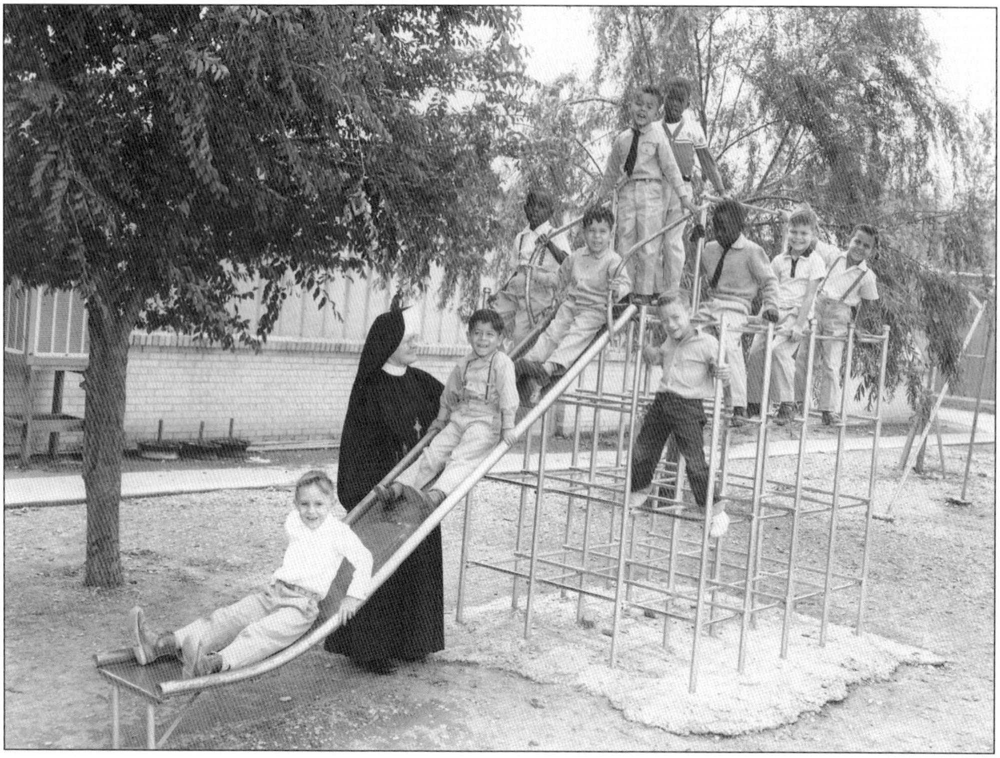

Sister Andrew and her class from St. Mary of Carmel in Dallas take a break from their schoolwork to get some exercise in 1963. The Sisters of the Holy Spirit opened this school in 1944, and by 1985 they also worked in parish religious education.

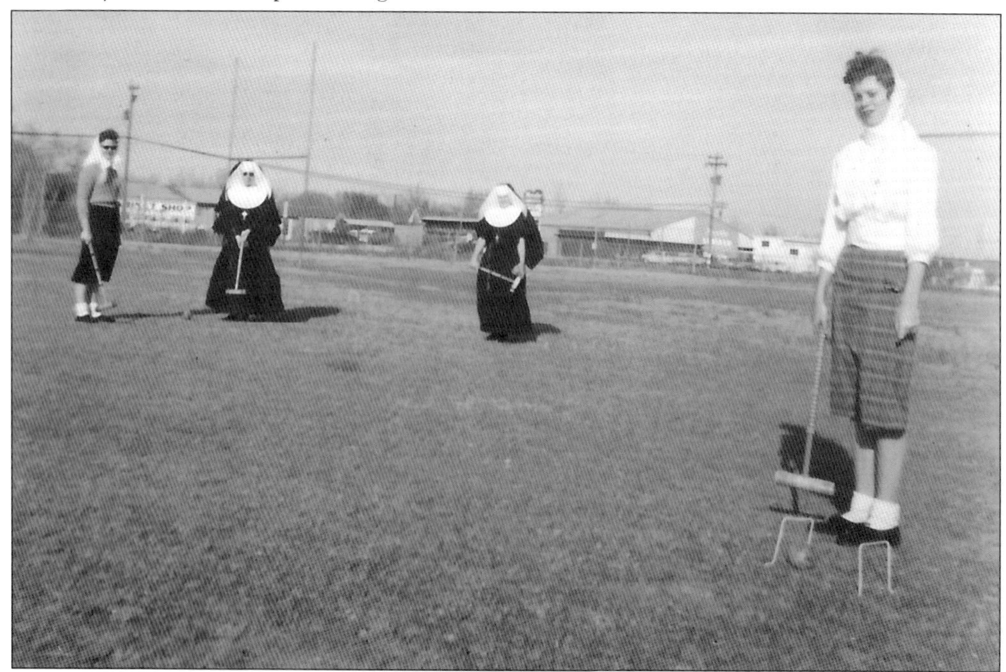

Sr. Teresa Nasche is pictured here enjoying a game of croquet in Dallas.

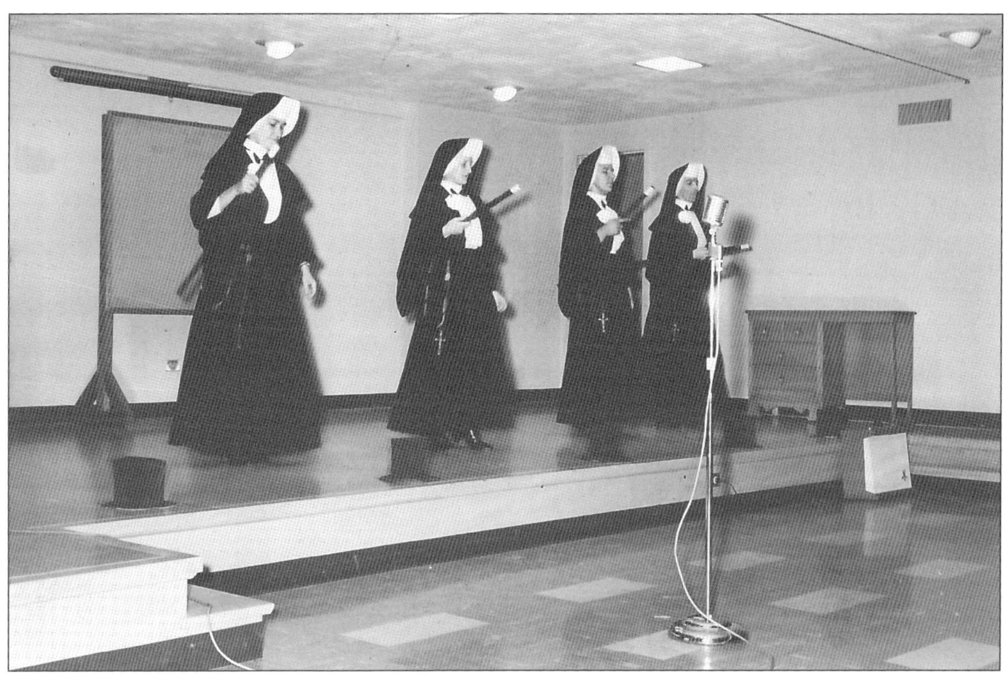

Srs. Leslie, Jarleth, Marguerite Ramirez, and Graciela Gallardo provide summer entertainment at the motherhouse on Yucca Street in San Antonio.

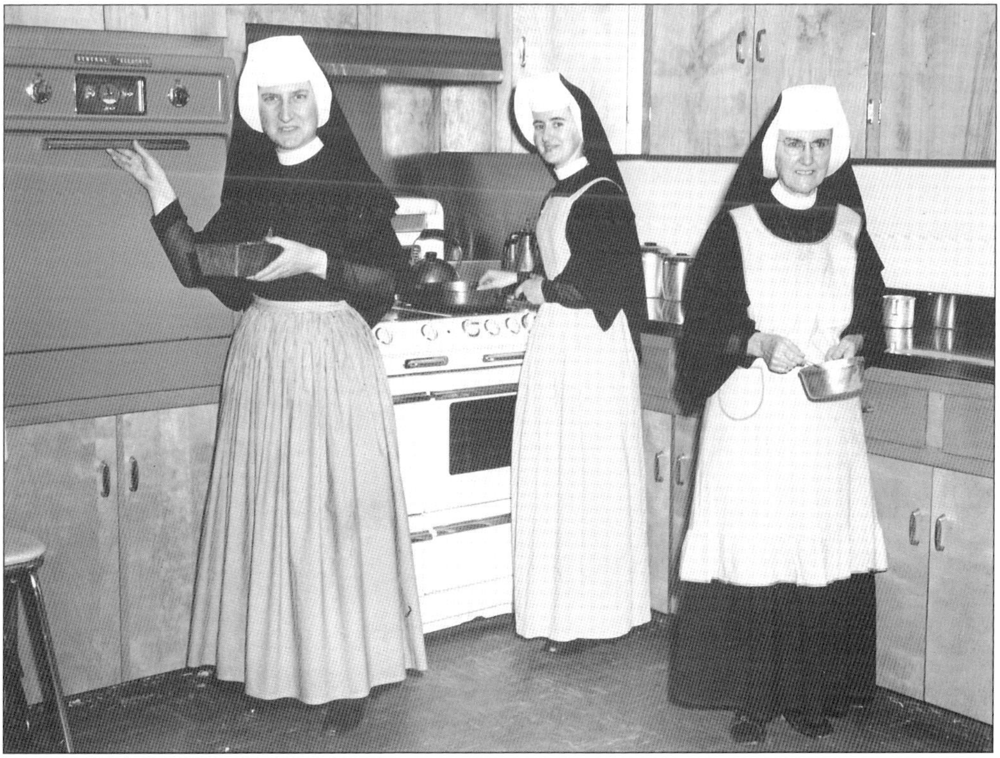

Sr. "Johnny" O'Rourke (right) prepares a meal and instructs Srs. Madeleine (left) and Rosaleen on the art of community cooking.

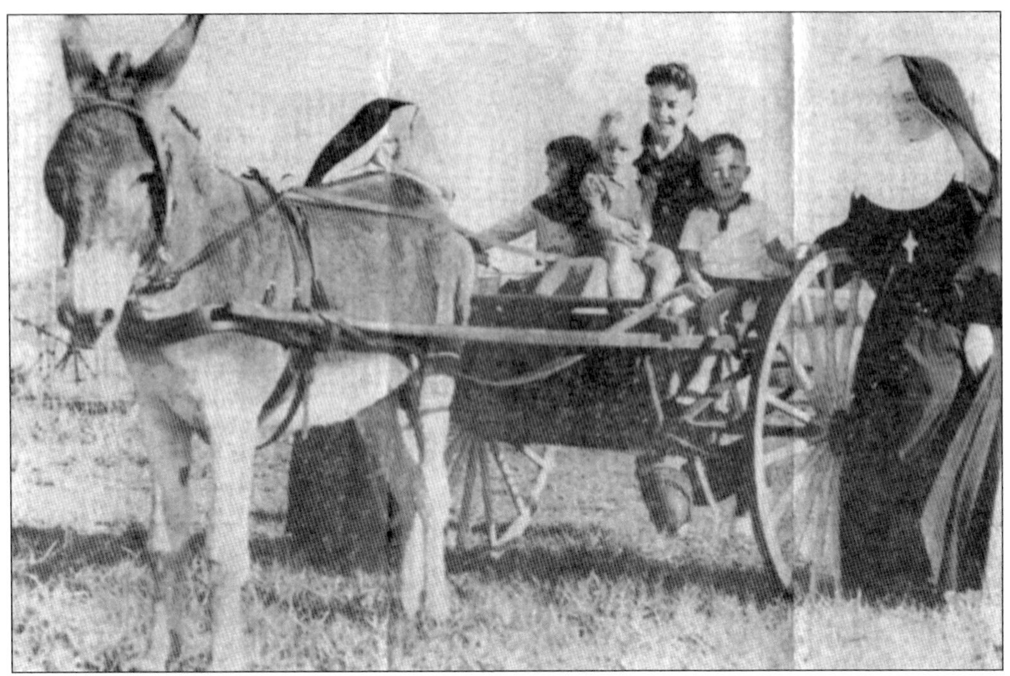

Srs. Sheila O'Sullivan and Eileen Mannion guide a donkey to carry the Blohms—Pamela, Patrice, and Mrs. George Blohm—along with Roy Olsen Jr. to the Holy Ghost Children's Carnival in Bellaire, Texas.

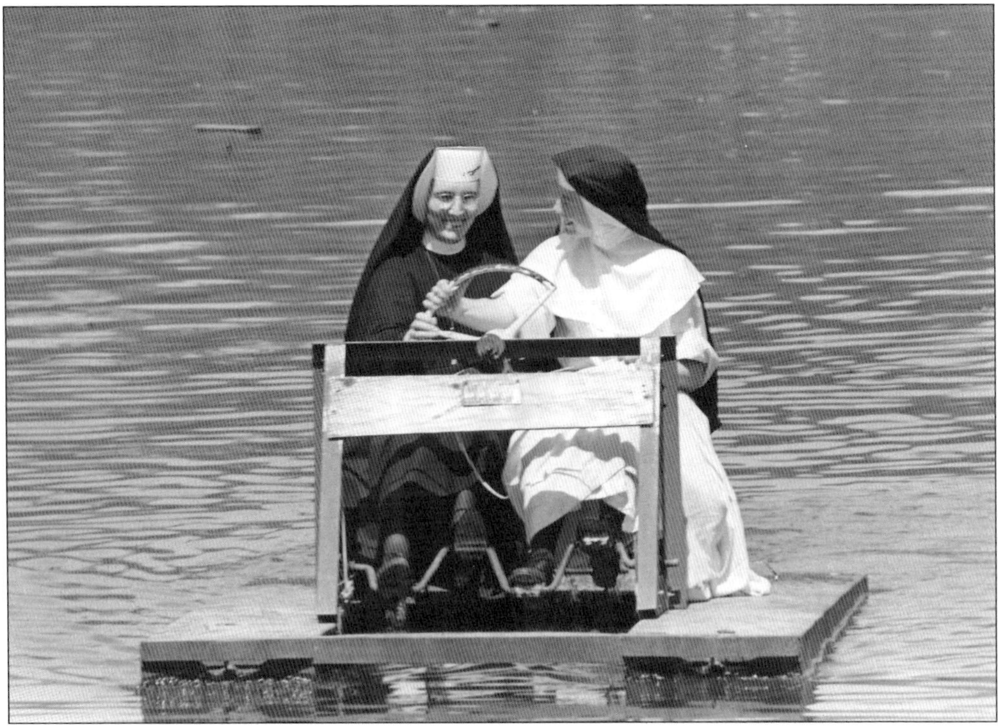

Sr. Laura Melody (left) and a Dominican sister take a leisurely paddleboat ride in 1967 at White Rock Lake near Dallas.

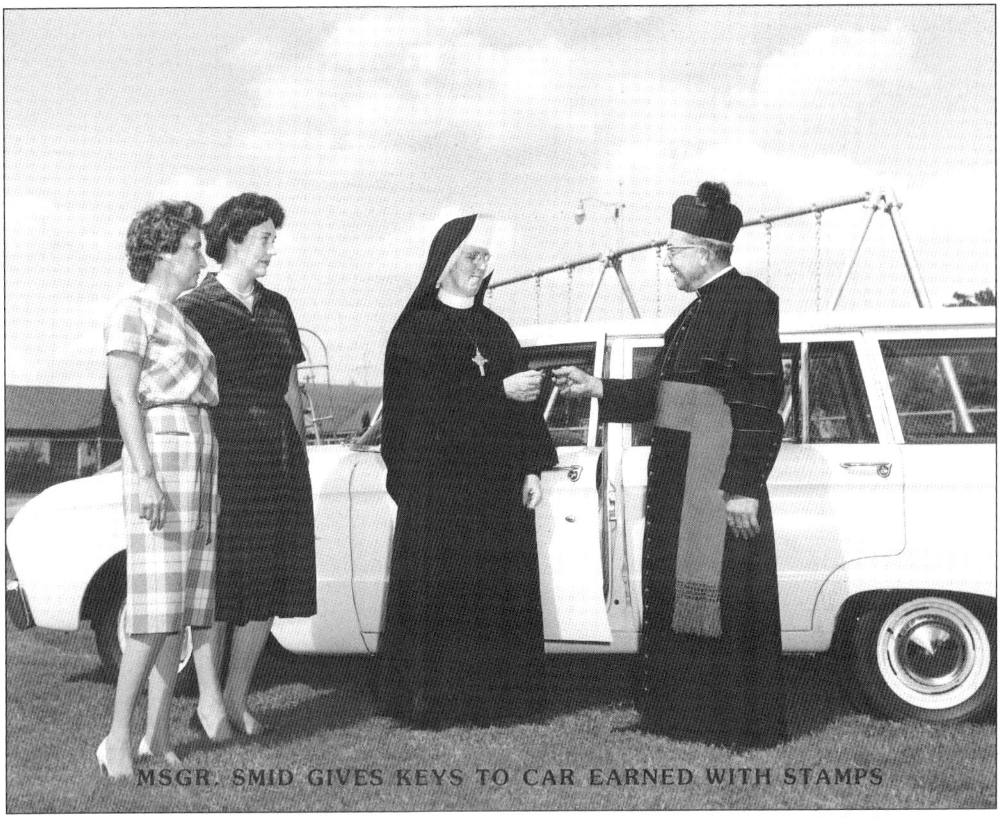

MSGR. SMID GIVES KEYS TO CAR EARNED WITH STAMPS

Monsignor Smid hands over the keys to this station wagon to Sr. Attracta Cahill, the principal at Good Shepherd School in Garland, Texas. The car was earned by collecting stamps.

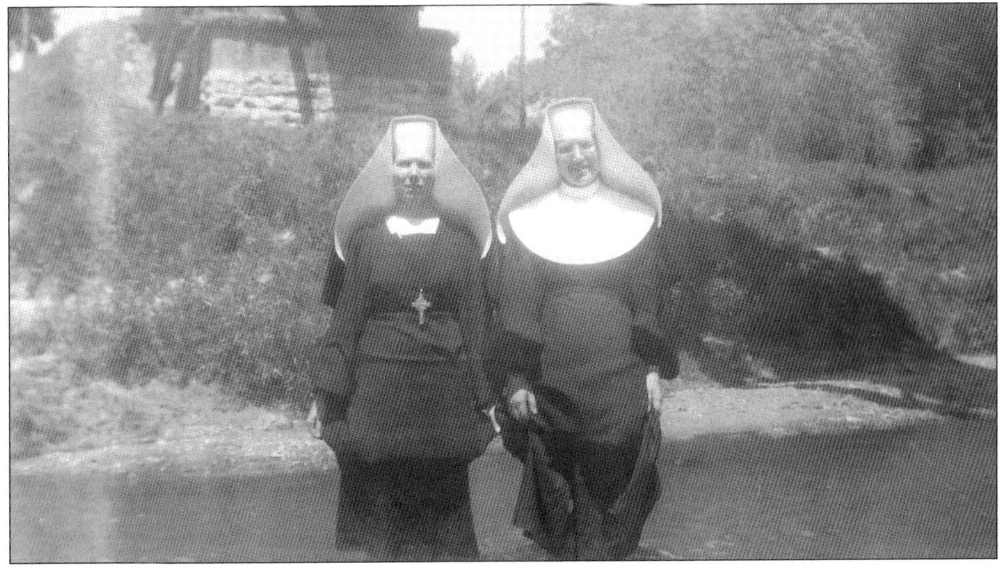

Srs. Regina and Aidan wade in the water at Harris Farm in Natchez, Mississippi.

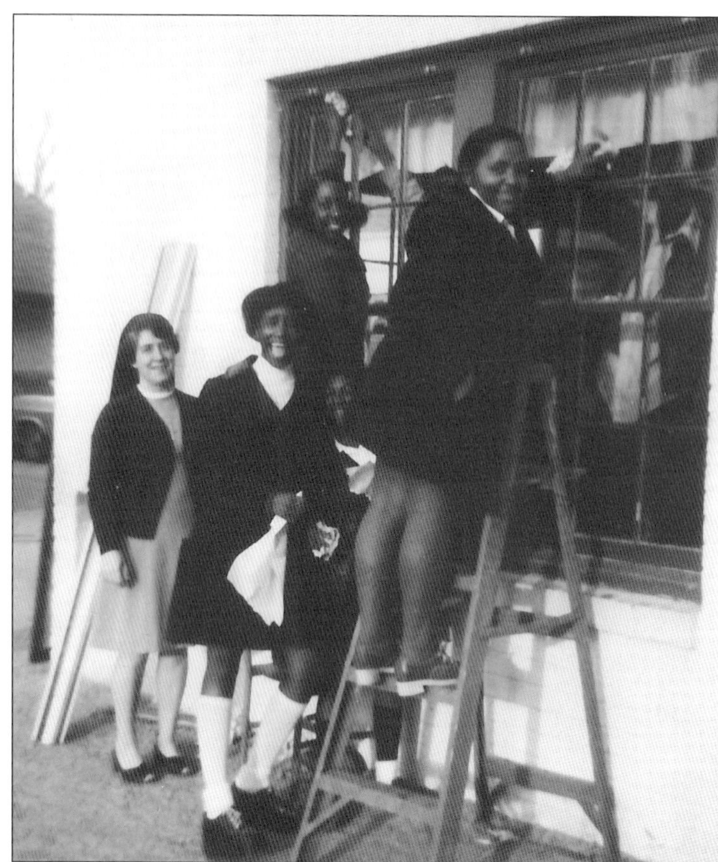

The budget was tight, so Sr. Philomena Connor and her students washed the windows at St. Peter School in Dallas themselves.

Sister Carmen participates in a bicentennial parade in Bellaire, Texas, for Holy Ghost Elementary School in Houston.

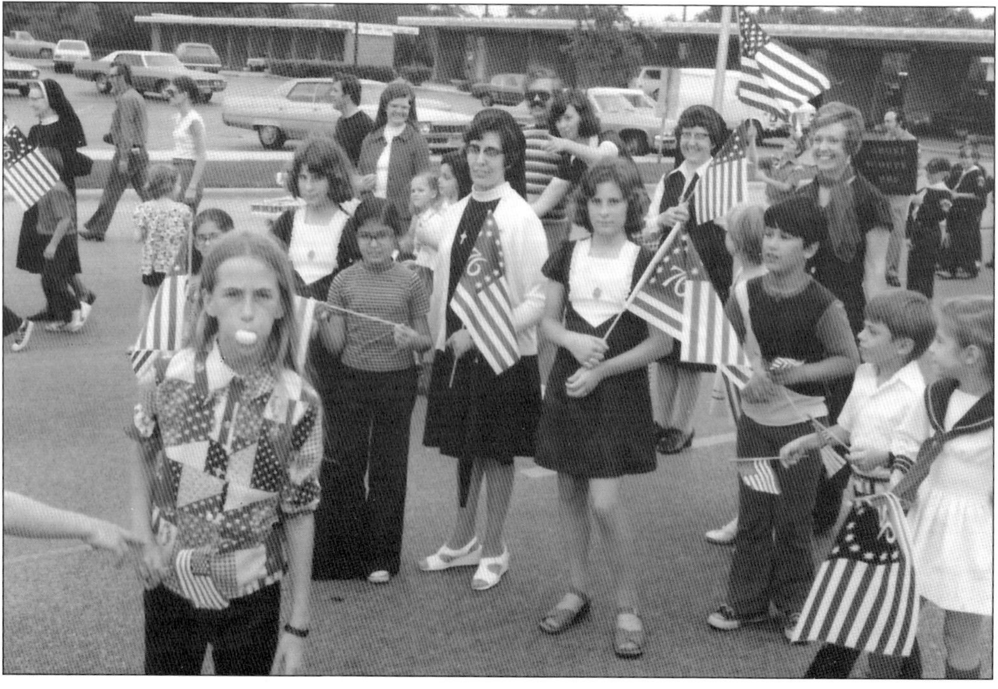

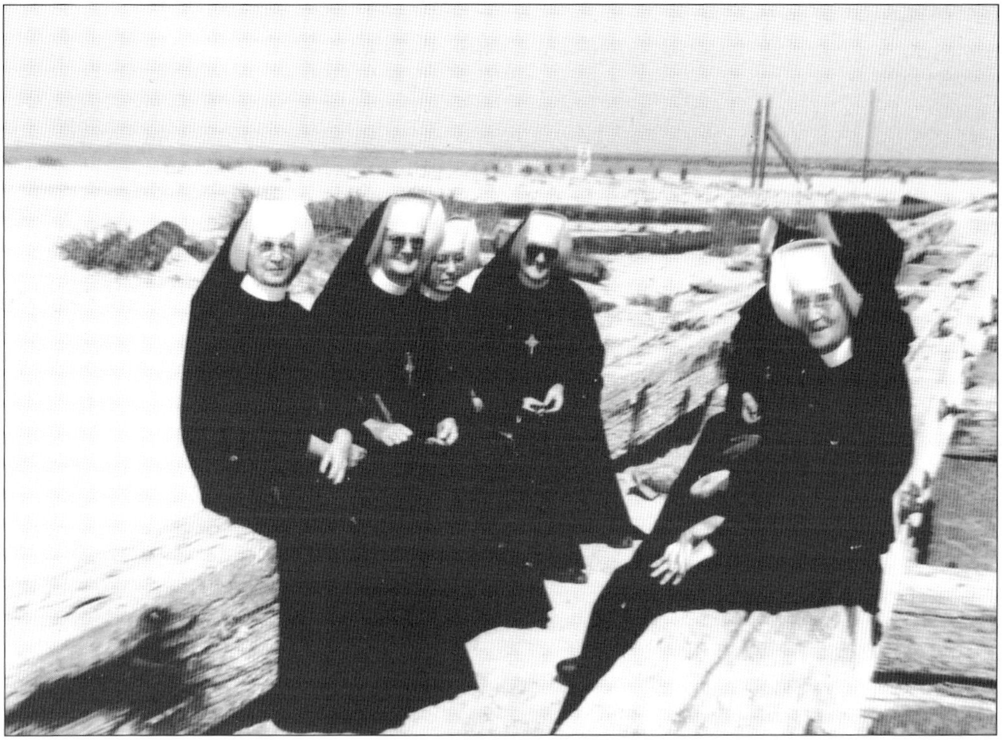

Srs. Ambrose, Immaculata, Columbanus, Camillus, and Aloysisus sit on a jetty at the beach.

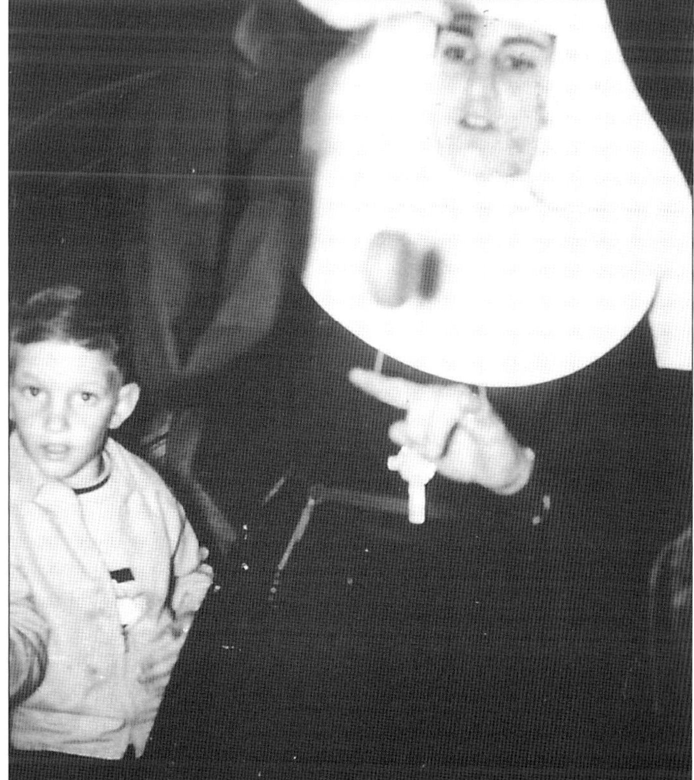

Sr. Teresa Nasche entertains her students with yo-yo tricks on a train trip from Austin to Good Shepherd School in Dallas for a school outing.

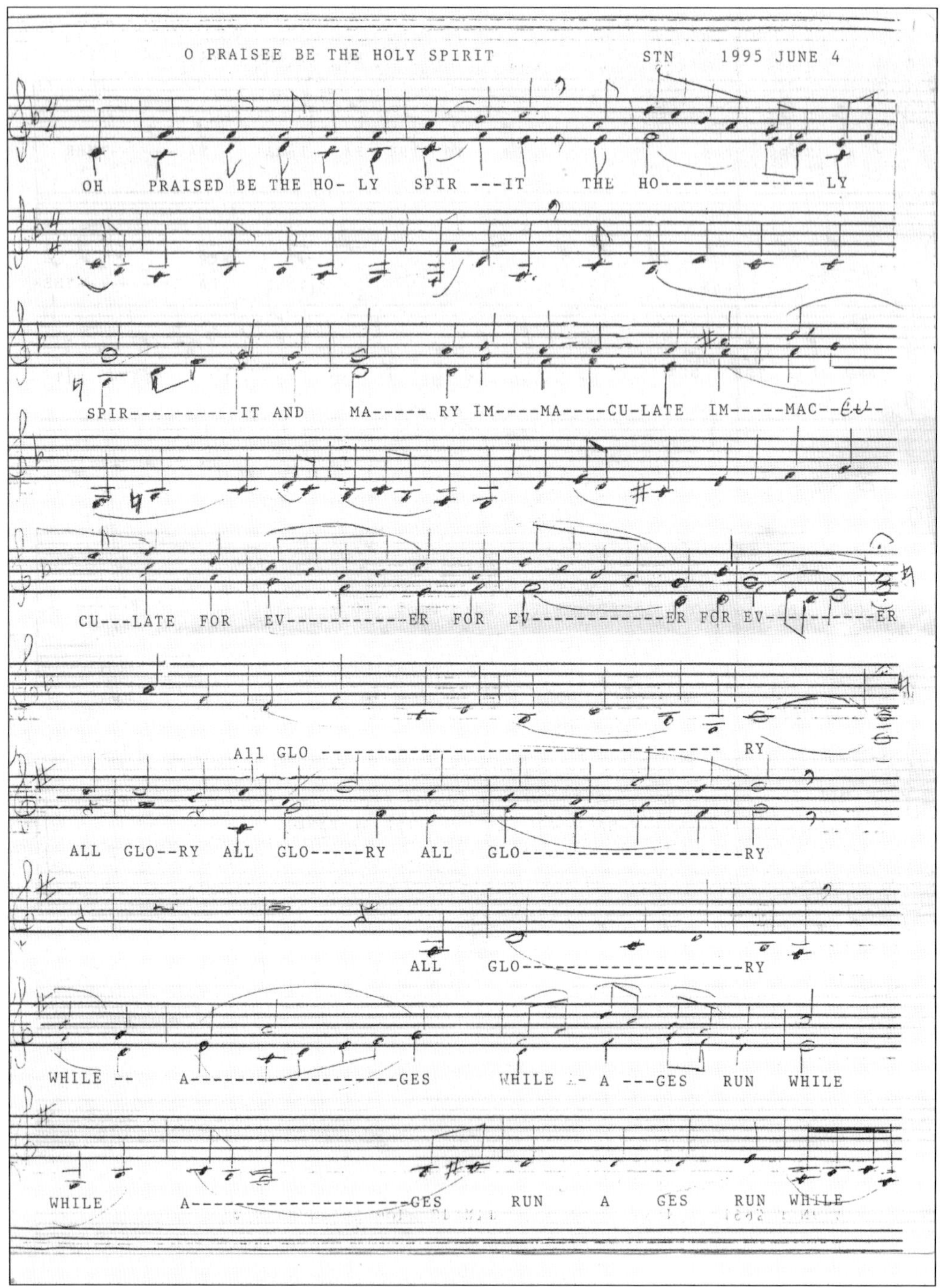

Sr. Teresa Nasche noted that the Sisters of the Holy Spirit celebrated Jubilee without any particular song, so she decided to write "O Praise Be the Holy Spirit," a song in three-part harmony and sung by the sisters for more than 50 years.

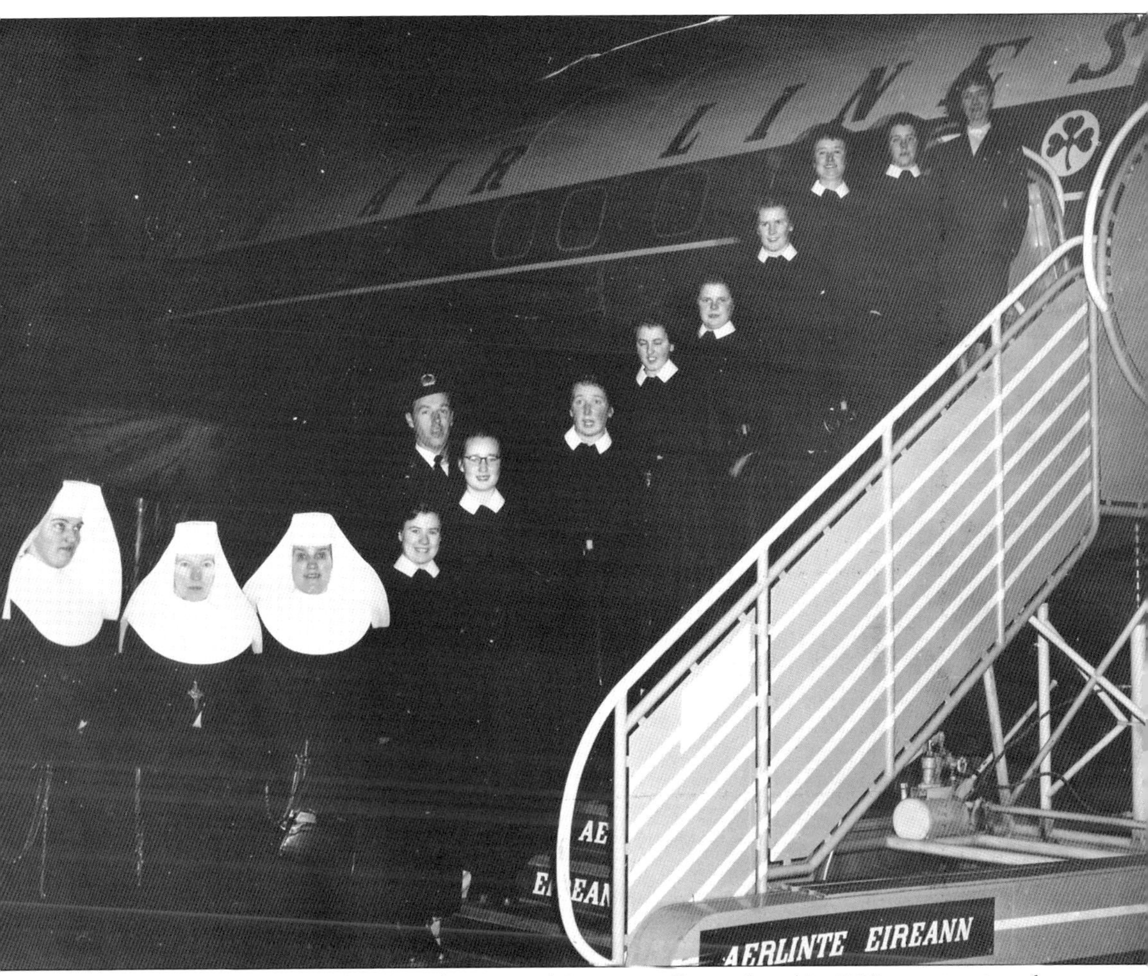

Postulants arrive from Ireland to the United States on December 16, 1958, just in time for Christmas. From left to right are Srs. Eileen Luby, Patrick Hughes, and Augustine McCurtain; and postulants Patsy McKee, Rita O'Sullivan, Anne Reynolds, Peggy Flaherty, Maureen Leonard, Vera Ruane, Brenda Cullen, and Nita Lohan.

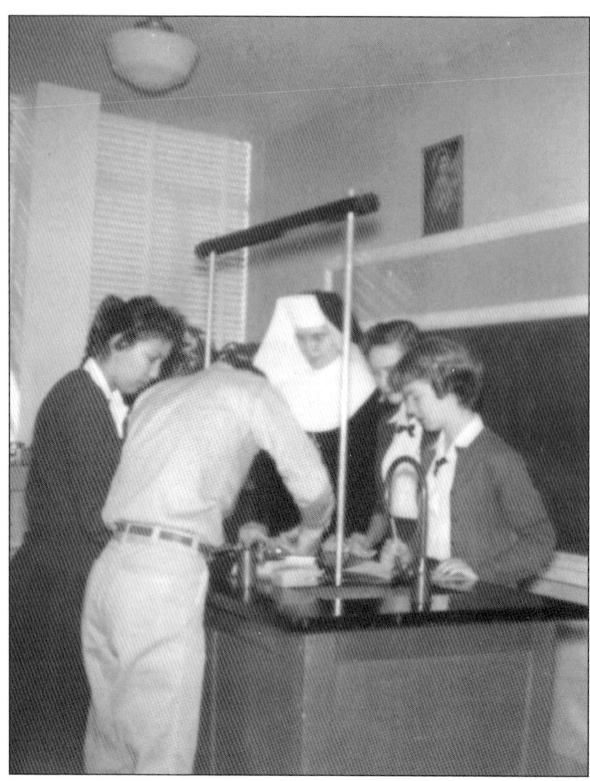

Sister Leocadia overlooks her science students while they dissect a frog in the biology lab at Little Flower School in San Antonio in Jan. 1959.

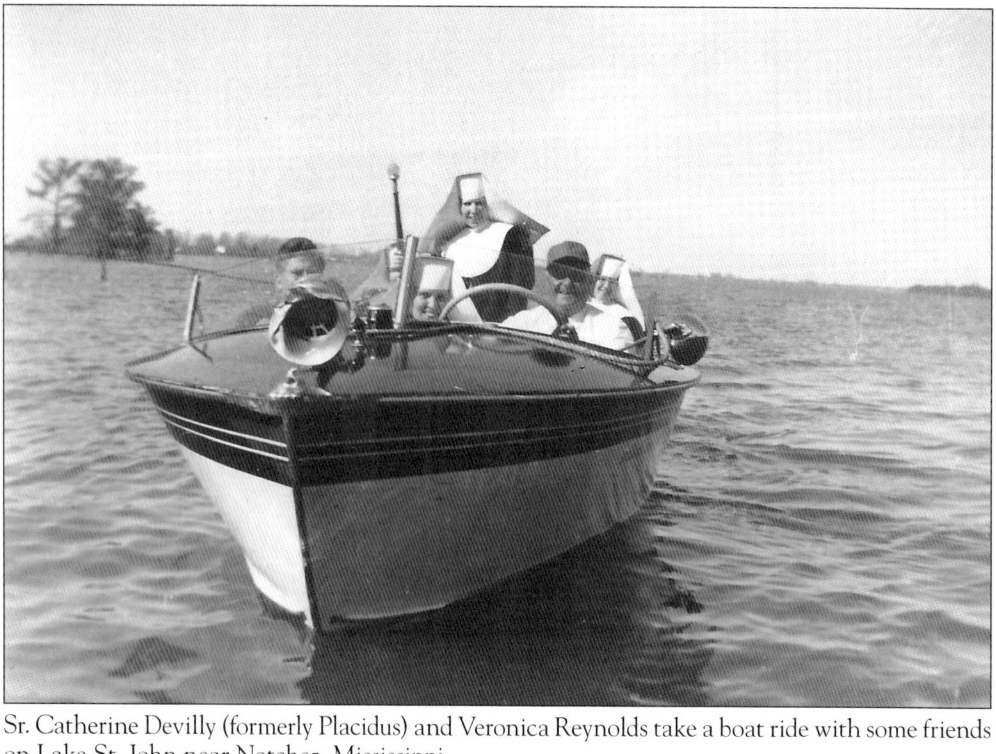

Sr. Catherine Devilly (formerly Placidus) and Veronica Reynolds take a boat ride with some friends on Lake St. John near Natchez, Mississippi.

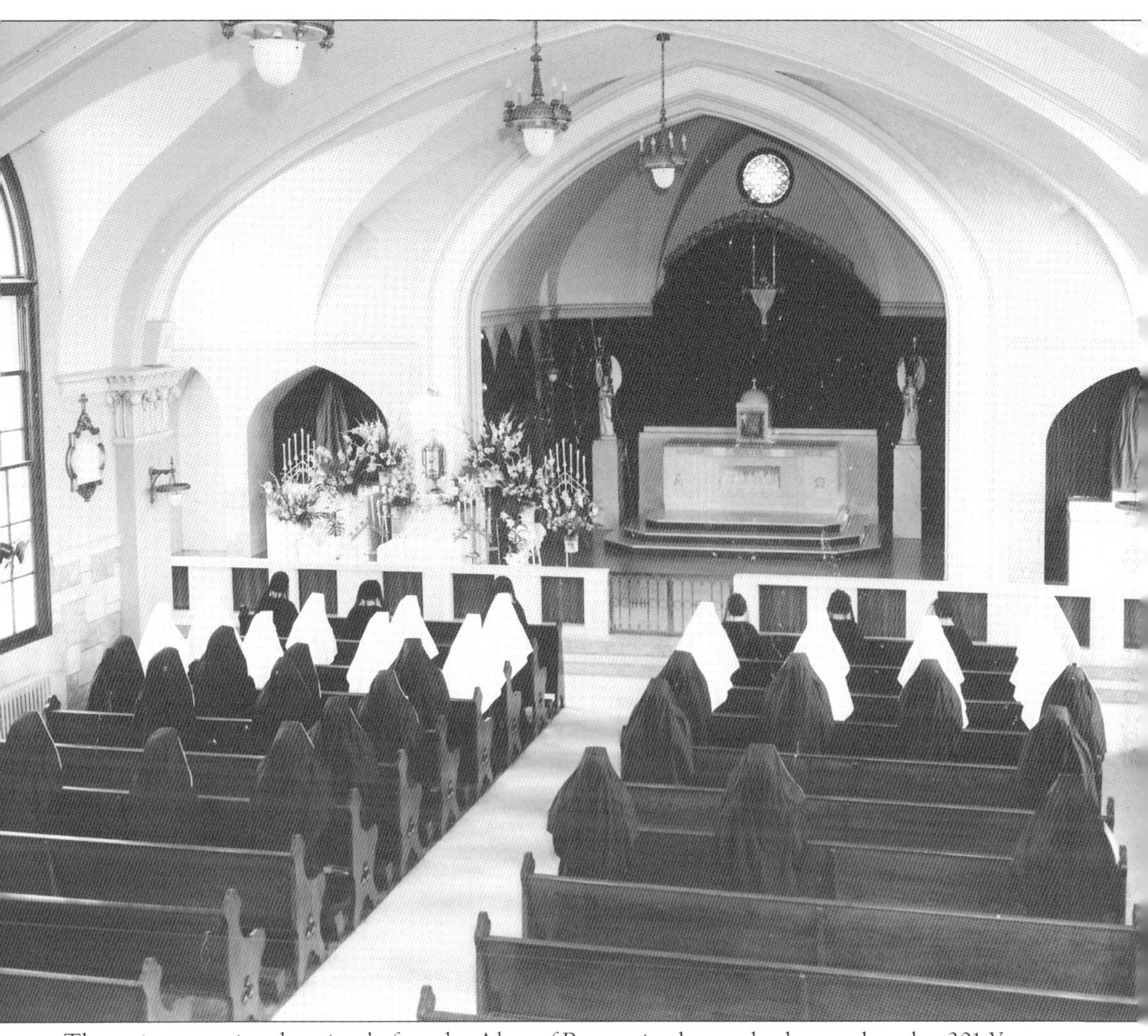

These sisters are in adoration before the Altar of Repose in the motherhouse chapel at 301 Yucca Street on Holy Thursday evening.

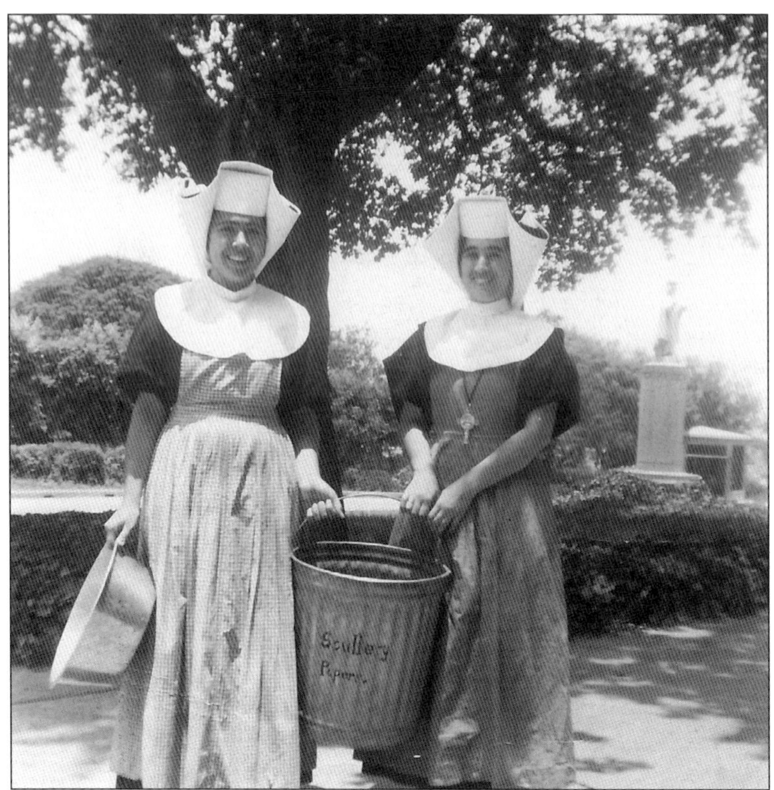

In June 1959, Sr. Irene Arrendondo and Sr. Lucia Marquez had trash duty after meals, so they pinned up their veils and fastened on their aprons to haul the trash. All the sisters in the house had chores to perform every day.

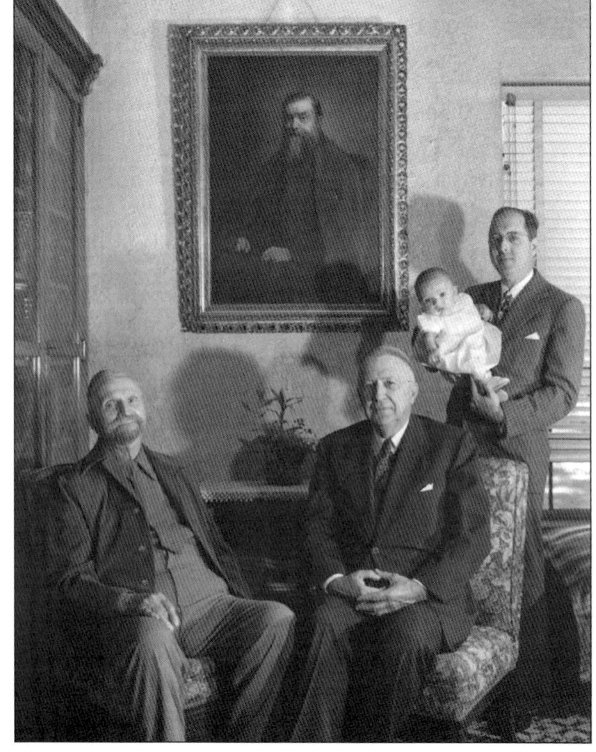

Dr. William M. Wolf Jr. is pictured holding a baby. He was the sisters' physician from 1920 to 1970. Wolf descended from prominent doctors in San Antonio. His father, Dr. William Wolf (seated right), was a physician there. His great-grandfather, Dr. Ferdinand Herff (in the painting) arrived in Texas in 1849 and performed surgeries under shade trees or in the brush, since many places in Texas did not have hospitals.

This photograph taken in 1963, just prior to Vatican II, shows the dress of the different stages of religious life leading up to temporary profession. Mary Ann Utz, an aspirant and a student, spent part of her high school years with the sisters and other young teenagers, studying and discerning. Peggy Kenny, shown in a long black dress, cape, and net veil, was a postulant in the community for a year, also studying and preparing to enter the novitiate. Teresa Imelda Mitchell entered the novitiate on August 14, 1962, and received the white veil of a novice. She became known as Sr. Miriam Mitchell. Sr. Christina Mitchell, a sister to Miriam, made temporary vows on August 15, 1962, and received the black veil as a professed sister.

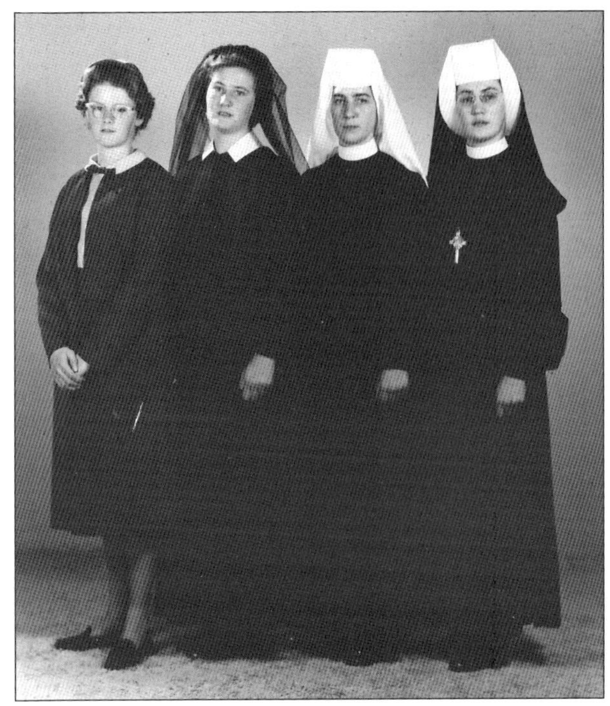

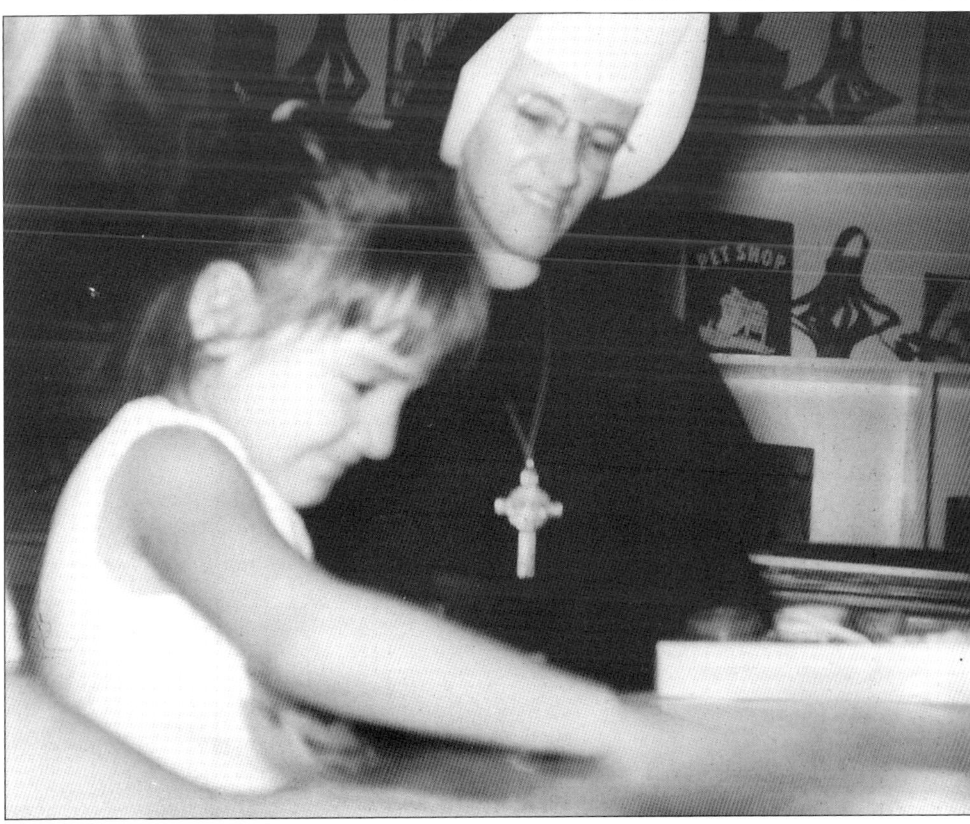

Sr. Marie Leonard looks over a student's project.

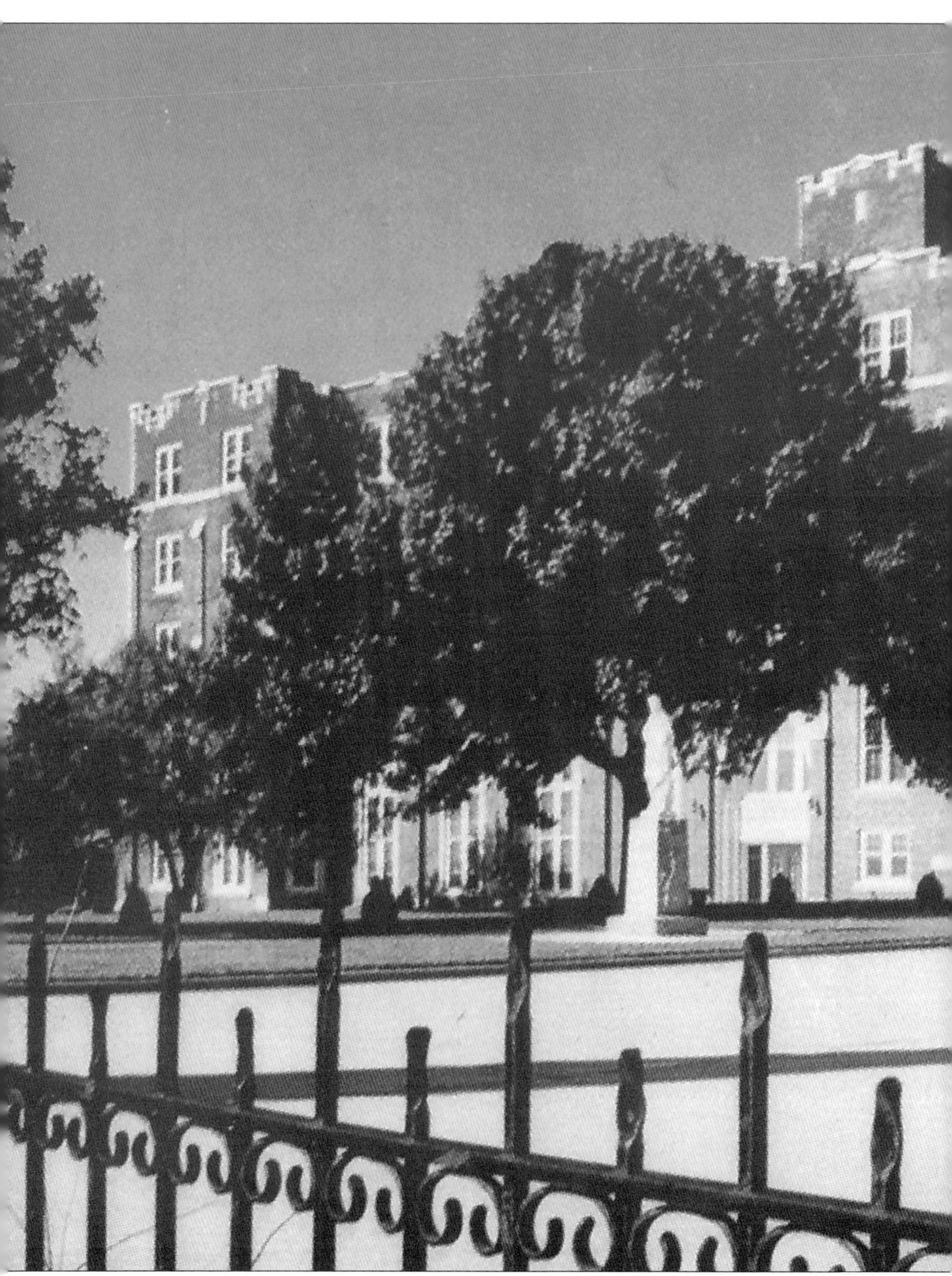

This photograph of the convent at 301 Yucca Street in San Antonio shows all of the additions

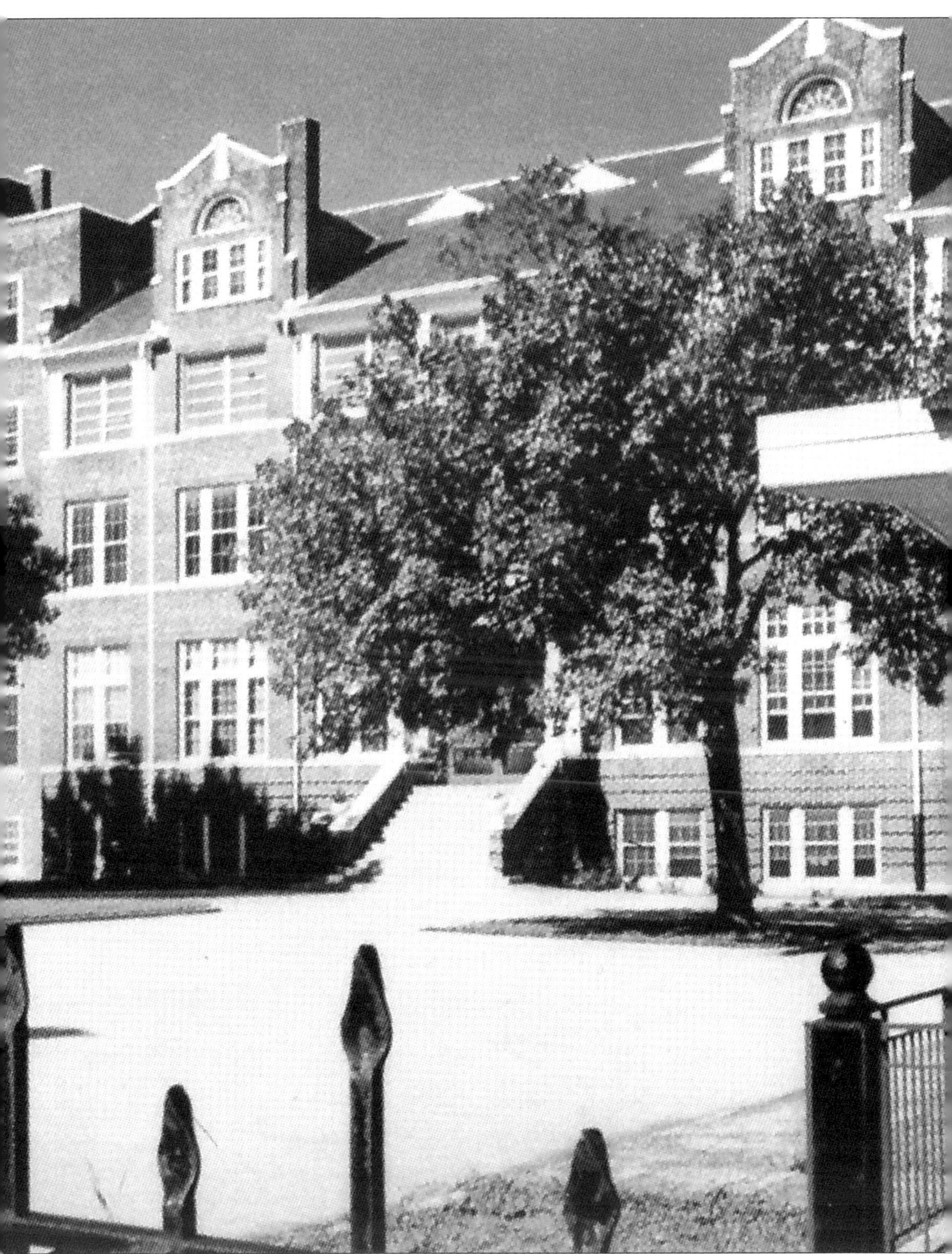

to the original 1922 building.

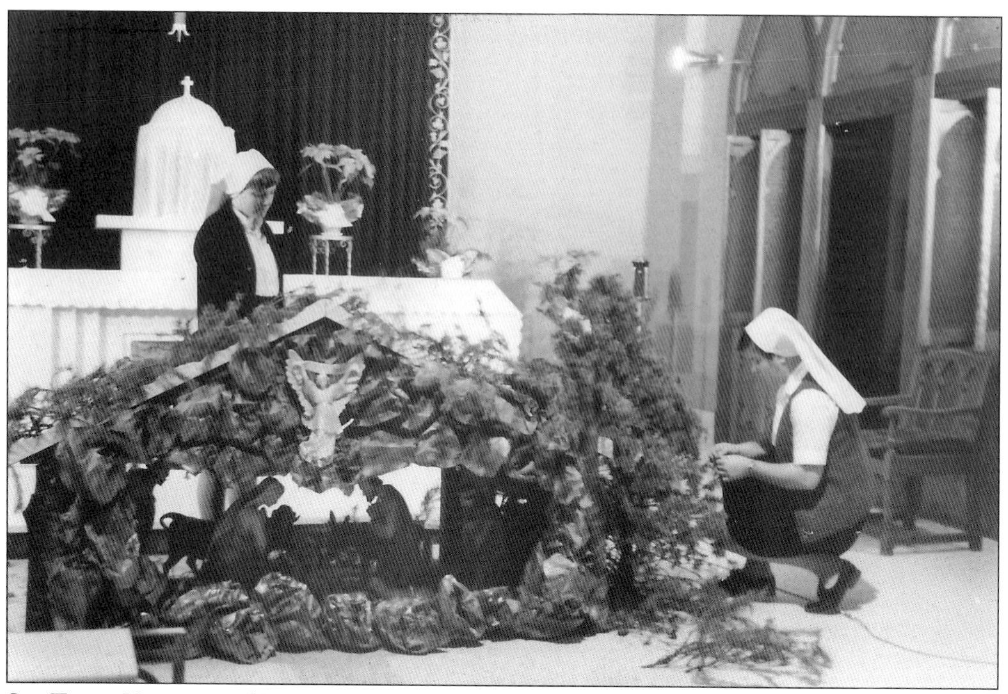

Srs. Teresa Harman and Mary Fagan are decorating the nativity scene at the altar of the chapel in the motherhouse in San Antonio.

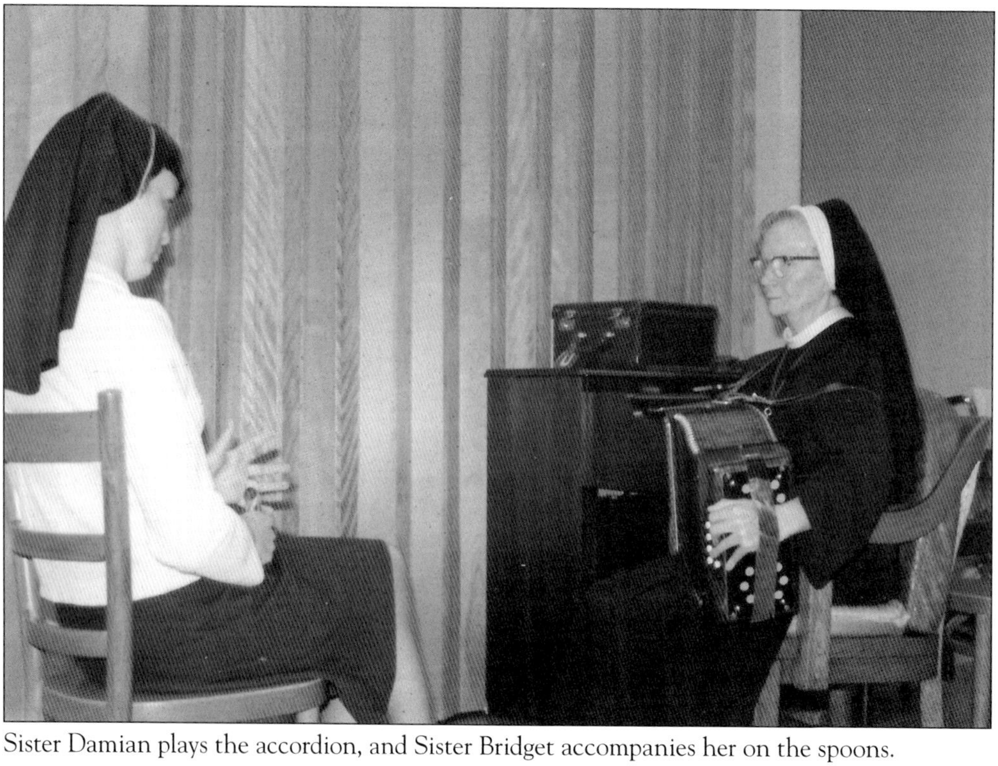

Sister Damian plays the accordion, and Sister Bridget accompanies her on the spoons.

Five

Imprinting a New Continent 1969–1993

By the 1970s, the Sisters of the Holy Spirit and Mary Immaculate experienced a decline in their numbers. They examined their mission, government, and spiritual life. During Sr. Bridget Mary Quinn's tenure (1975–1983), they studied the missions where they worked and left several schools because they did not comply with their mission. The congregation also continued to diversify their ministries into parish work and health care. Since many of the sisters also needed nursing care, the second floor of the convent was remodeled for the growing needs of the community.

Another project underway was rewriting and updating the congregation's constitution. It was finally approved by Rome during Sr. Monica Carroll's administration (1983–1991). Sister Monica moved the Community Cemetery to its present Yucca Street location, next to the motherhouse. She also donated land next to the convent to be used for Habitat for Humanity housing. Her tenure, coupled with Sr. Anne Finnerty's (1991–1999) tenure, drew the sisters to reassess their mission and expand it to deal with emerging social justice issues. To broaden their geographic reach, they added missions in Mexico and flew to another continent when they established a mission in Zambia.

This tumultuous time in the congregation found the sisters harking back to their original mission, even though it was out of the United States. The celebration for their 100 years of service in 1993 was a memorable event. The congregation celebrated in both the United States and Ireland. In Ireland, both in Galway and Cahirciveen, ceremonial plaques were placed, one in the back of Daniel O'Connell Church and the other outside St. Philip's Convent.

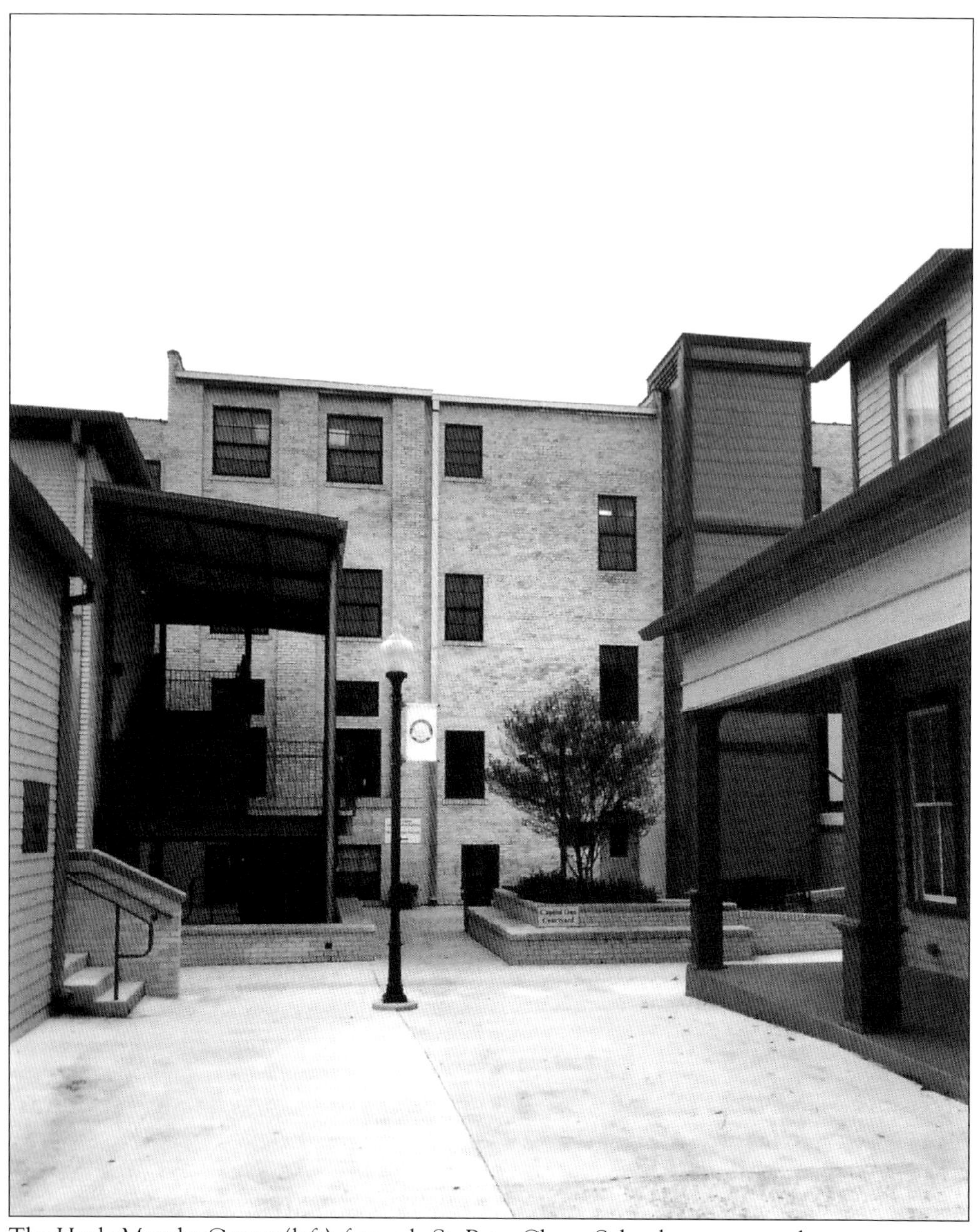

The Healy-Murphy Center (left), formerly St. Peter Claver School, now serves the community as an alternative high school. The school was incorporated in 1969 by Sister Boniface and operated by a board of directors and chartered by the State of Texas. It is also a member of the Southern Association of Colleges and Secondary Schools.

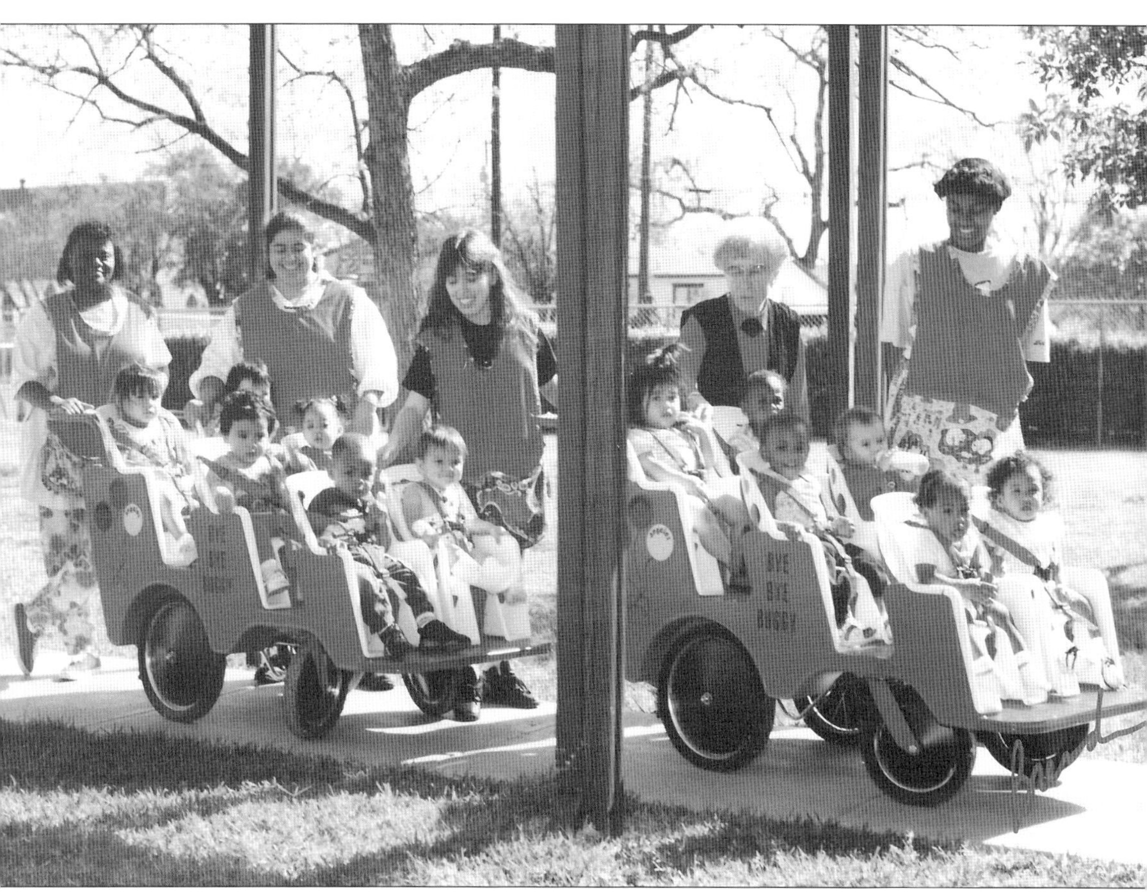

Sister Boniface pushes children in a buggy used by the Healy-Murphy Day Care Center. The center, located across from Healy-Murphy High School, caters to children through kindergarten. The facility provides a health clinic and holds child development classes, as well as infant care. Several sisters teach at the school, and retired sisters volunteer to care for the babies.

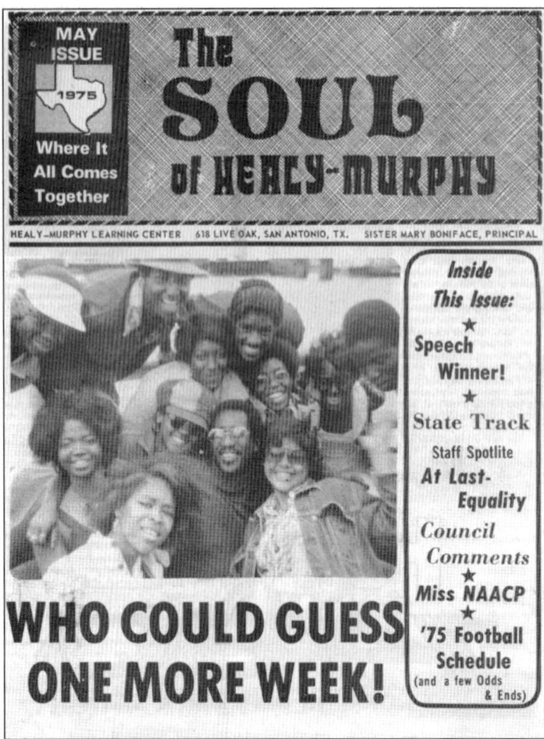

MAY ISSUE 1975

Where It All Comes Together

The SOUL of HEALY-MURPHY

HEALY-MURPHY LEARNING CENTER 618 LIVE OAK, SAN ANTONIO, TX. SISTER MARY BONIFACE, PRINCIPAL

Inside This Issue:

★ Speech Winner!

★ State Track

Staff Spotlite

At Last- Equality

Council Comments

★ Miss NAACP

★ '75 Football Schedule

(and a few Odds & Ends)

WHO COULD GUESS ONE MORE WEEK!

When St. Peter Claver School repurposed itself as an alternative high school, the students produced this paper under the guidance of Sister Boniface. This cover highlights the different activities the students participated in at the Healy-Murphy Center.

Srs. John Berchmans, Brendan, Imelda, Agatha, Frances, Hughes, Bernard, and Alphonsus pose with the Carmelite Fathers of Little Flower in San Antonio. The group was celebrating the feast of Little Flower.

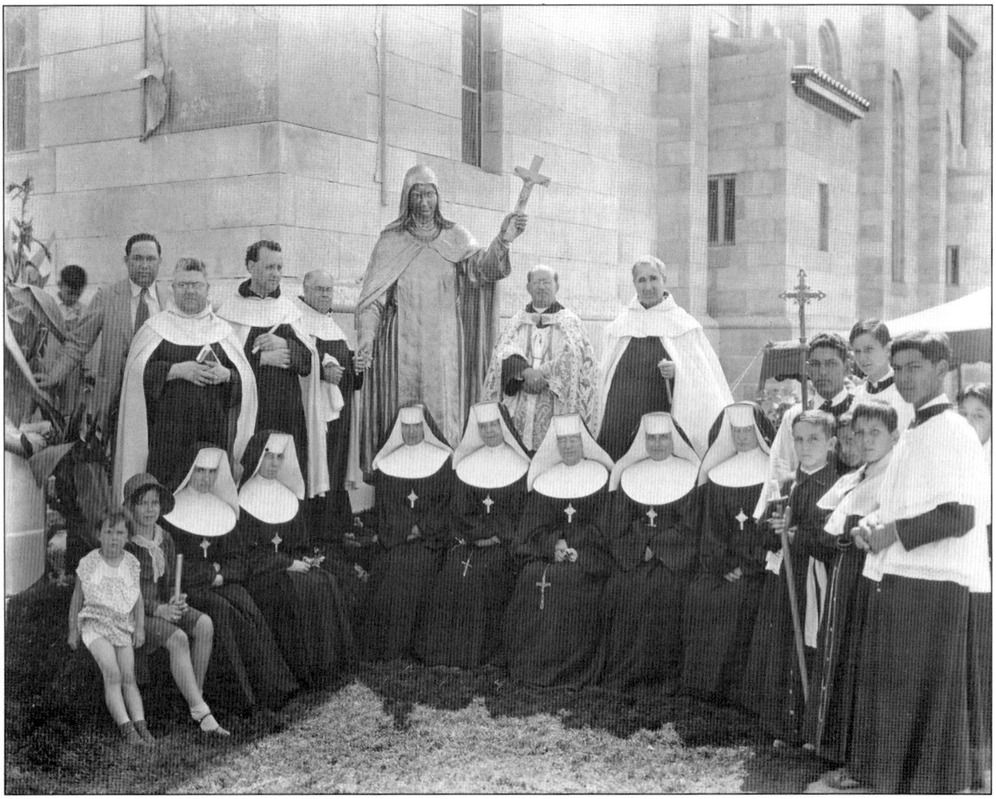

During the summer, Srs. Kathleen O'Connell, Betty Higgins, and Ellen Dempsey ministered in Oaxaca, Mexico, with Sr. Magdalen Kilbane. The sisters toured Casa de Cuna to see the oil painting *Las Irlandesas* by Sister Cecilia, which depicted four sisters: one reading a letter and another holding a baby, while the other two overlook the document. The painting portrays an incident when a woman sent a letter to the sisters asking them to care for her infant.

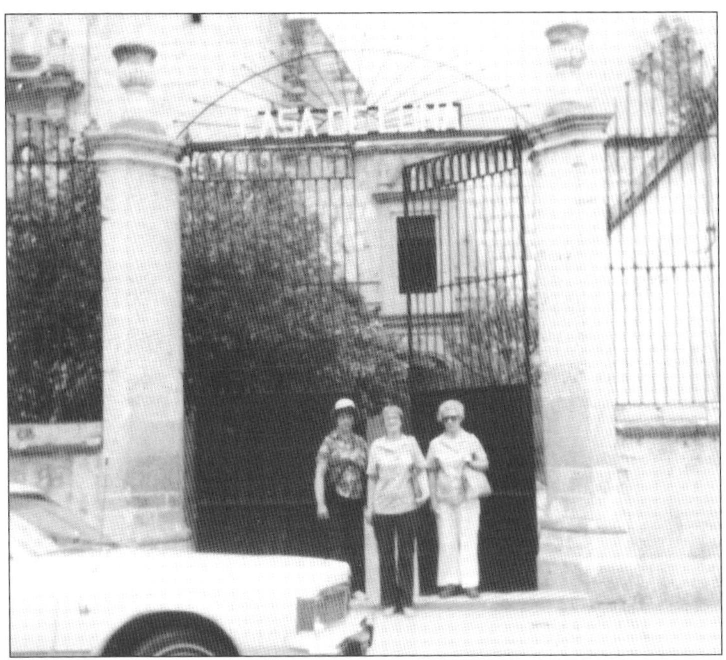

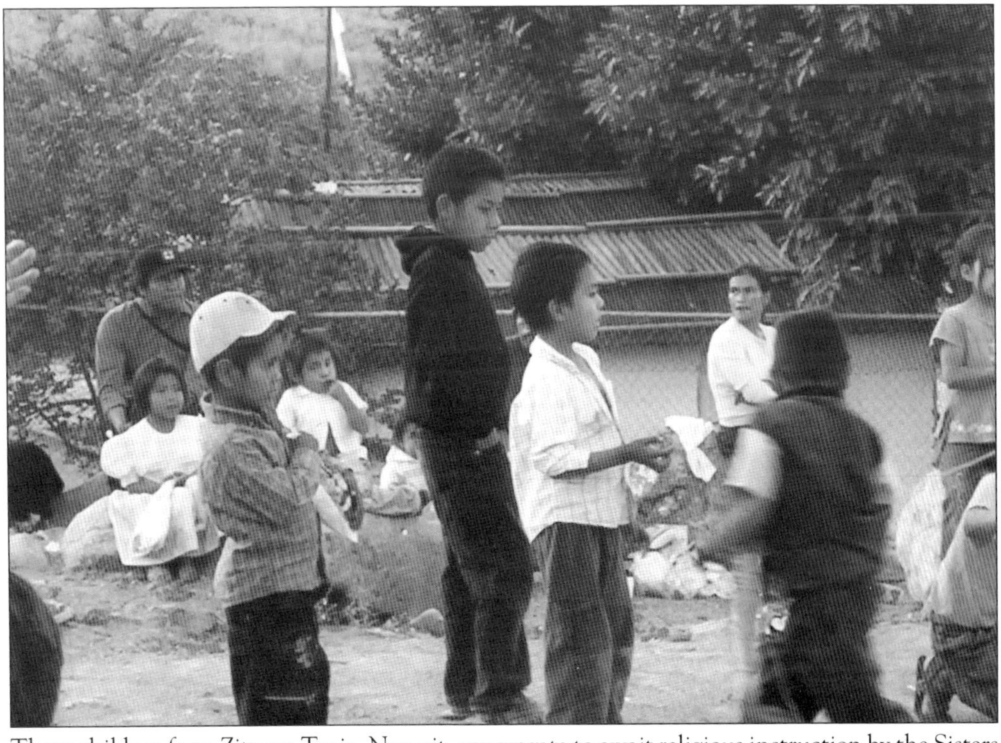

These children from Zitaqua Tepic, Nayarit, congregate to await religious instruction by the Sisters of the Holy Spirit and Mary Immaculate. The sisters taught the Huichol indigenous community in Mexico for several years.

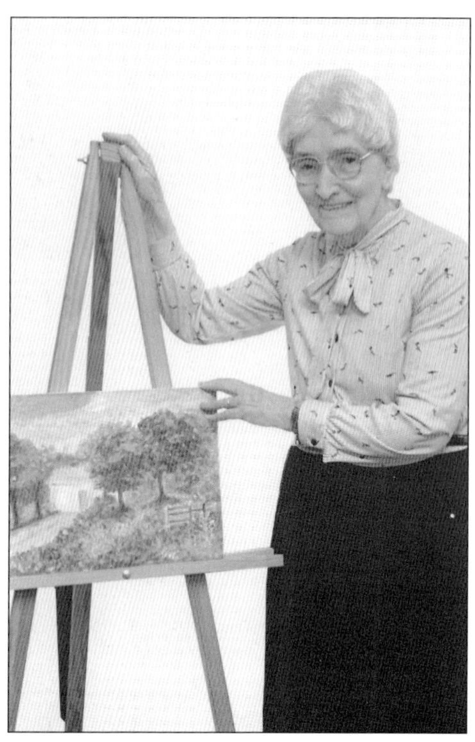

Sr. Laura Melody poses with one of her paintings. Sister Laura had a talent for painting outdoor scenes of the Texas landscape. Her artwork decorates the walls of the Sisters of the Holy Spirit convent.

From left to right, Srs. Regina, Magdalen, Emmanuel, and Isabel pose with a snowman they built in 1975 at Notre Dame School in Shreveport, Louisiana.

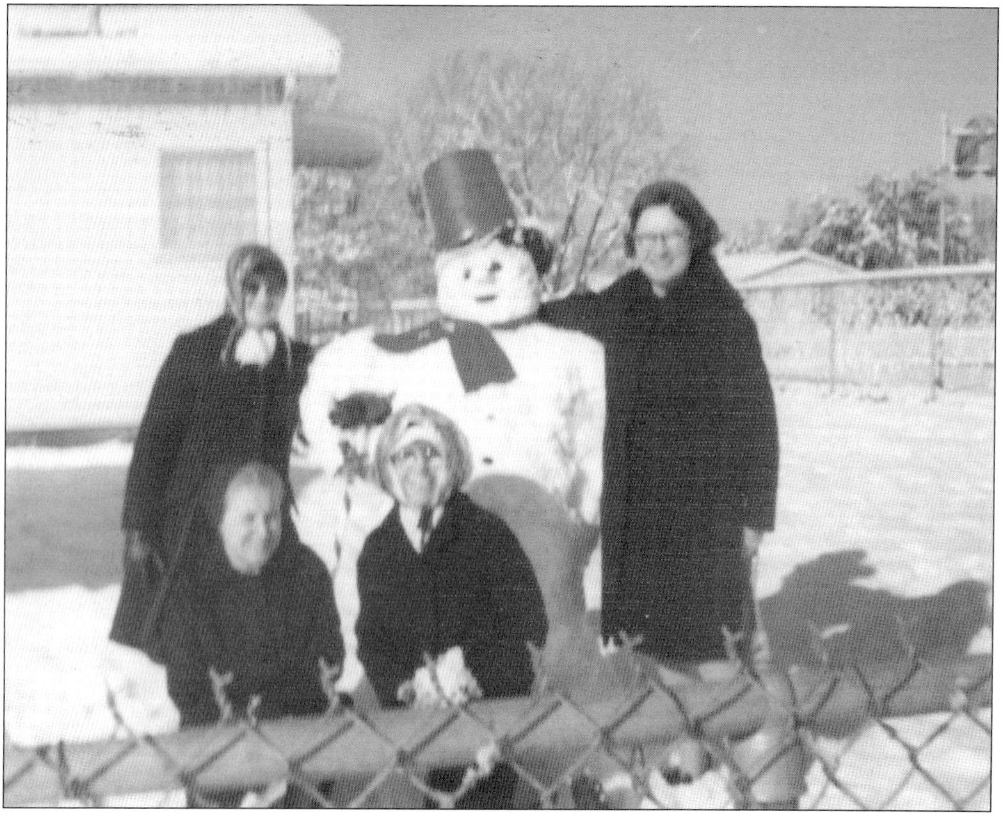

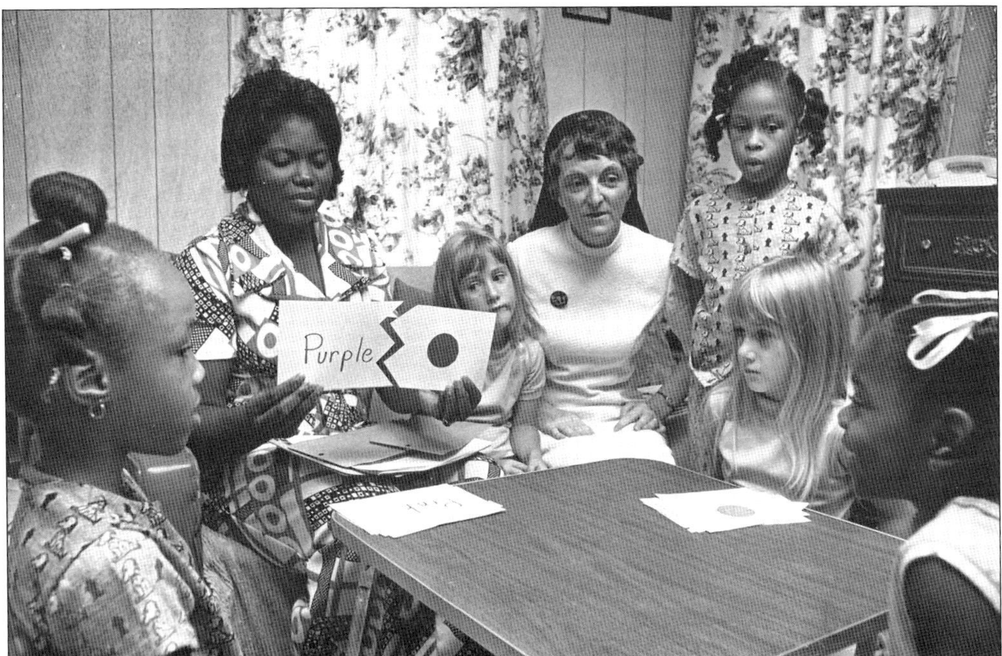

In 1972, Sr. Rosario O'Connell began social work at St. Lucy Day Care Center in Houma, Louisiana. She soon realized that some of the children required more help than the day care could provide, so the sisters converted the bottom floor of their home into a licensed child care center for abused children. The facility expanded and annexed another home. By 1988, another home was acquired to accommodate the growing number of children.

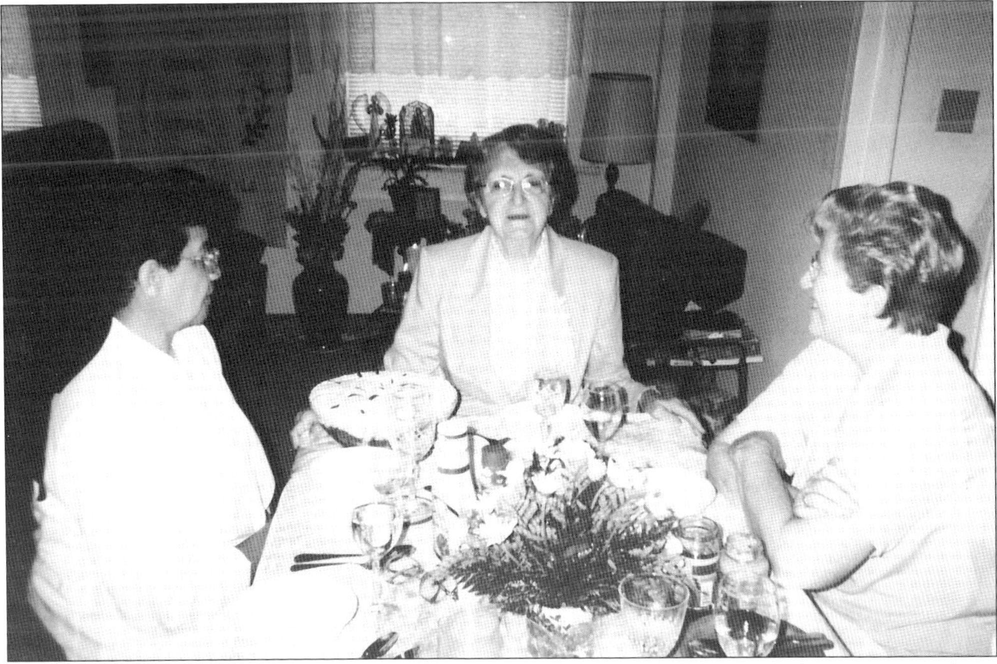

Sr. Rosario O'Connell (center) worked at the Louis Infant Center for more than 47 years. She is pictured here awaiting a delicious meal for Srs. Martha and Carmelita.

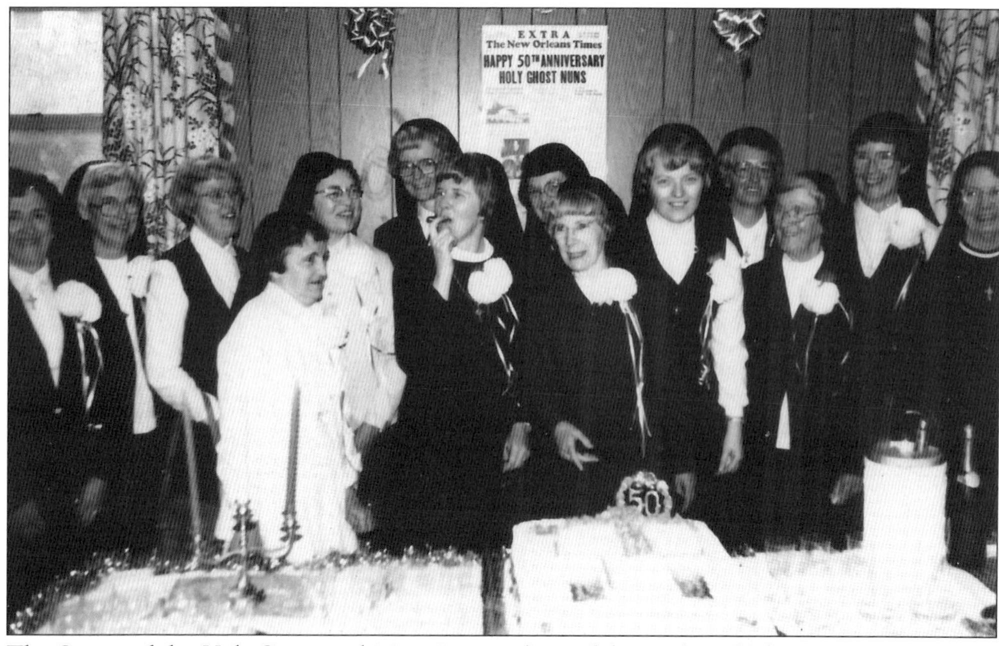

The Sisters of the Holy Spirit and Mary Immaculate celebrate their 50th anniversary at Holy Redeemer Parish in New Orleans, Louisiana (1932–1982). Pictured are Srs. Fidelma Healy, Bernadette McNamara, Rose McHugh, Rosario O'Connell, Isabel Rush, Lucy Collins, Carmelita Mulry, Rita Mannion, Bridget Mary Quinn, Veronica Cahill, Kay Jo Evelo, Philomena Daly, Theresa O'Toole, and Hilda Mangan.

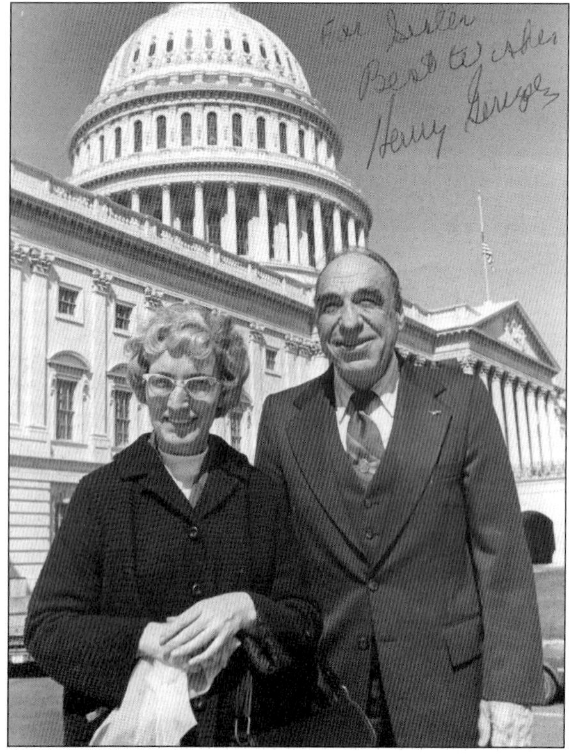

Sr. Laura Melody and Texas representative Henry B. Gonzalez attend a conference in Washington, DC.

Sr. Jo Murray stands beside a baobab tree in Ghana. The tree is an iconic symbol of the African Sahara and has a smooth shiny bark, which makes it difficult for animals to climb up and feast on its leaves. Sister Jo lived in Ghana for three years, serving as a nurse in the local community.

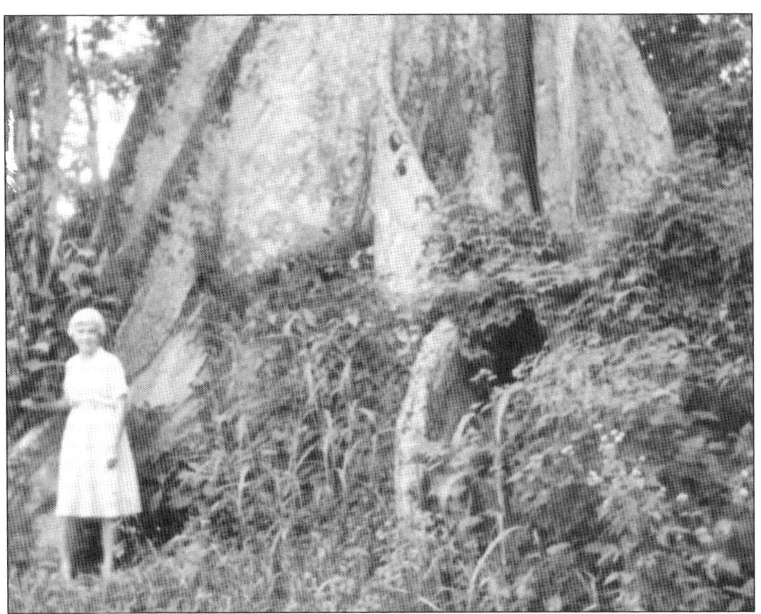

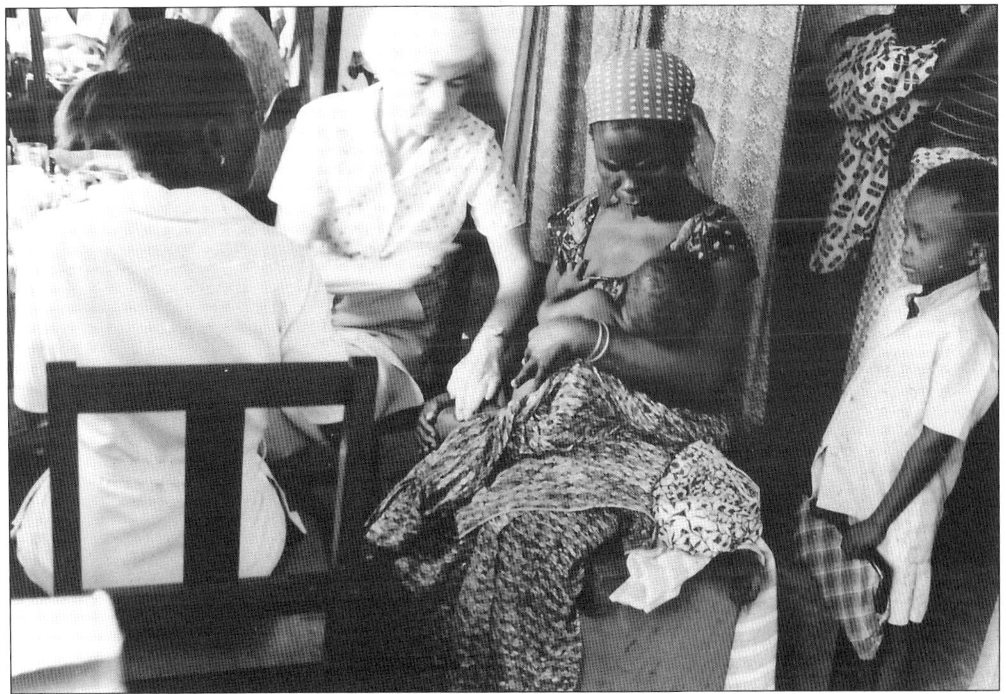

In 1981, the Sisters of Notre Dame asked Sister Jo Murray to fill in for their Sister Bernice, SSND, who had to leave. Sister Jo agreed to fill in and remained until Sister Bernice returned. The three years Sister Murray worked there proved to be enriching for her. She loved learning about the Ghanaians' rich culture and customs, but acclimating to the climate was a challenge.

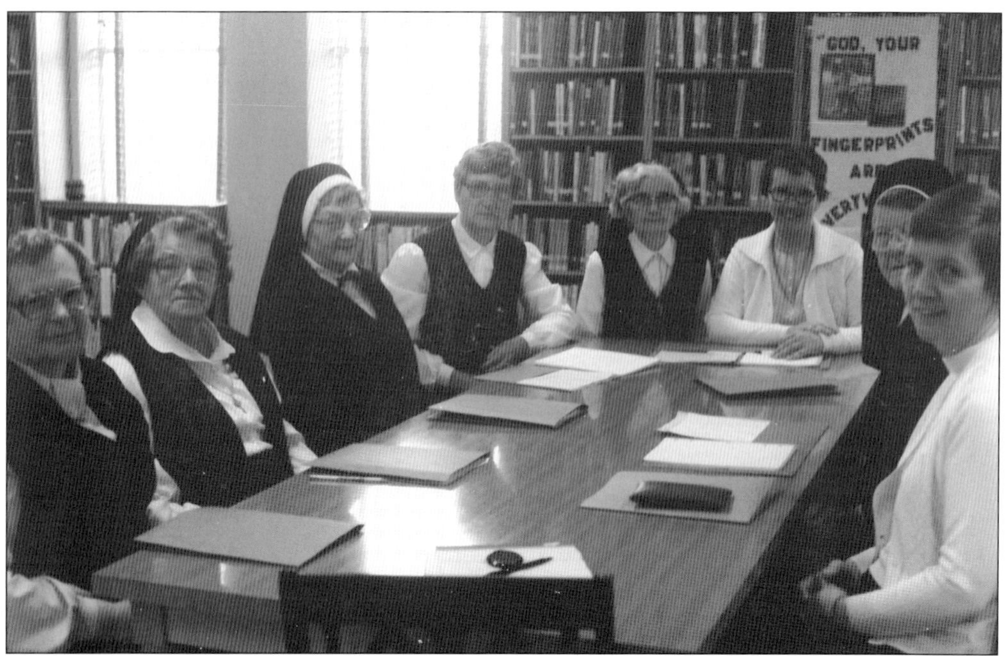

The general assembly meets in the library for a discussion group. Pictured from left to right are Srs. Josephine Burkimsher, Mary Kieran Donlon, Concepta Clarken, Madeleine Cannon, Ferdinand Connerney, Kathleen Lynch, Andrew O'Connor, and Anne Finnerty.

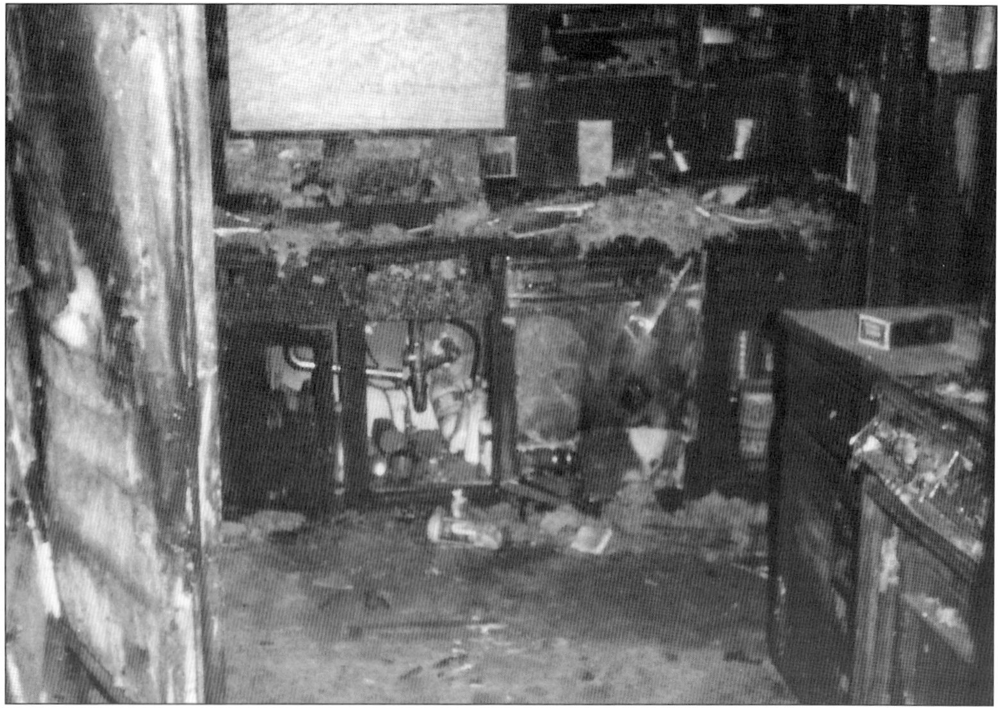

On January 21, 1985, at St. Mary of Carmel Convent in Dallas, a fire destroyed the convent kitchen. The sisters were displaced for eight months before they could get back to some semblance of home.

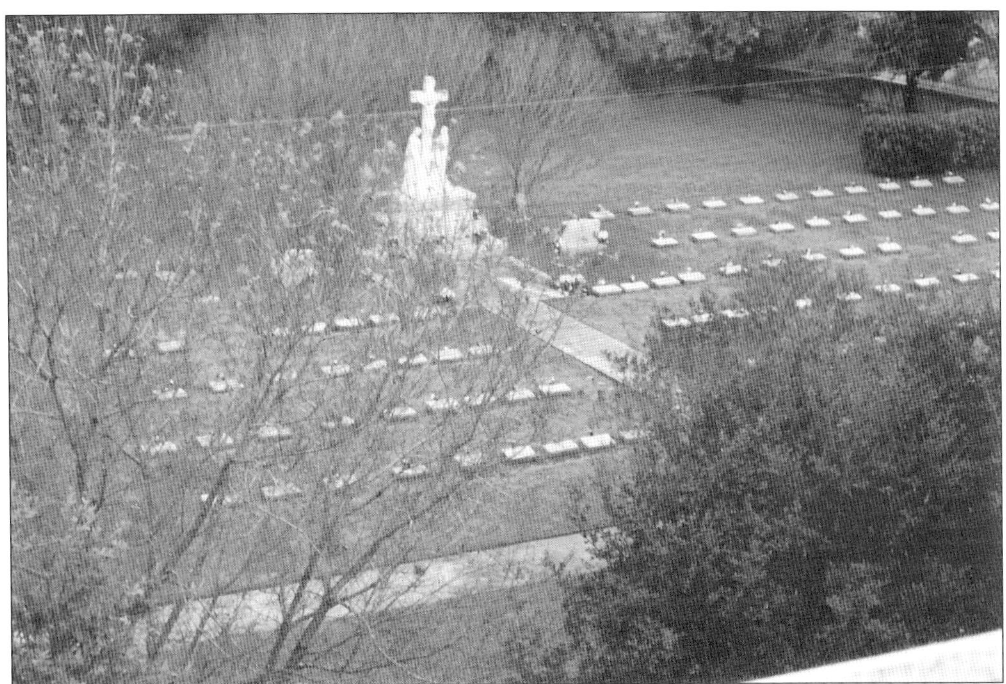

This is the cemetery for the Sisters of the Holy Spirit and Mary Immaculate, located next to the 1922 convent located at 301 Yucca Street in San Antonio. This photograph was taken by Sr. Eugenius Gallagher from a window in the convent that overlooked the cemetery.

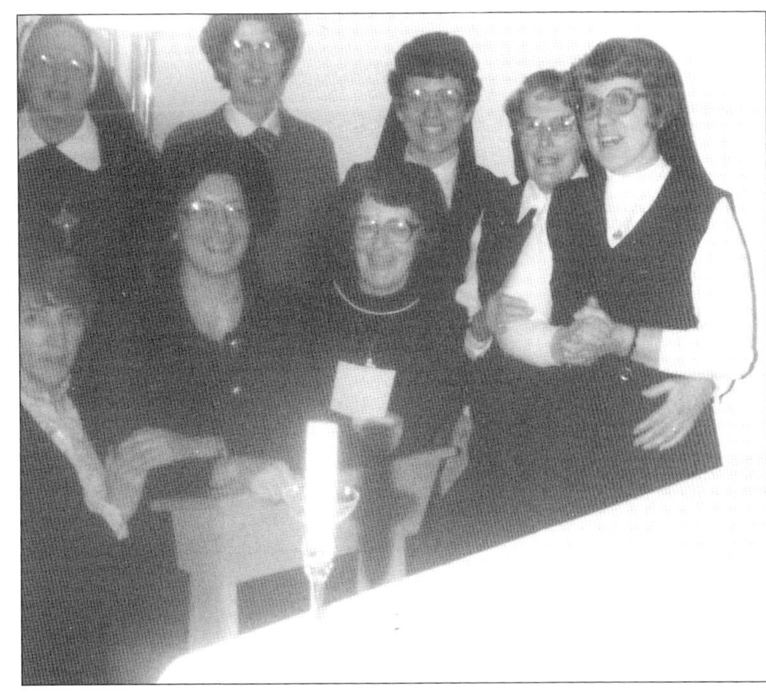

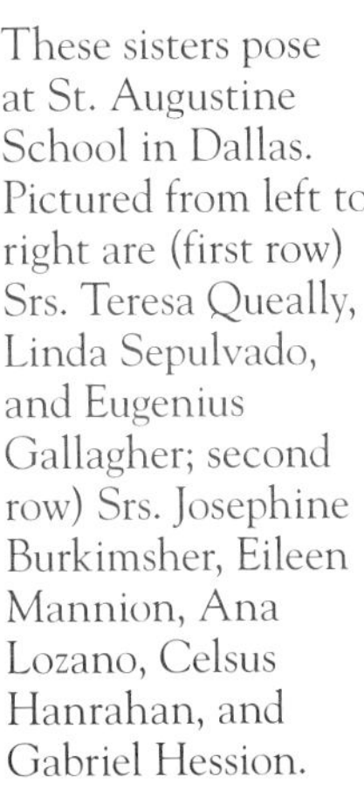

These sisters pose at St. Augustine School in Dallas. Pictured from left to right are (first row) Srs. Teresa Queally, Linda Sepulvado, and Eugenius Gallagher; second row) Srs. Josephine Burkimsher, Eileen Mannion, Ana Lozano, Celsus Hanrahan, and Gabriel Hession.

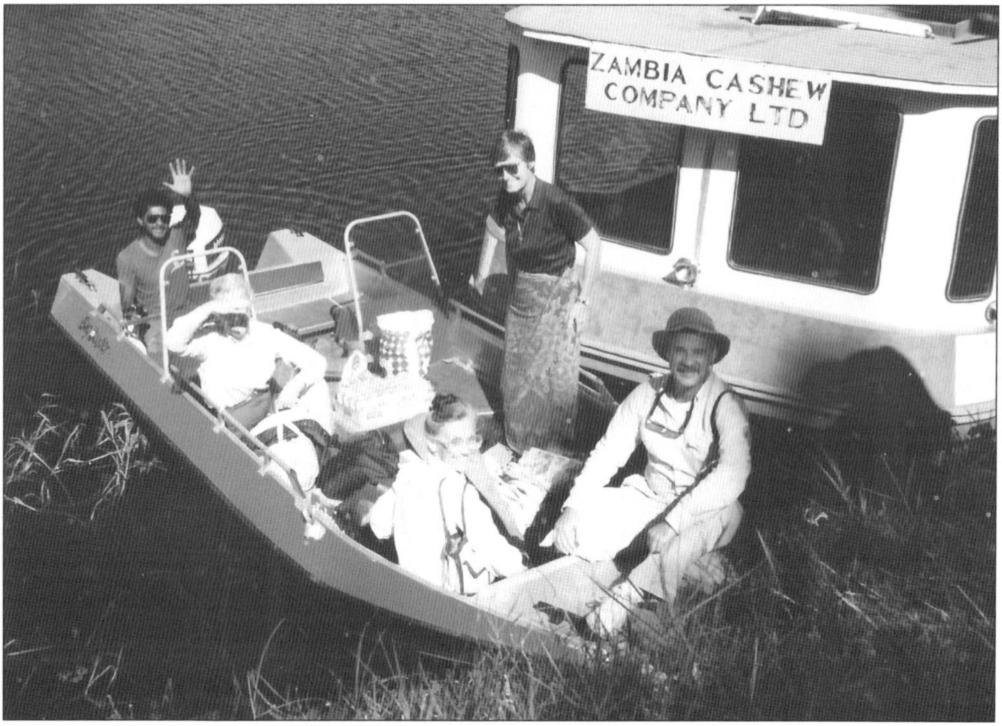

These passengers are getting ready to take off from Mongu Harbor heading to Kalabo. From left to right are Renaud Heviamoorima, Srs. Rose McHugh, Christina Mitchell, Geraldine Klein (standing), and Brian Wallace.

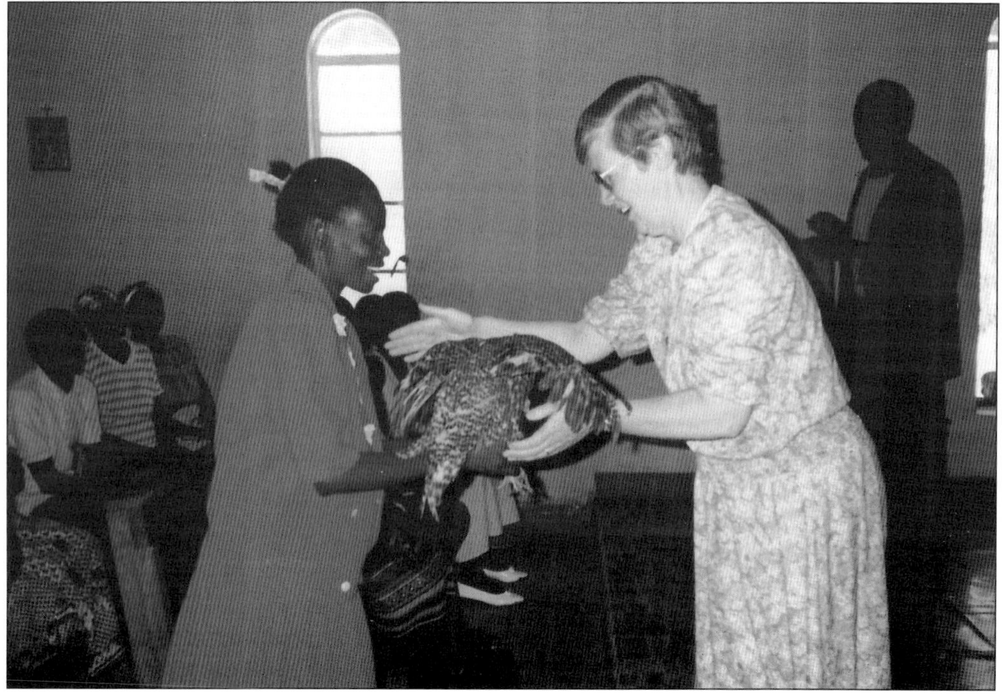

Sr. Anne Finnerty received a significant gift of a chicken from a Shihole parishioner.

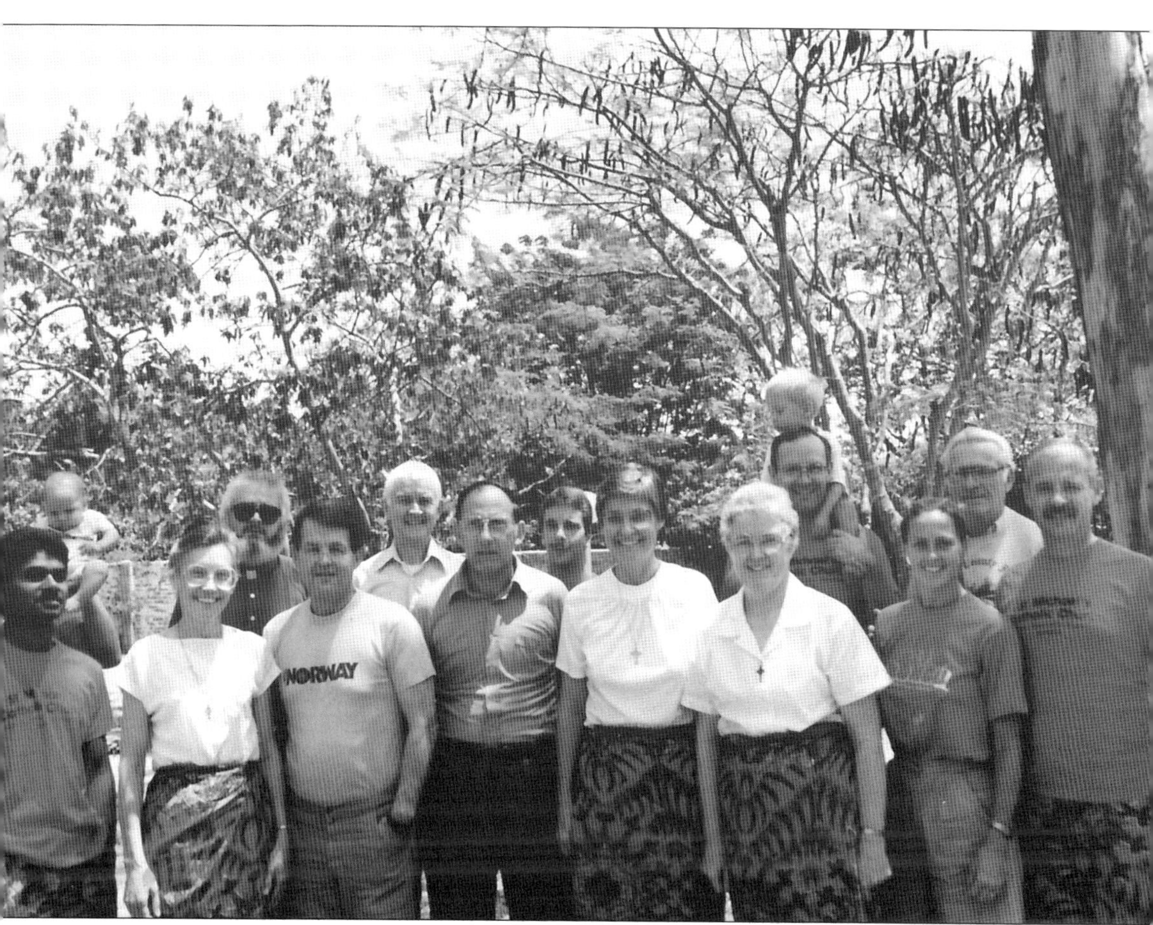

This photograph was taken when the Sisters of the Holy Spirit and Mary Immaculate first arrived in Zambia in 1988. The *sitengi* material that was made into shorts for the men and wrap-around skirts for the sisters was a gift from the oblates. They are seen on the people in the front row. From left to right are (first row) Renaud Heviamoorima; Sr. Christina Mitchell; Fr. Jack Joyce, OMI; Fr. Ron Walker, OMI; Sr. Geraldine Klein; Sr. Rose McHugh; Jeanie Ritter; and Fr. Brian Wallace, OMI; (second row) Bill Ritter (holding Abe); Fr. Ed Matthews, OMI; Fr. Paul Duffy, OMI; Billy Fuller; Fr. Pat Gitzen, OMI (holding Augie Ritter); and unidentified.

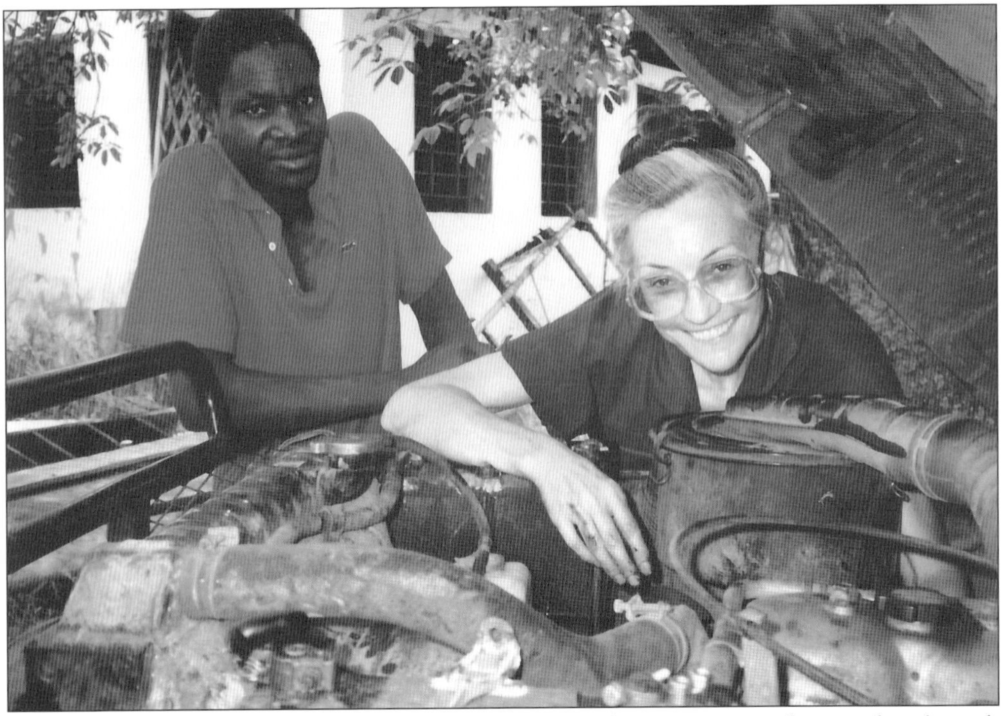

Sr. Christina Mitchell and Pelekelo, an employee at the mission, work on a diesel truck in Kalobo.

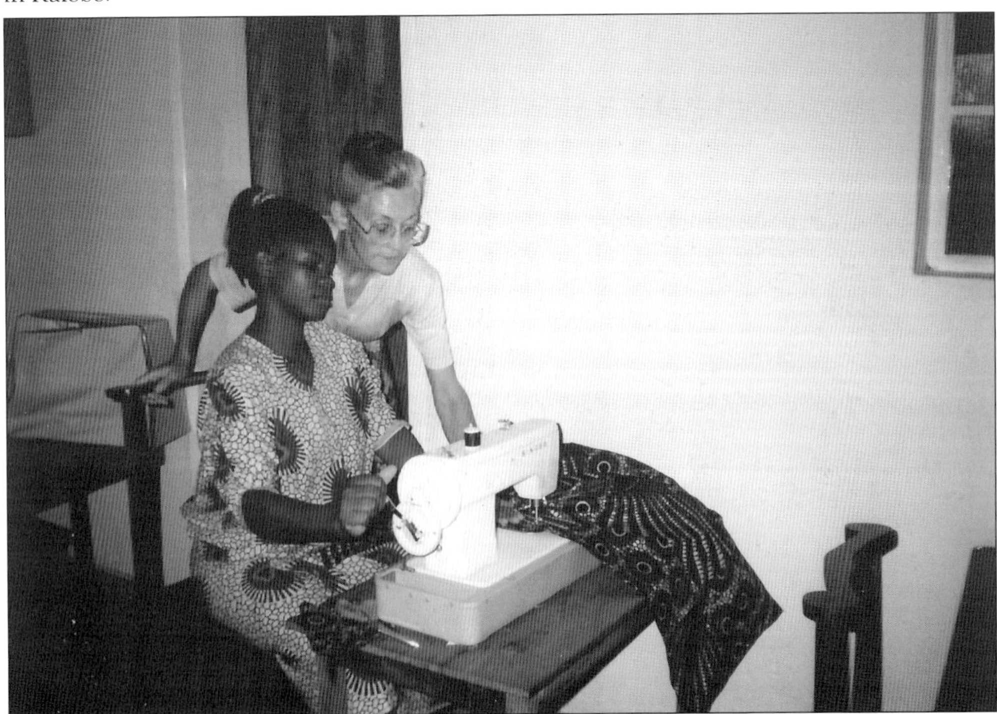

Sr. Christina Mitchell is as comfortable working on a truck as she is on a sewing machine. Here, Sister Christina guides a student in a sewing lesson.

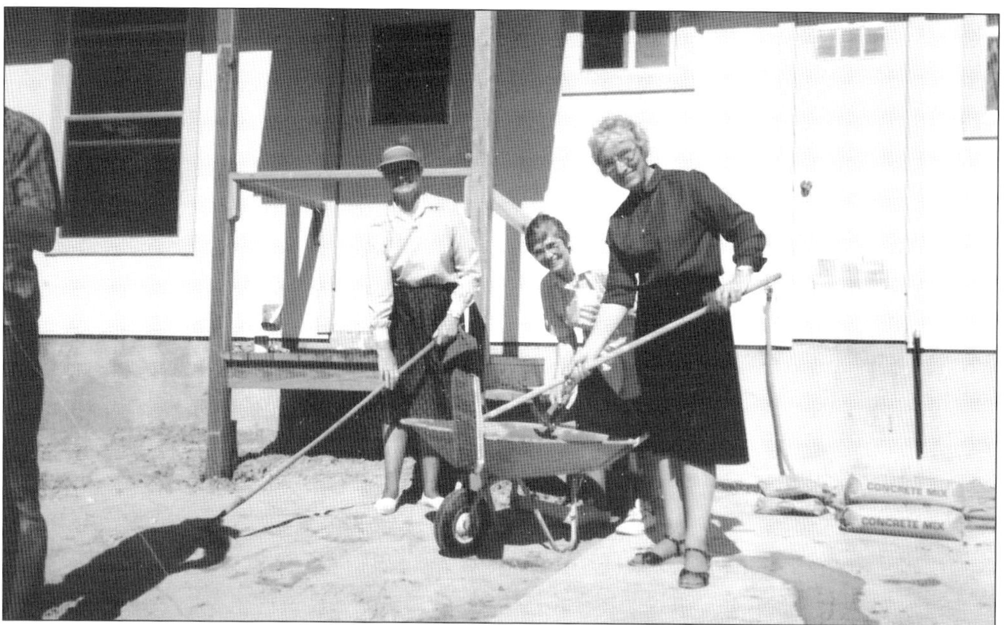

Srs. Teresa Healy, Vera Ruane, and Laura Melody are working on the "Miracle House." The home received this name because it was constructed in one week through the Habitat for Humanity program. Sister Melody served for many years on the board of this organization and was an avid supporter of the program.

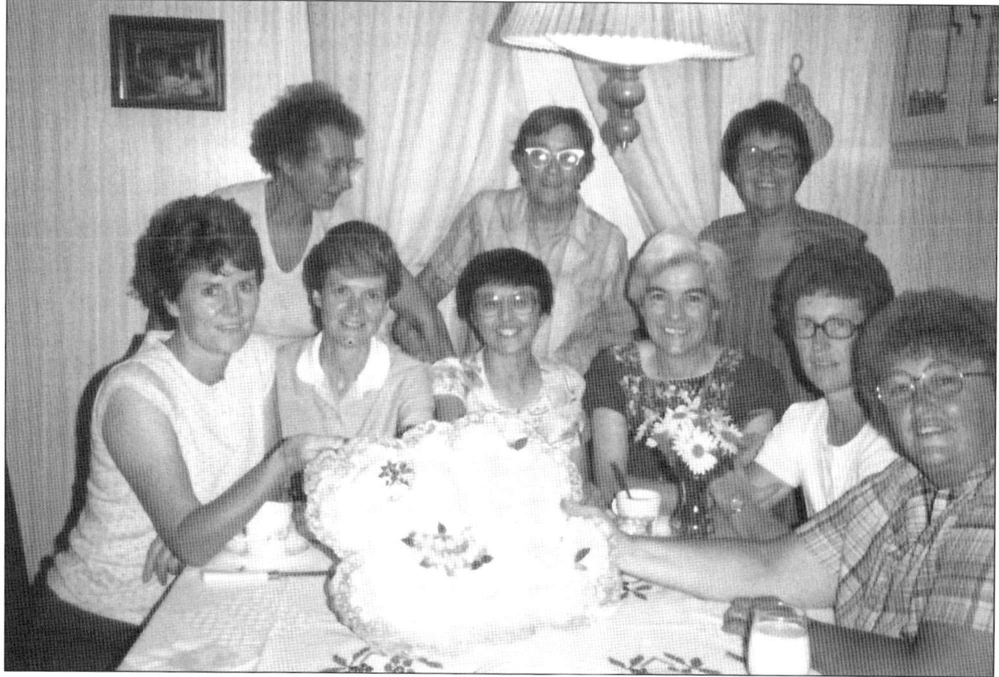

Seated from left to right, Srs. Vera Ruane, unidentified, Peggy Flaherty, and Jo Murray sit around a table with the midwives in Weslaco, Texas. The sisters and the midwives worked at the Holy Family Birth Center in town. They were accompanied by several other congregations of sisters who also worked at the center.

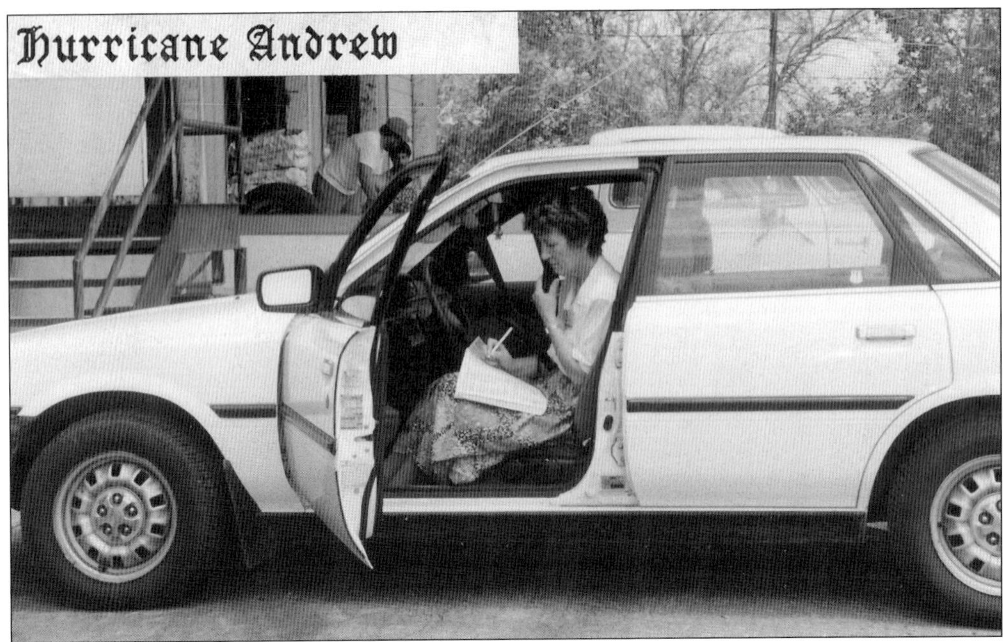

Sr. Miriam Mitchell sits in her car taking some notes during the relief effort for Hurricane Andrew, which hit Houma-Thibodaux Diocese, Louisiana. This storm devastated the area, and the relief effort was hampered by the lack of cell phones. However, the manager of Mobiletel provided cell phones for first responders who went into the Bayou Communities. Although these early phones were large and not easily to carry, they helped the responders provide aid to the victims of this category 4 hurricane.

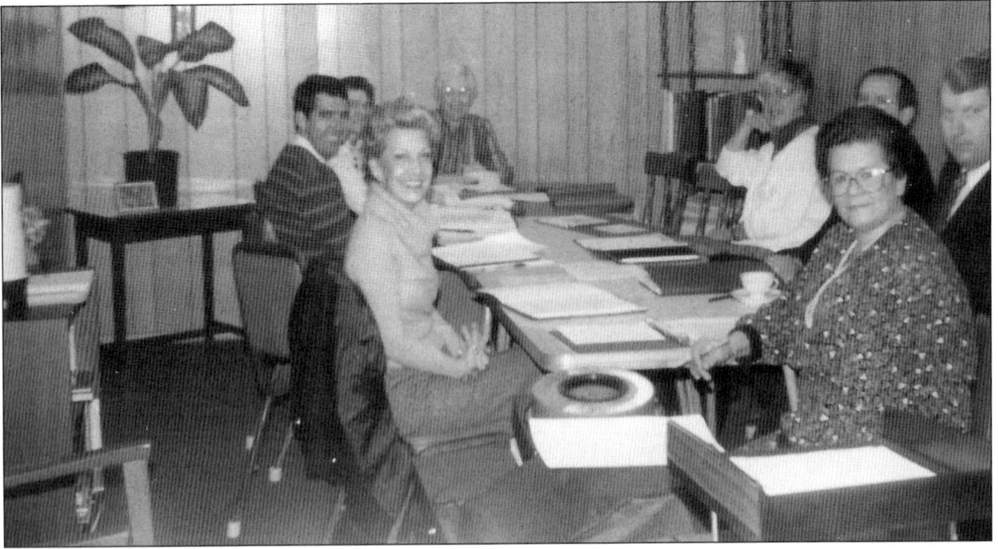

The board of Mother of Perpetual Help meets for an organizational meeting in the fall of 1988. This Brownsville, Texas, nursing home established by Nora Kelley in 1922 began as a "charity house." The Sisters of the Holy Spirit and Mary Immaculate purchased and ministered in this nursing home and later served on the board of directors. Pictured from left to right are Nena Roser, Blanca Vela, James Gomez, Sr. Jane Frances, Sr. Monica Carroll, unidentified, Marshall Ray, Joan DeLeon, and Jack Cowley.

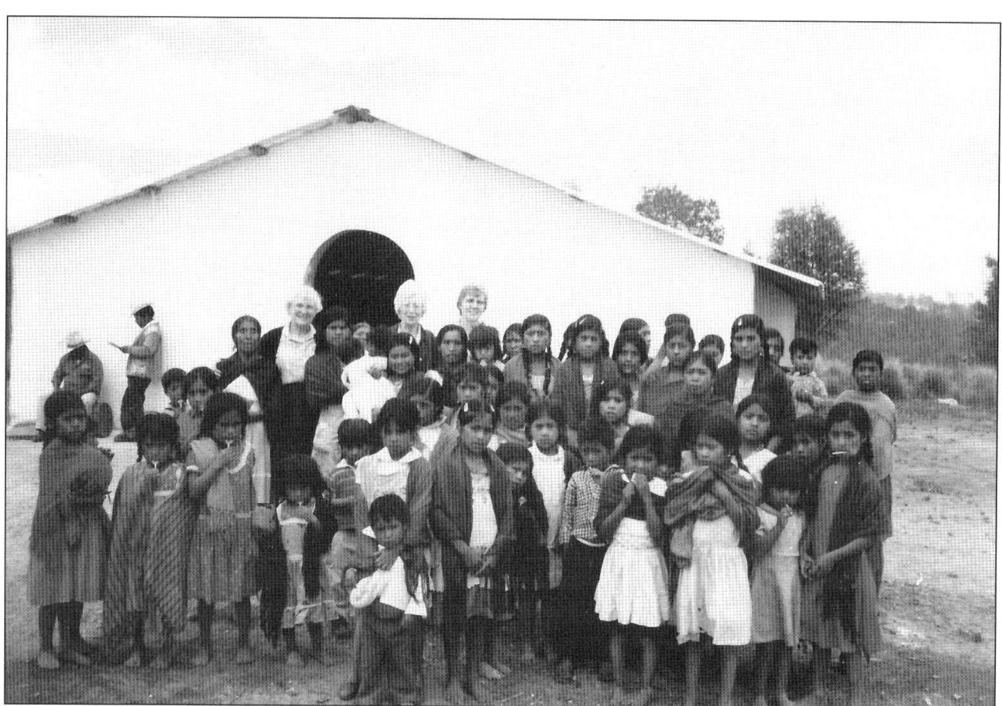

Srs. Magdalen Kilbane, Monica Carroll, and Anne Finnerty visit the indigenous mission of Santa Cruz Mixtepec in April 1989.

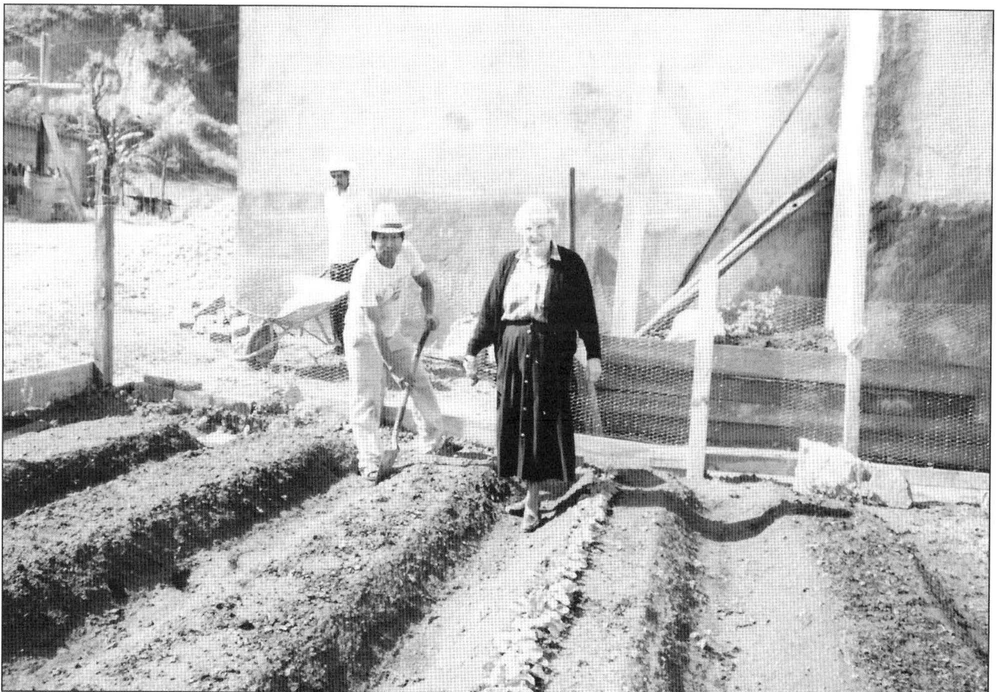

Sr. Magdalen Kilbane traveled into the Sierra Nevada Mountains near Oaxaca, Mexico, and worked with the indigenous peoples on a gardening project. She purchased seeds and helped start local gardens in the area.

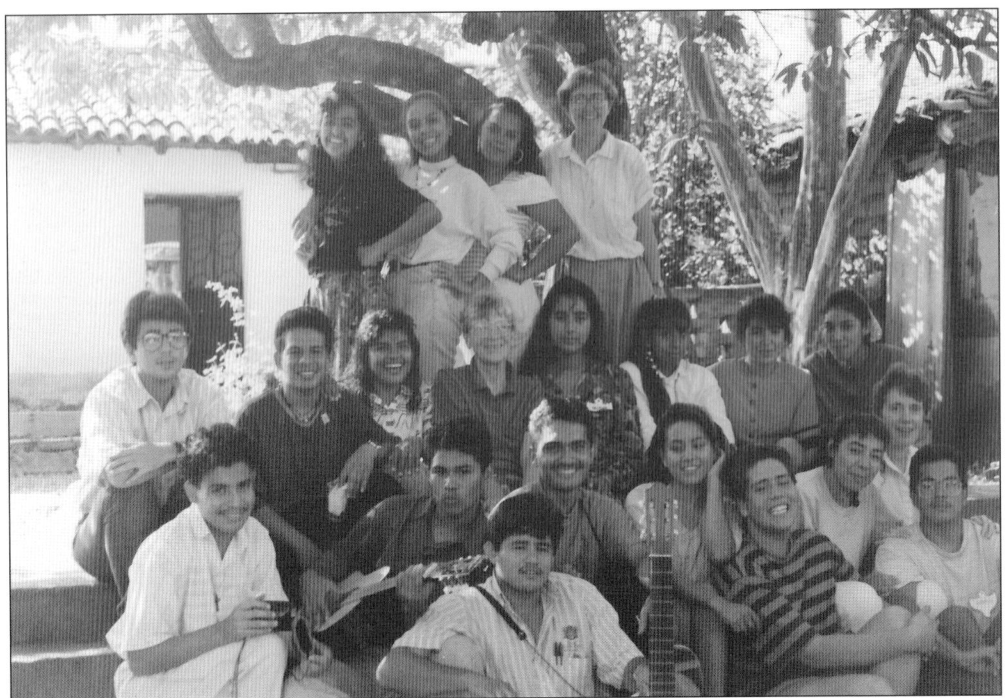

This photograph was taken in front of the house in Santa Maria del Oro, Nayarit, Mexico, around 1992. The youth group from Puerto Vallarta, Jalisco, Mexico, and Santa Maria del Oro, Nayarit, Mexico, came for a weekend youth workshop. Pictured are Srs. Rita Nealon (right, on the middle step), Beatrice Donnellan (center, seated on the top step), and Loretta Armand (right, standing).

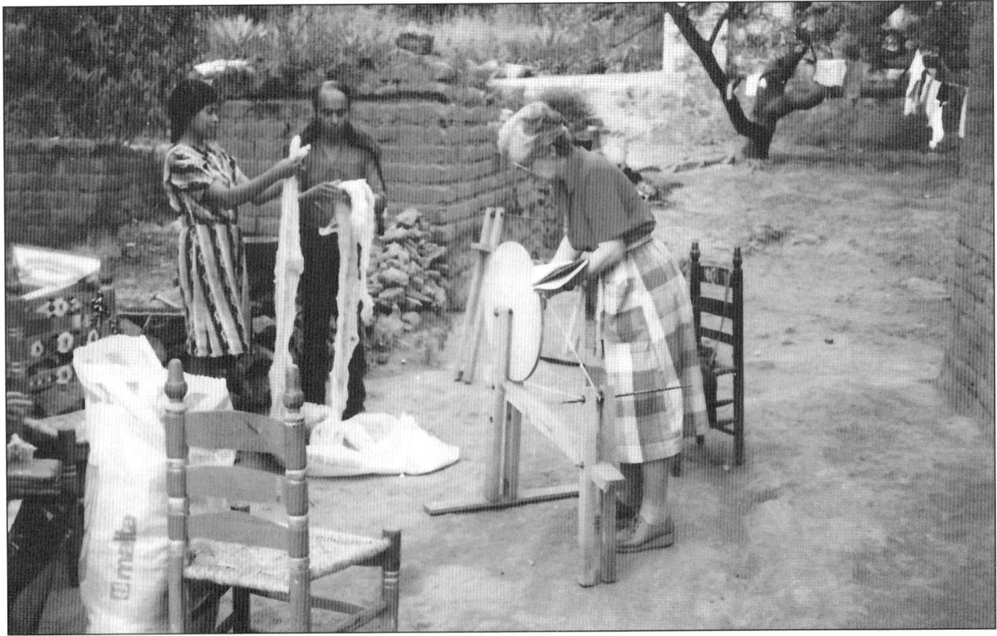

Sr. Beatrice Donnellan (center) works on a spinning wheel at a weaving cooperative in Malinalco, Mexico State, Mexico.

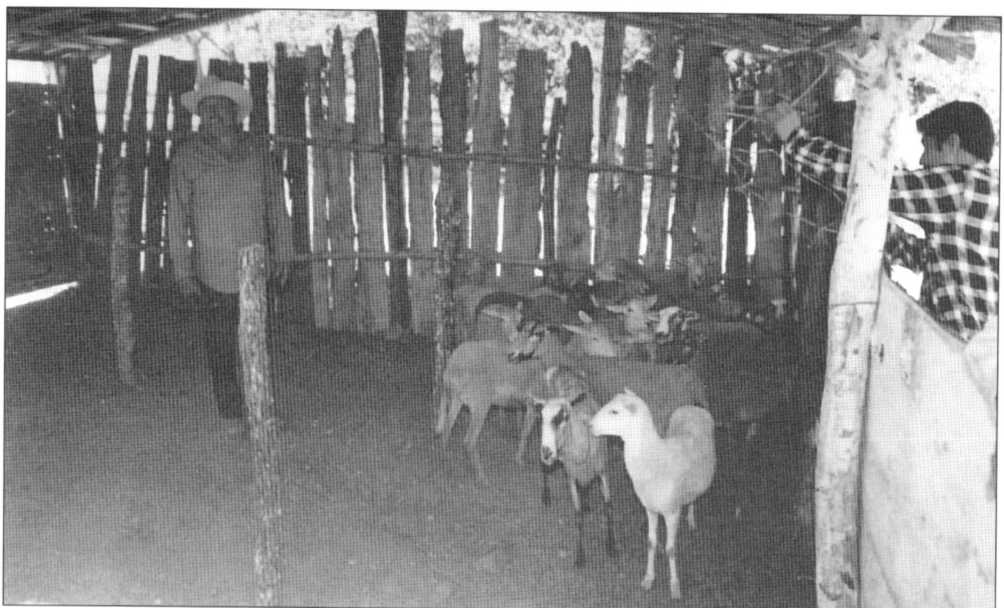

Sister Marian introduced the Heifer International Program to assist people in the rural area of Nayarit. She wanted to assist the poor farmers and help improve the livelihood of the community. This program provided each farmer with sheep or goats. They would feed and care for the animals, and when they reproduced, the young animals were given back to the community. After the initial offspring replaced what the farmer received, they could retain the future progeny.

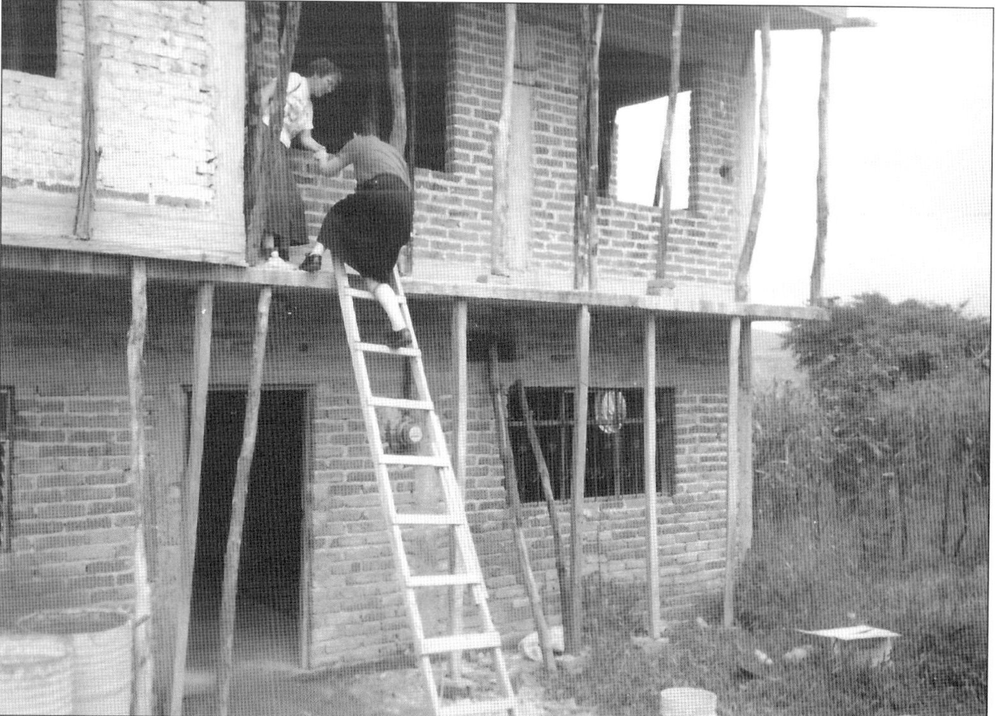

Sr. Loretta Armand gives Sr. Dympna Clarke a hand climbing up the ladder to review the remodeling of this building in Nayarit, Mexico.

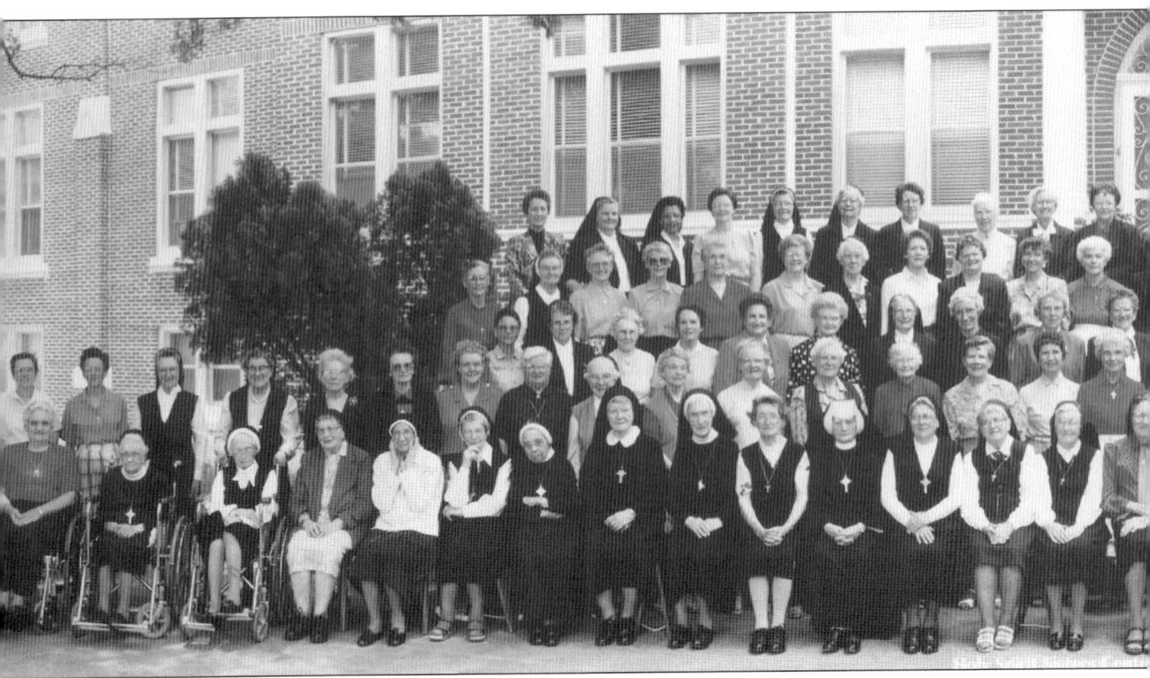

The Sisters of the Holy Spirit and Mary Immaculate celebrated their 100 years of service in 1993.

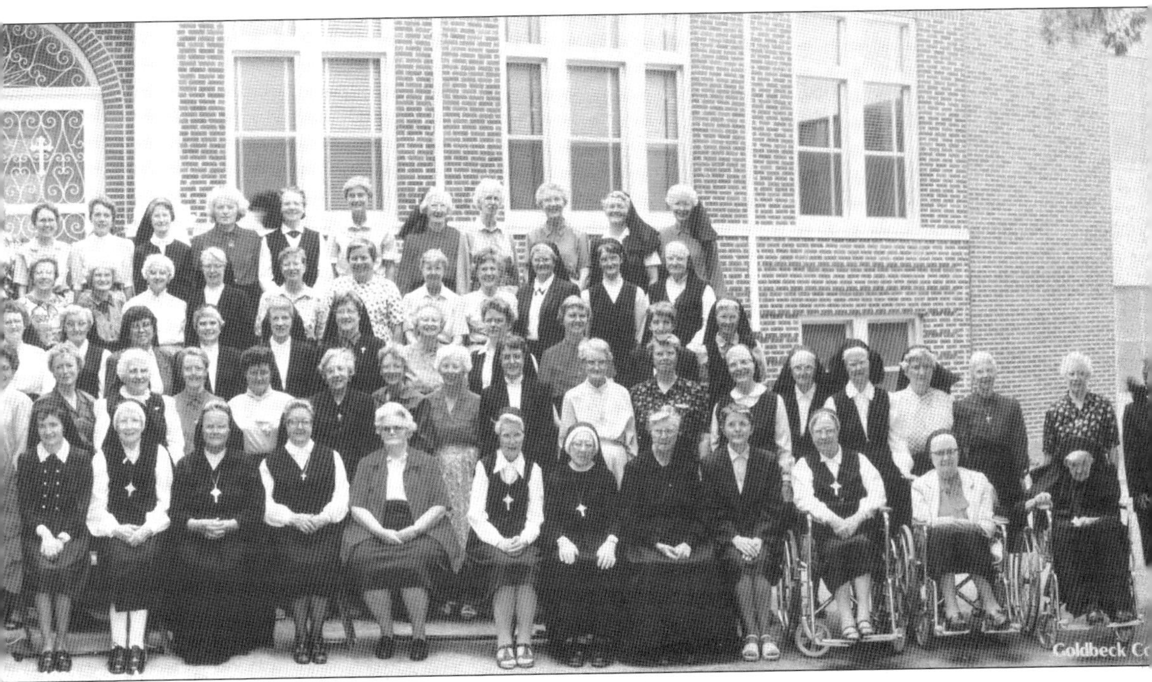

The community posed for this picture in front of the 1922 convent.

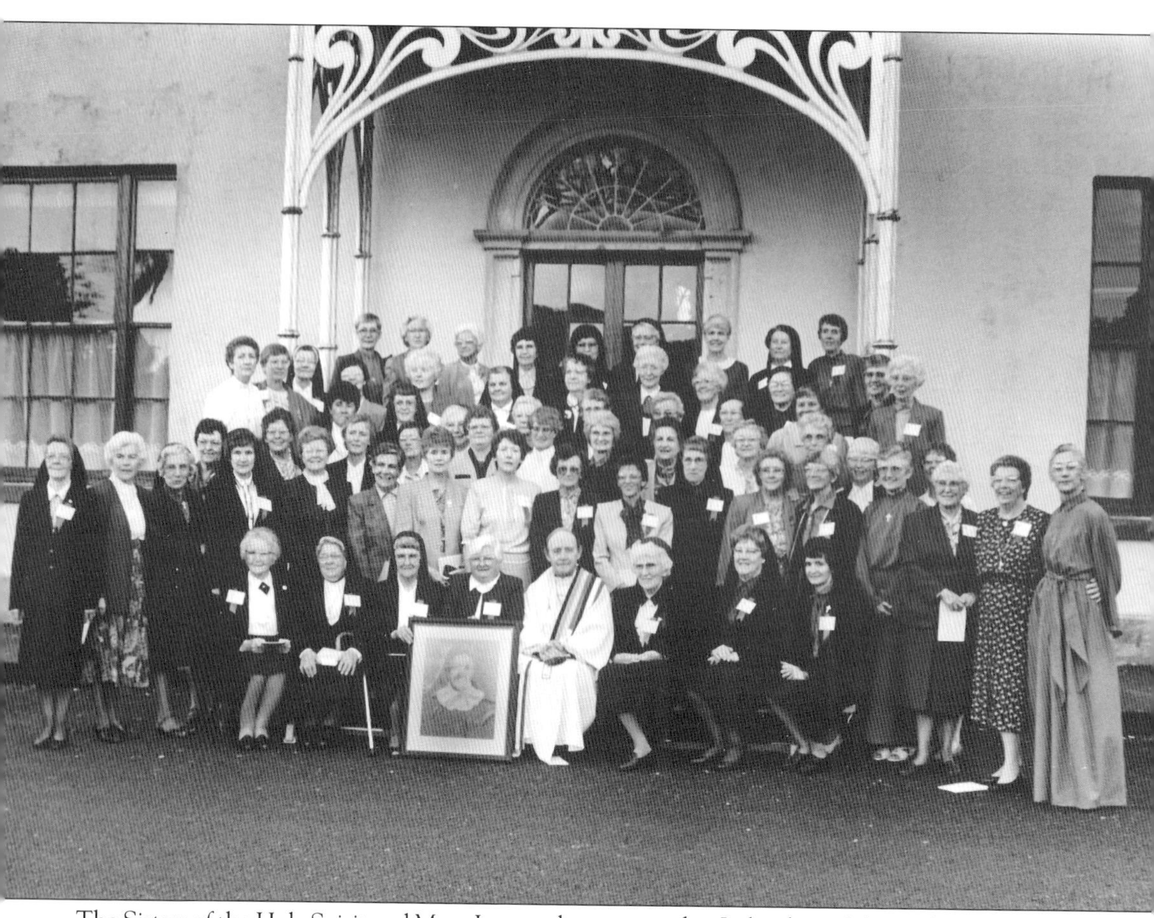

The Sisters of the Holy Spirit and Mary Immaculate returned to Ireland to celebrate their 100 years of service in Galway, Ireland. They are pictured here in front of their old convent and school.

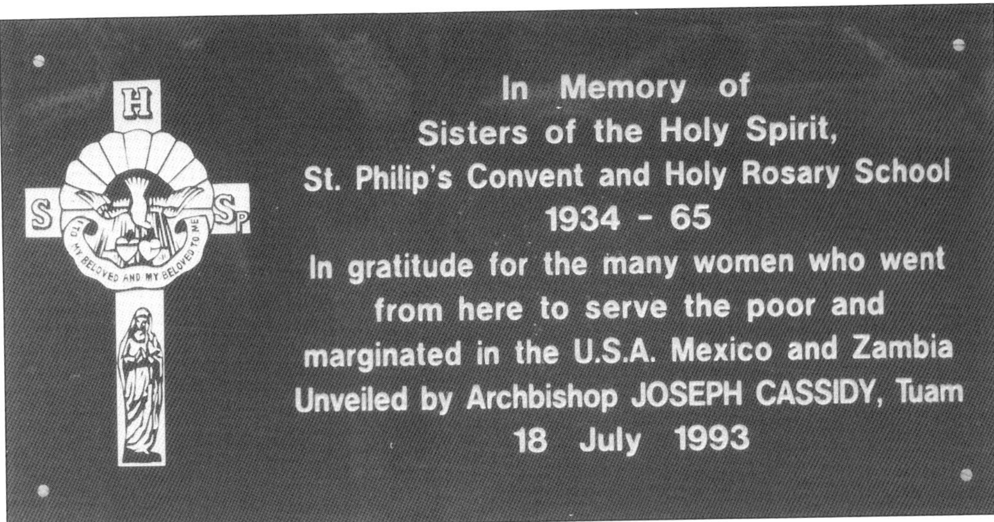

During their 100-year celebration of service, the Sisters of the Holy Spirit and Mary Immaculate had a plaque mounted on a wall commemorating their anniversary at Mount Bellew, the home of their convent and school in Ireland. A similar plaque also hangs on the back wall of the church in Cahirciveen, Ireland, where Margaret Mary Healy Murphy was born.

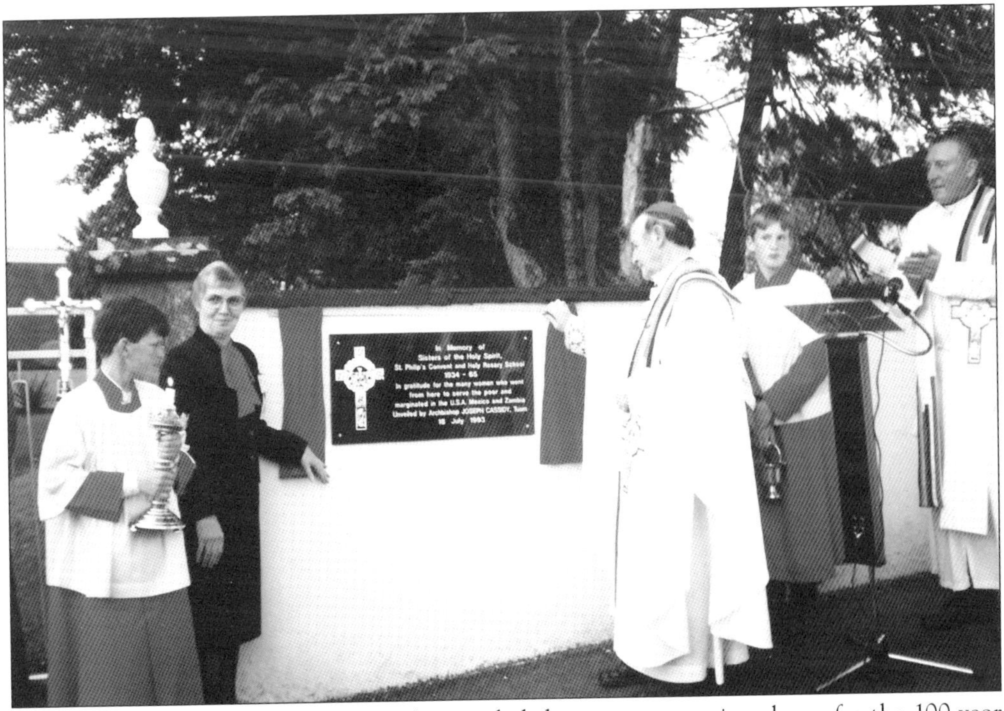

Sr. Anne Finnerty and Bishop Cassidy unveiled the commemorative plaque for the 100-year celebration of service, which was hung on the wall of St. Philip's Convent and School at Mount Bellew, County Galway, Ireland.

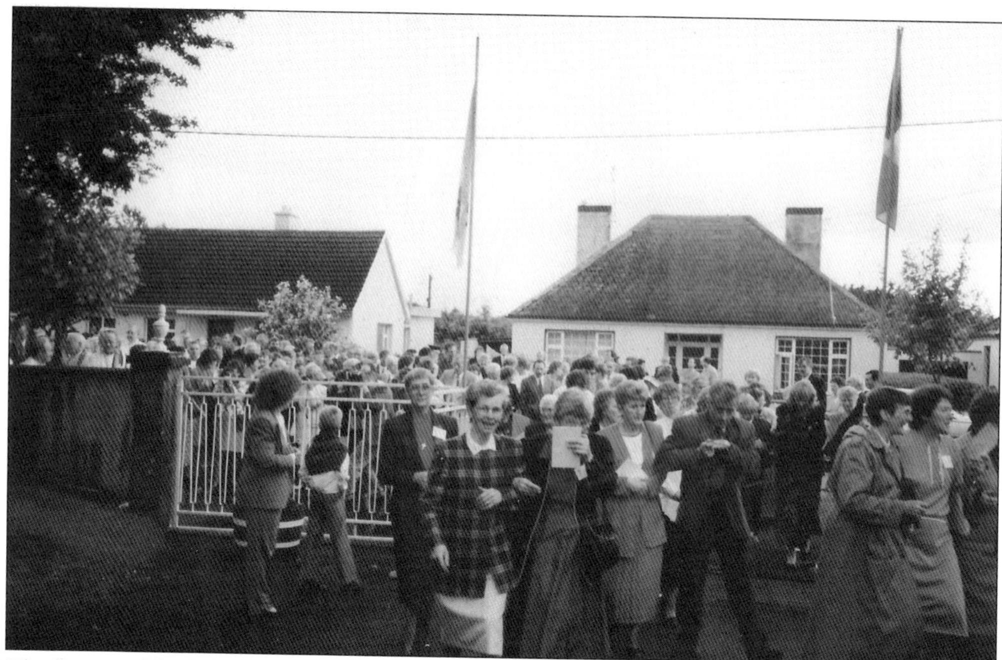

The Sisters of the Holy Spirit and Mary Immaculate are walking with the people of Mount Bellew, County Galway, Ireland, to celebrate a century of service.

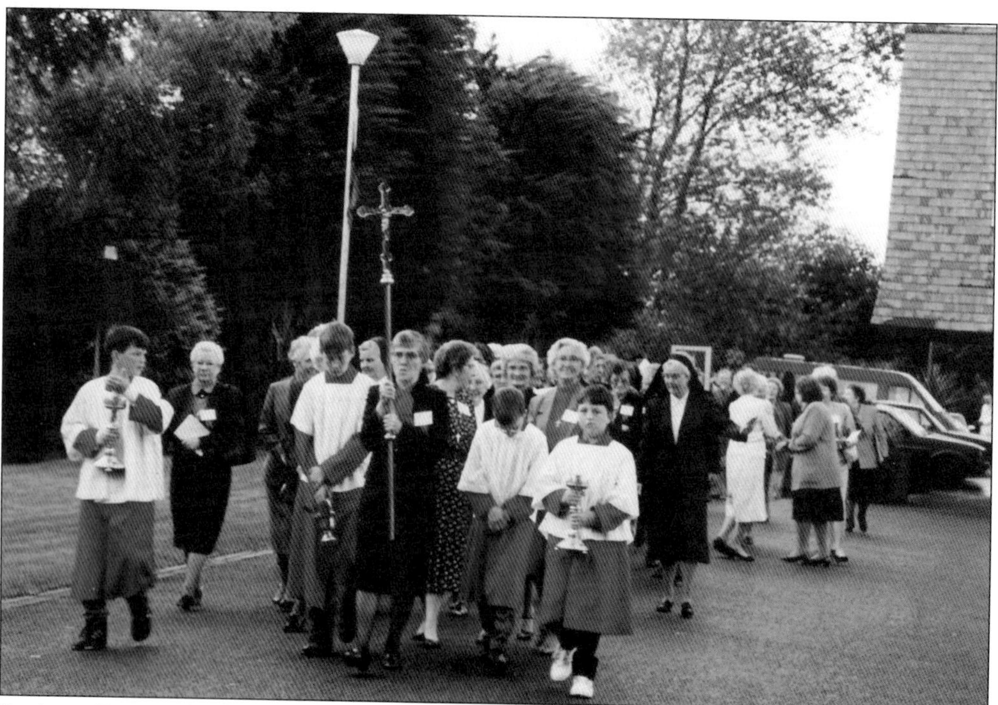

Sr. Anne Finnerty leads a procession celebrating the 100-year celebration of service in Cahirciveen, County Kerry, Ireland.

Six

Looking Back and Celebrating 125 Years 1994–2018

The Sisters of the Holy Spirit and Mary Immaculate found their next 25 years as a congregation even more enlightening and fulfilling. The remaining general superiors, Sr. Anne Finnerty (1991–1999), Sr. Veronica Cahill (1999–2007), Sr. Miriam Mitchell (2007–2015), and Sr. Geraldine Klein (2015–) elected during this time were energetic, dynamic religious women with the foresight to lead the congregation into areas where they were much needed.

The 100 years of service celebration carried the euphoric community for the next several years. They reviewed their history with Sr. Anne Finnerty's work documenting their ministries, producing a pamphlet about their founding and establishing a Heritage Room.

The dawning of a new millennium found the sisters leaving several schools. The mission in Zambia in the Mongu Diocese, however, expanded. One of their projects in Limulunga was the infant at-risk program for orphans. The sisters had three communities in Zambia: Limulunga, Moya OKenile House, and St. Gabriel Parish, Namushakende. In Mexico, they were still in Oaxaca and with the indigenous Tepic peoples.

Several sisters retired, and Sister Veronica encouraged volunteer ministries. Their expertise and dedication increased their community presence in San Antonio, and they also lent their talents to various nonprofit boards. The major decision of this administration was to sell the old convent and build a new motherhouse across the street.

Sr. Miriam Mitchell had the daunting task of implementing this decision by selling the old motherhouse, building the new motherhouse, and moving into the new building. She also carried out another decision made during Sister Veronica's administration to provide monetary support for programs working with the poor for empowerment and training. In light of this new direction, the sisters supported the building of a house for bruised and battered women in Zambia as one of several projects they funded. They also received the SANKOFA Award, which was in recognition of "Lifelong Dedication to Education in the Black Community."

With Sr. Geraldine Klein's administration, the sisters continue to be active on several boards. The missions of the sisters are now confined to Texas, Louisiana, Mississippi, and Zambia. Consequently, the goal of this administration is to attract vocations. They are still active at the Healy-Murphy Center and gave a substantial gift for the purchase of land and the building of a new Child Development Center at the high school. They continue to diversify their ministry with immigrants, the poor, and incarcerated. The sisters continue to teach and work with parish and hospital ministry, as well as hospice.

In 2018, they celebrated 125 years of service and the construction of a Mother Margaret Calvary Shrine next to their motherhouse.

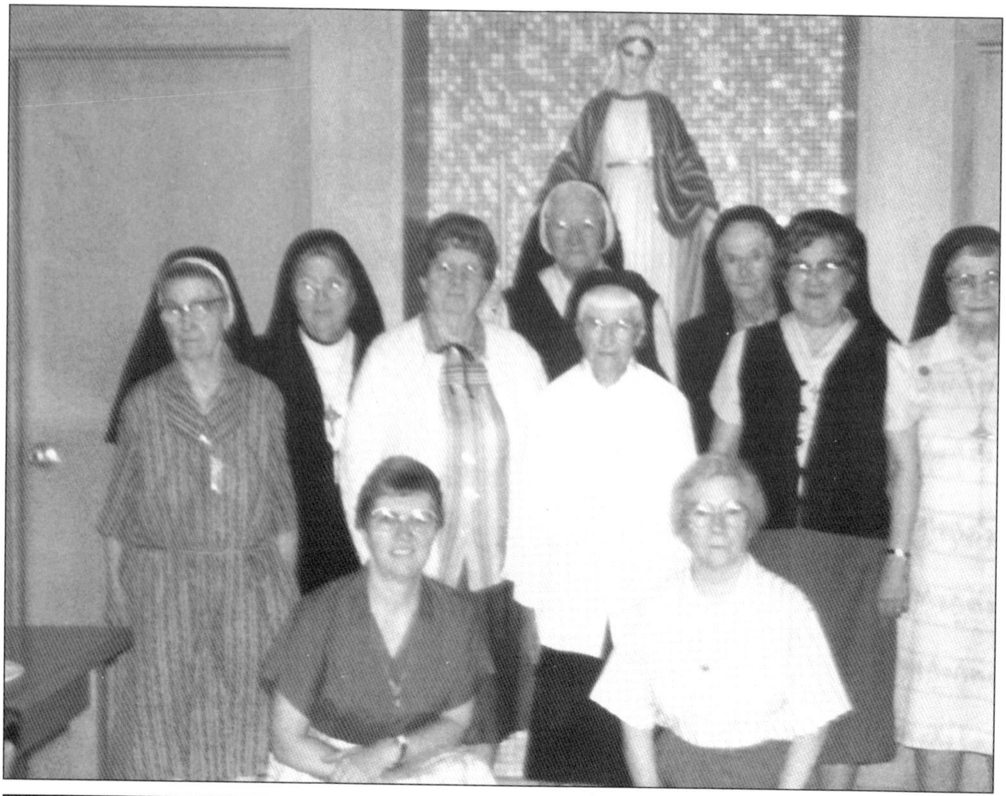

The Sisters of the Holy Spirit and Mary Immaculate who taught in St. Joseph, Missouri, gathered for this photograph in July 1990. From left to right are (first row) Anne Finnerty, John Berchmans O'Rourke, and Betty Higgins; (second row) Srs. Angela Stanton, Margaret Murray, Germaine DeMar, Joachim Kelly, Aloysius Kelly, Anna Theresa Connella, and Eugene Newton.

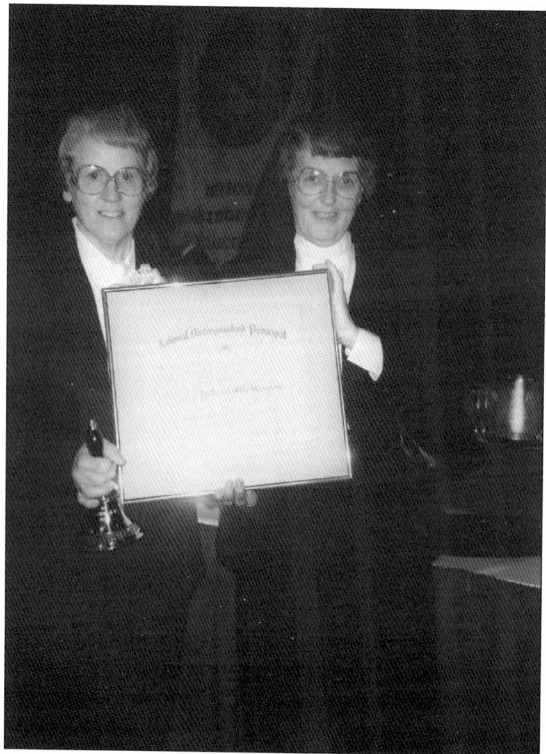

Sr. Eugenius Gallagher helps Sr. Gabriel Hession hold an award presented to her. Sister Gabriel traveled to Washington, DC, to receive the National Distinguished Principal Award from the US secretary of education on October 13, 1995.

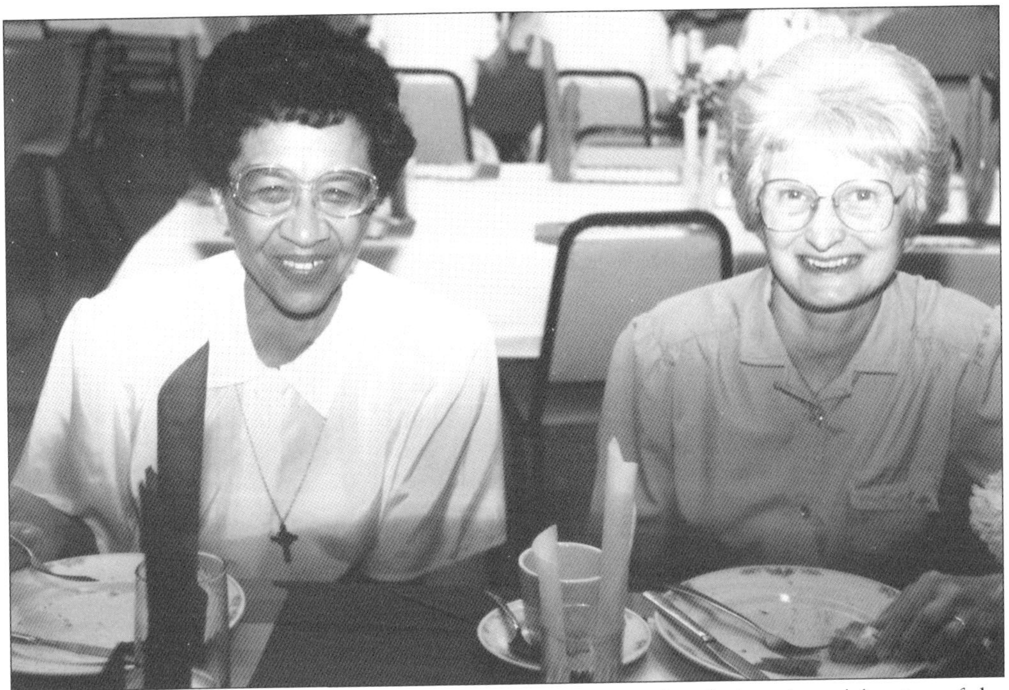

Sr. Martha Readore and Sr. Rosetta Leonard enjoy time together during the celebration of the centenary at the motherhouse in June 1993. Martha and Rosetta enjoyed many years serving in the ministry of education in Louisiana.

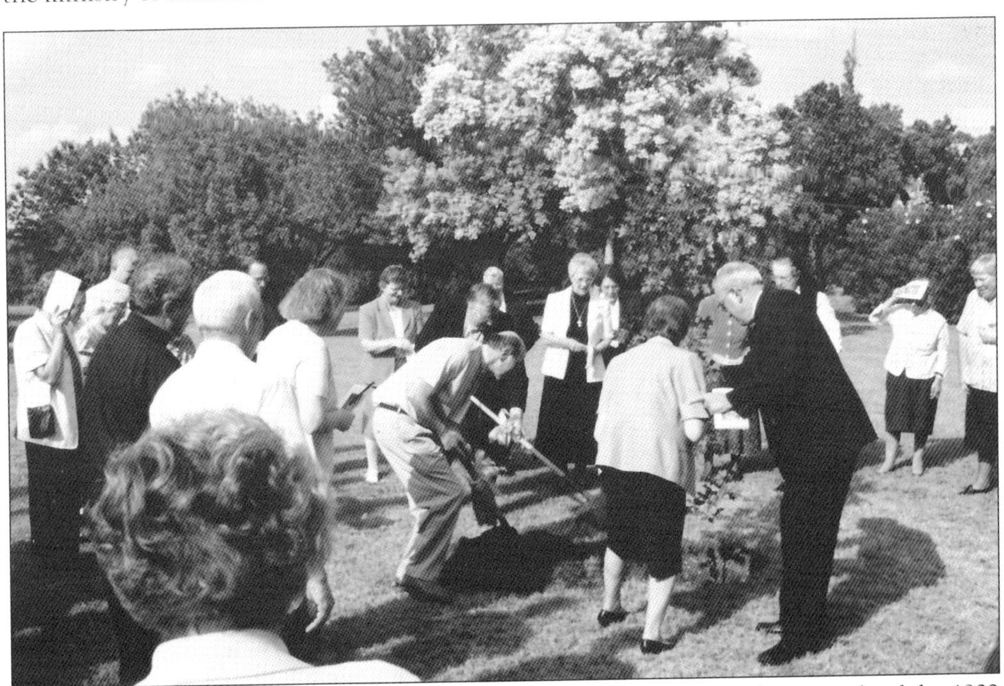

The Sisters of the Holy Spirit and Mary Immaculate plant a tree on the grounds of the 1922 convent at 301 Yucca Street in San Antonio. They were celebrating the installation of leadership in 2003.

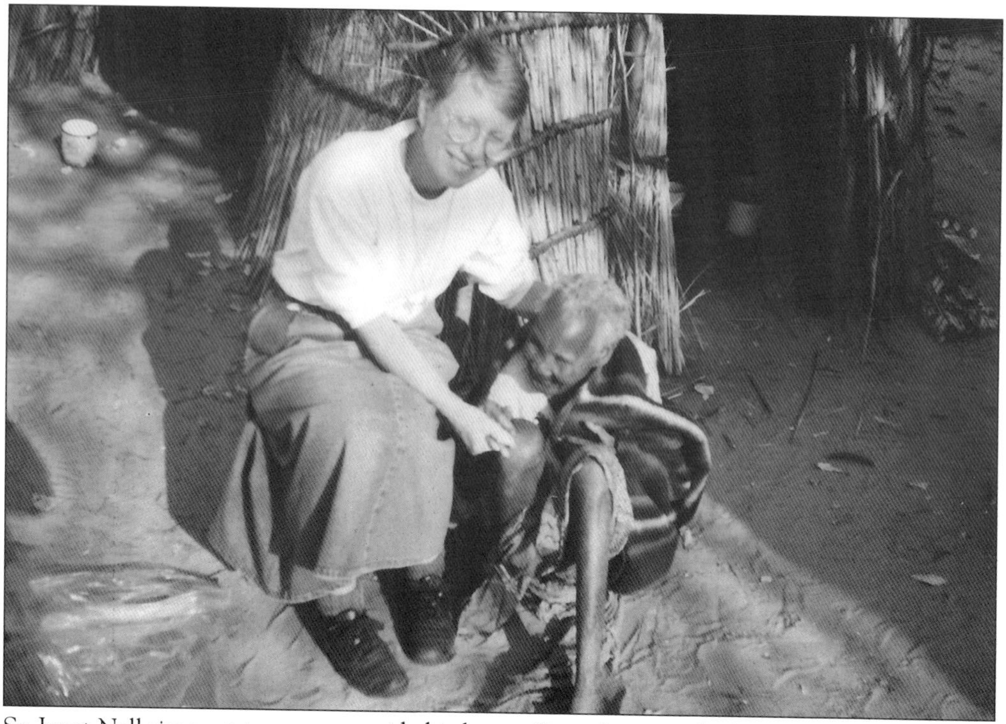

Sr. Janet Nall sits next to a man outside his home. Sister Janet worked with home-based care, a Zambian program in response to the HIV/AIDS crisis. The program sought to help eliminate severely crowded hospitals. This program provided simple medicines, wound care, and sometimes food and transportation to the clinic with emotional and spiritual support for those who were terminally ill.

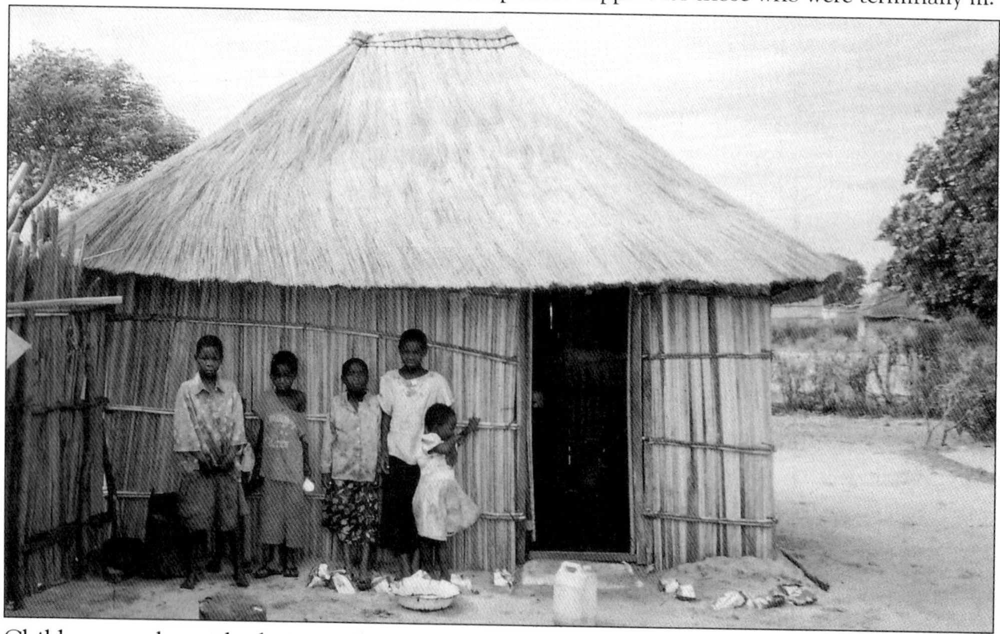

Children stand outside their new home in Zambia that the sisters helped build. The Sisters of the Holy Spirit and Mary Immaculate built these homes with the help of donations from several individuals.

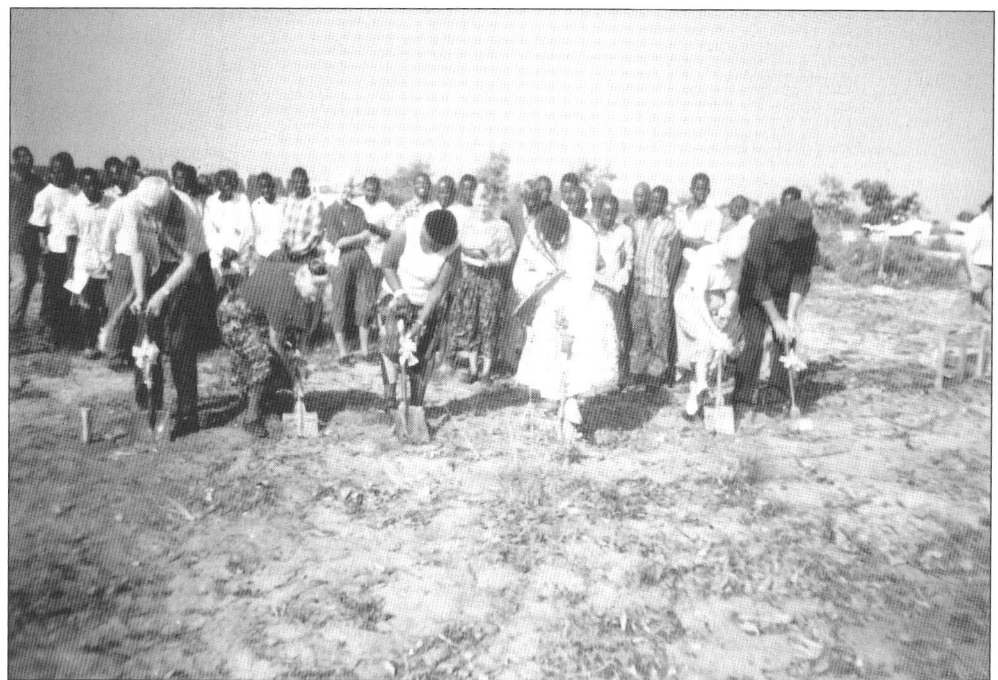

From left to right are (in front, with shovels) Bishop Paul Duffy, OMI; Sr. Christina Mitchell; Princess Mbuywana; Prince Kusigo Liwanika; Sr. Monica Carroll; and Winfred Dieter breaking ground for a new formation house for the sisters in Mongu, Zambia. The land is traditional royal land that was donated by Princess Mbuywana for this house.

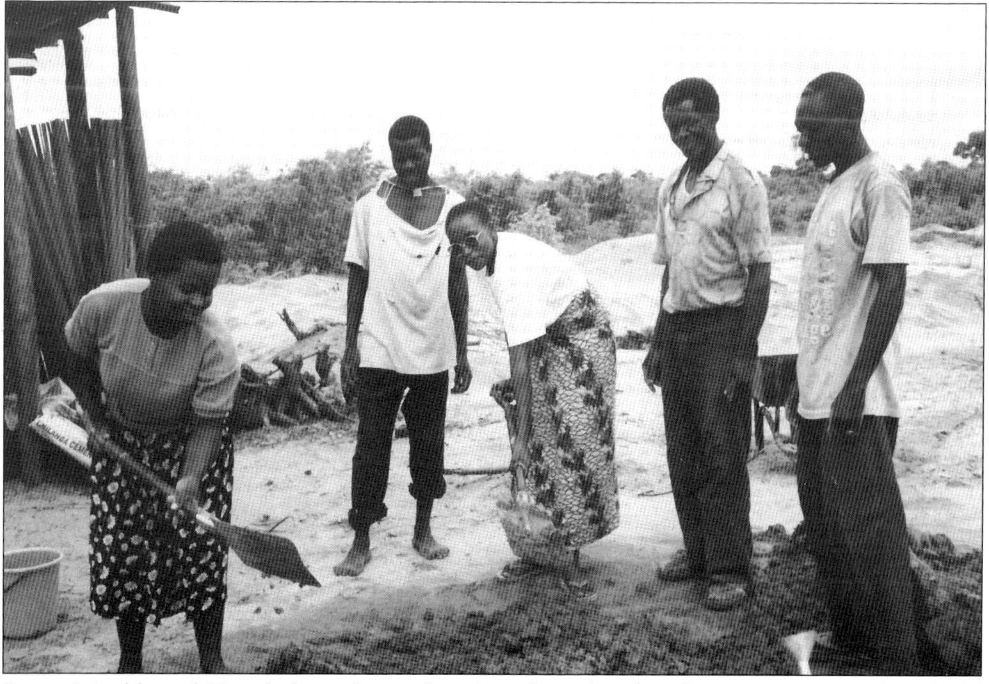

Sisters Matilda and Maimbolwa take up shovels and try their hand at mixing materials to build blocks for the construction of the formation house in Mongu, Zambia.

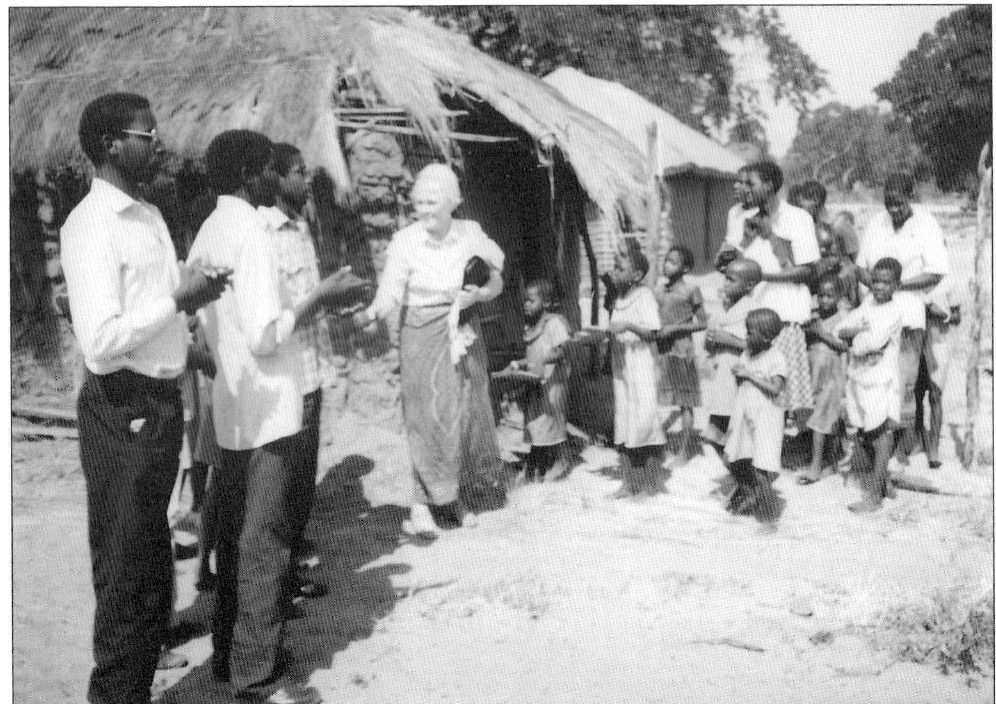
Sr. Rose McHugh visits one of the villages near Kalabo. This small town rests on the western banks of the Zambezi River in Zambia. Surrounding Kalabo are lesser villages with minor populations that form "Mass centers," where they rely on missionaries for religious instruction.

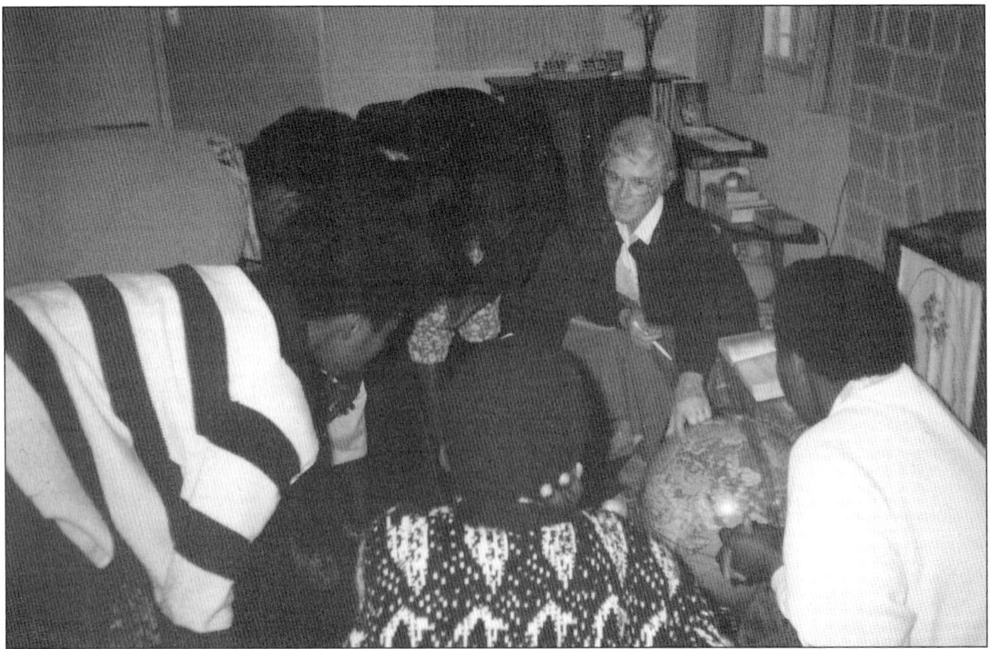
Sr. Rose McHugh sits with students in 1994 for religious education in Zambia. The Sisters of the Holy Spirit and Mary Immaculate arrived in Zambia in 1988. They concentrated their efforts in one of the poorest areas in the new Diocese of Mongu.

Sr. Janet Nall holds a young child in Zambia. Sister Nall participated in a program for infants at risk for malnutrition. She started this program in 2000 after a parishioner requested help for starving twins. The program grew when mothers and guardians came forward to ask for help. Infant formula was given to mothers who could not feed their children because of various illnesses.

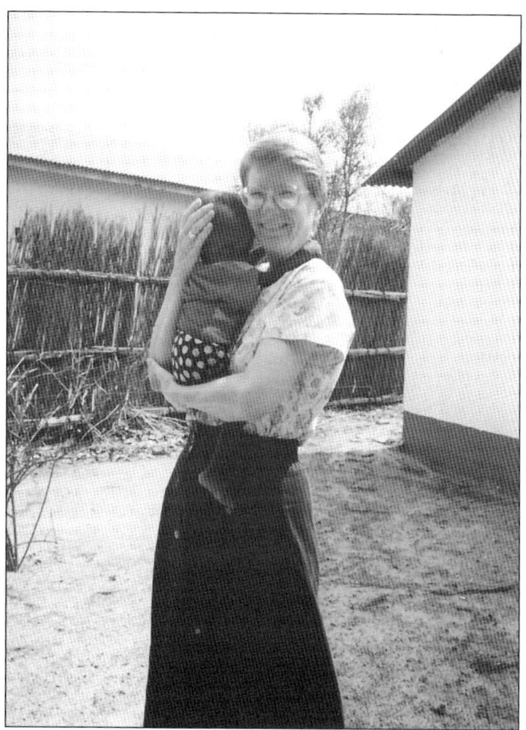

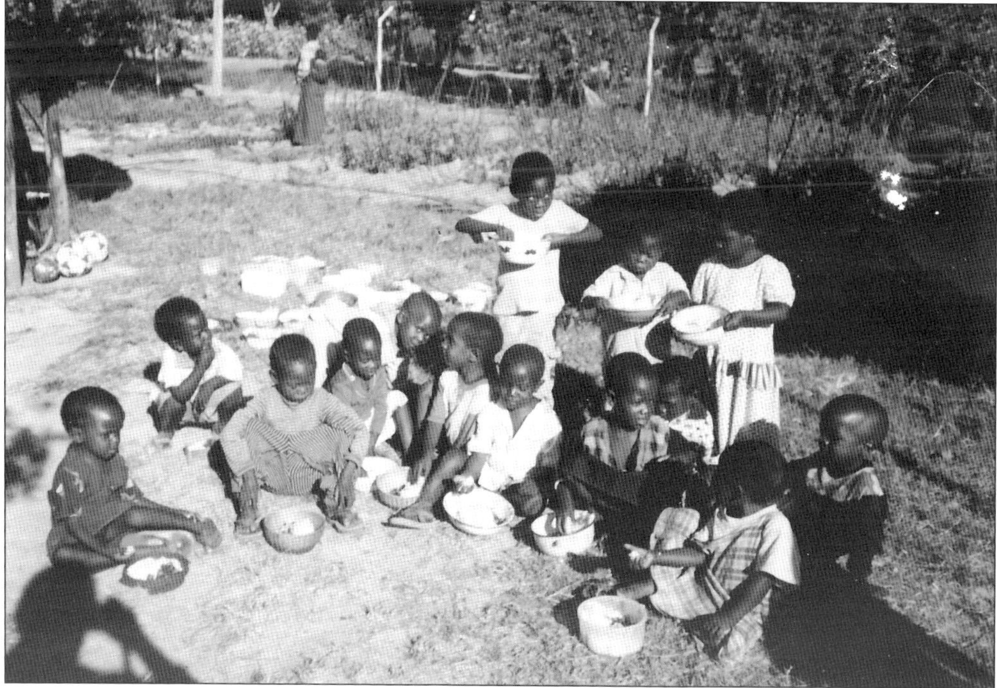

These children are part of the Zambian orphan program in which the Sisters of the Holy Spirit and Mary Immaculate participated. From four years of age through kindergarten, these children would come to the center for preschool and lunch every day. The sisters started a garden, as seen in the background of this photograph, to help feed them.

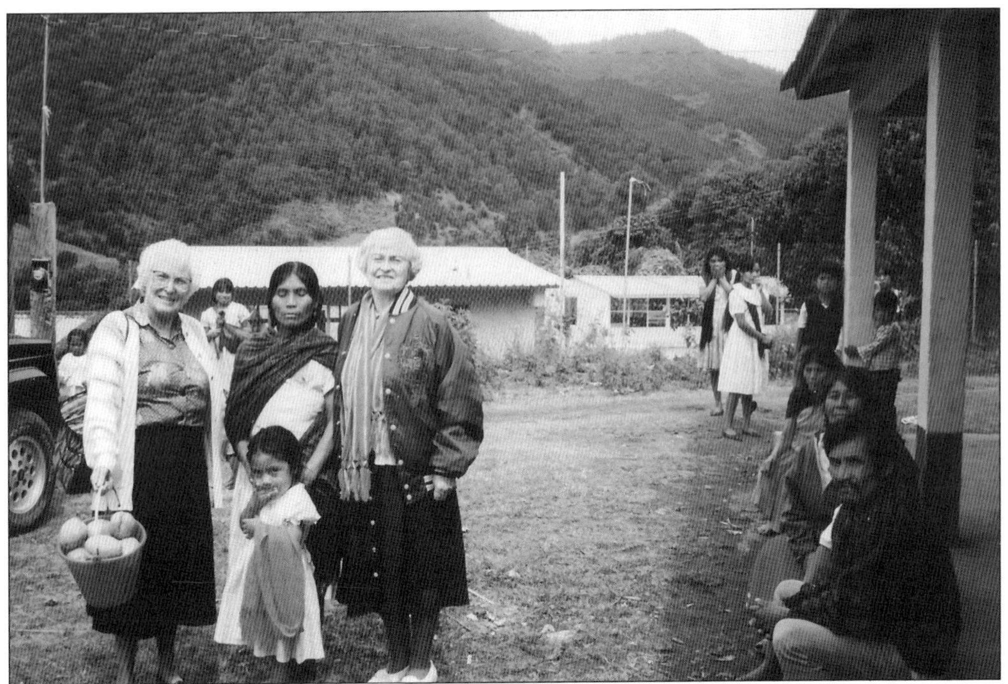

Srs. Magdalen Kilbane and Kathleen O'Connell visit with the indigenous populations in Mexico.

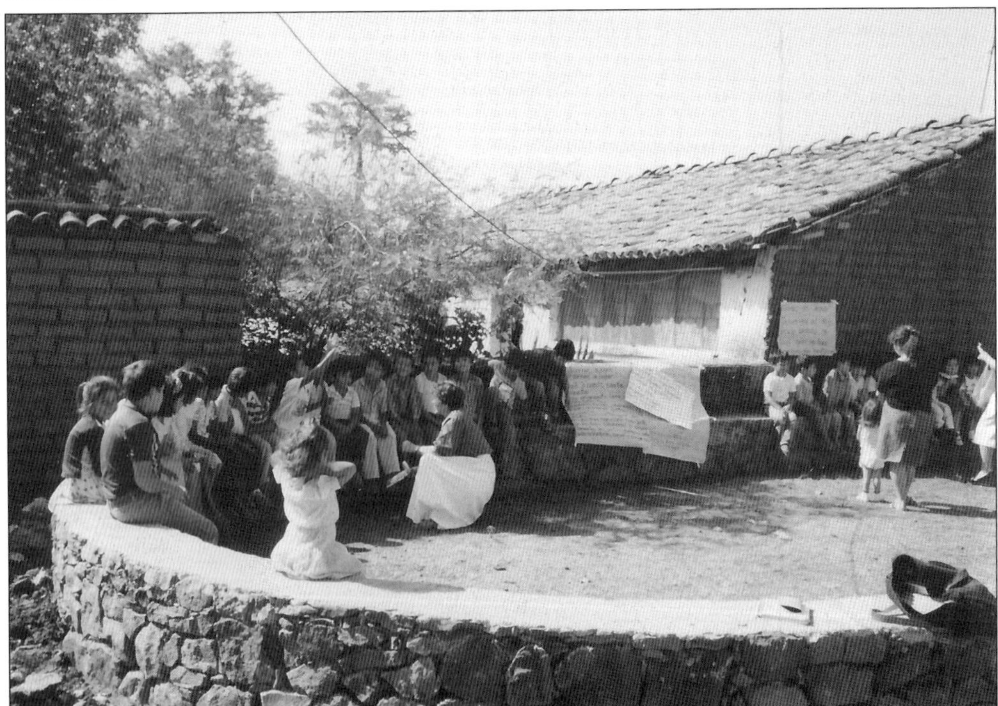

Sr. Marian Murray provides religious education to the village children in this outdoor classroom in Nayarit, Mexico. She uses the adobe walls to hang her visual aids to help the children in their studies.

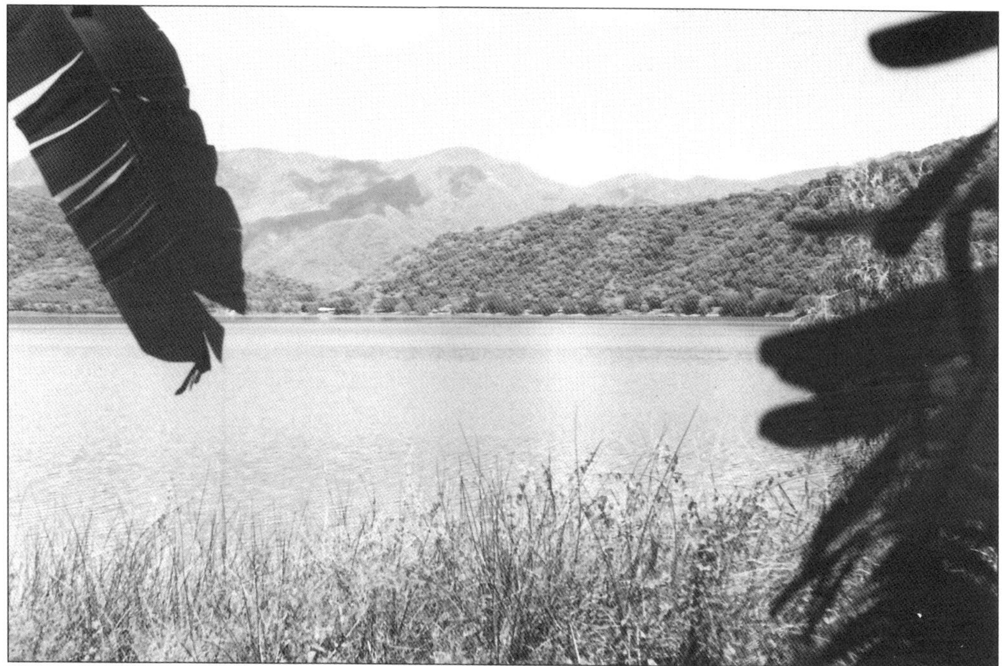

La Laguna de Santa Maria del Oro in Nayarit, Mexico, was formed by a volcanic crater. The lake skirts the mountainous region of the Sierra Madre Occidental. This reservoir provides the area with numerous recreational opportunities. The sisters traveled to the lake during their free time.

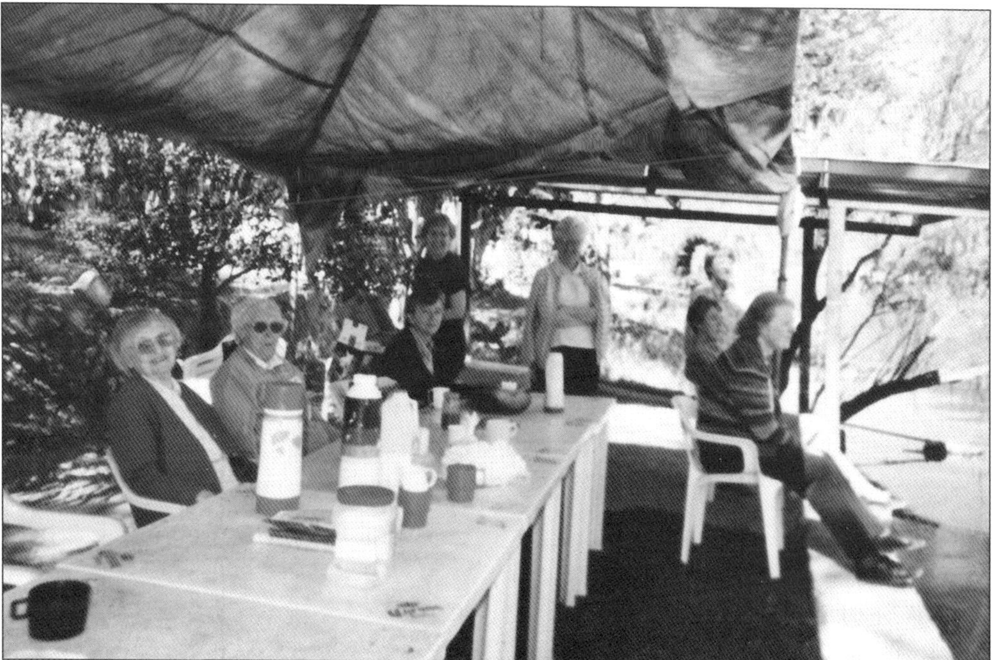

In this March 2004 photograph, the sisters are enjoying a breakfast at La Laguna de Santa Maria del Oro. From left to right are (seated) Srs. Kathleen O'Connell, Magdalen Kilbane, and Marian Murray; (standing) Srs. Loretta Armand, Therese Cunningham, and Peggy O'Flaherty; (seated at right, looking at lake) Srs. Veronica Cahill and Rita Nealon.

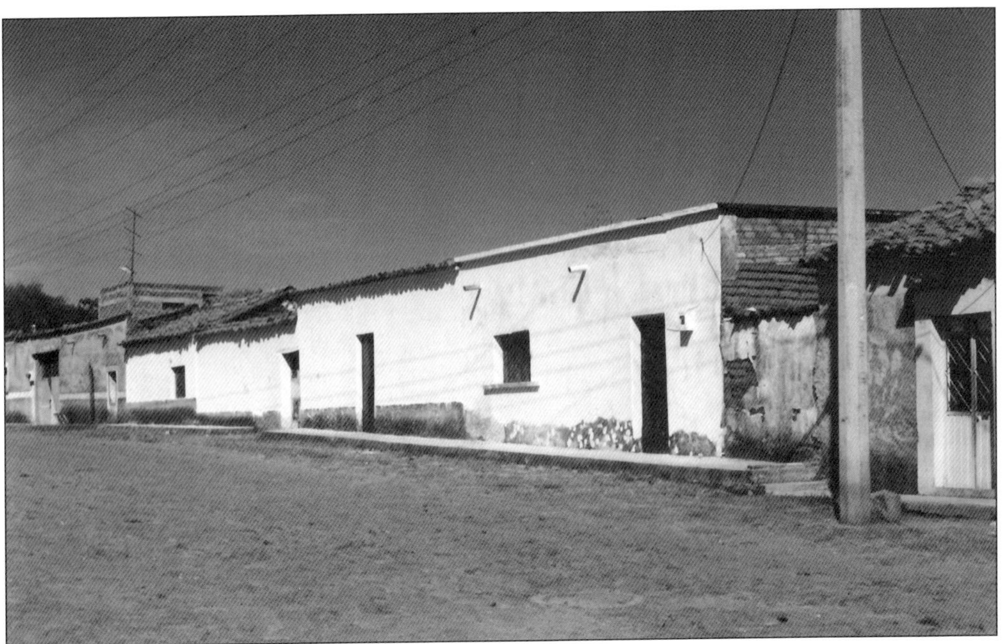

This was the first house in Nayarit where Srs. Marian Murray and Beatrice Donnellon lived in Santa Maria del Oro from November 6, 1990, through June 1, 1991. The sisters worked in religious education, natural medicine, and therapy, as well as different housing projects.

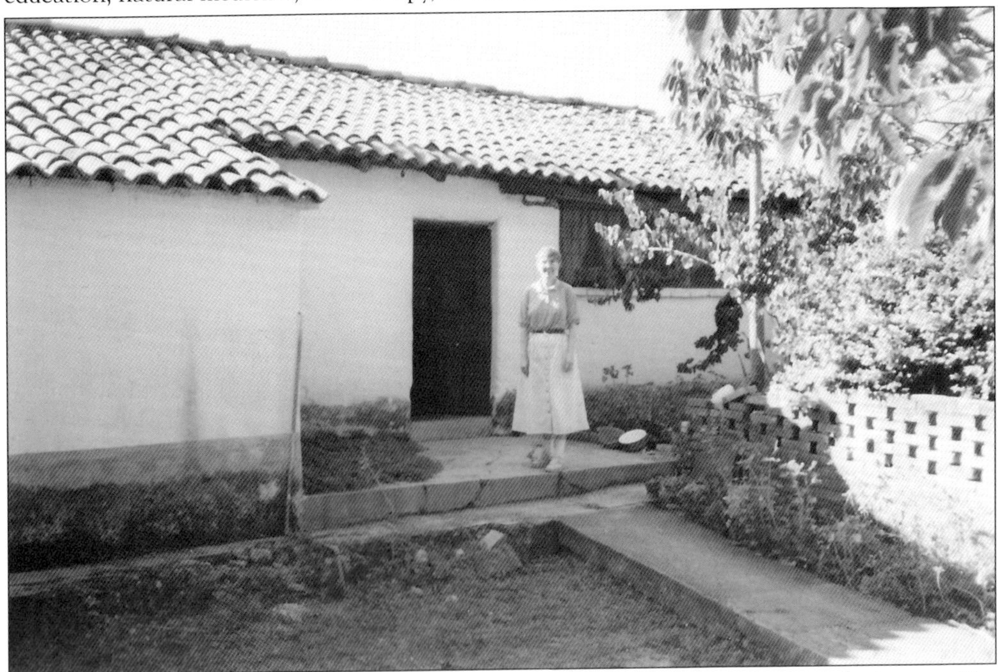

Sr. Loretta Armand is standing in front of their second home (1991–1994) in the *barrio* of La Quinta in Santa Maria del Oro, Nayarit, Mexico. The sisters performed main ministries in the barrios. The parish, El Senor de la Ascension, had about 25 villages where the sisters ministered. They also served in religious education and helped with Fiesta preparation, which proved to be a key event for evangelization.

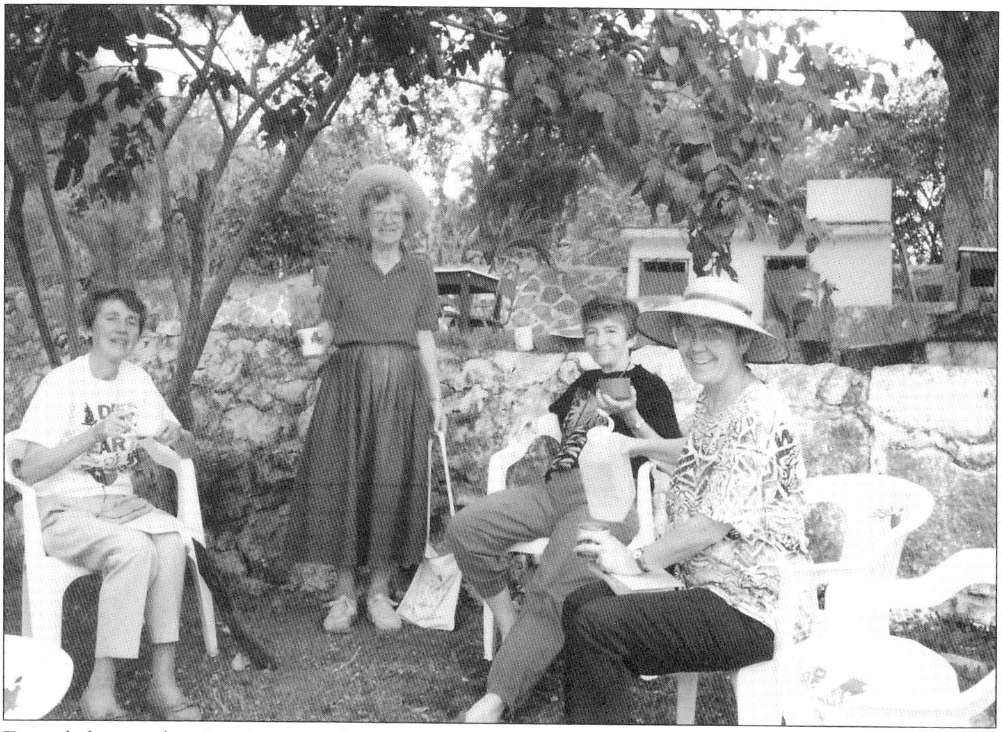

From left to right, Srs. Rita Nealon, Beatrice Donnellon, Marian Murray, and Loretta Armand are relaxing and keeping cool in La Laguna de Santa Maria del Oro.

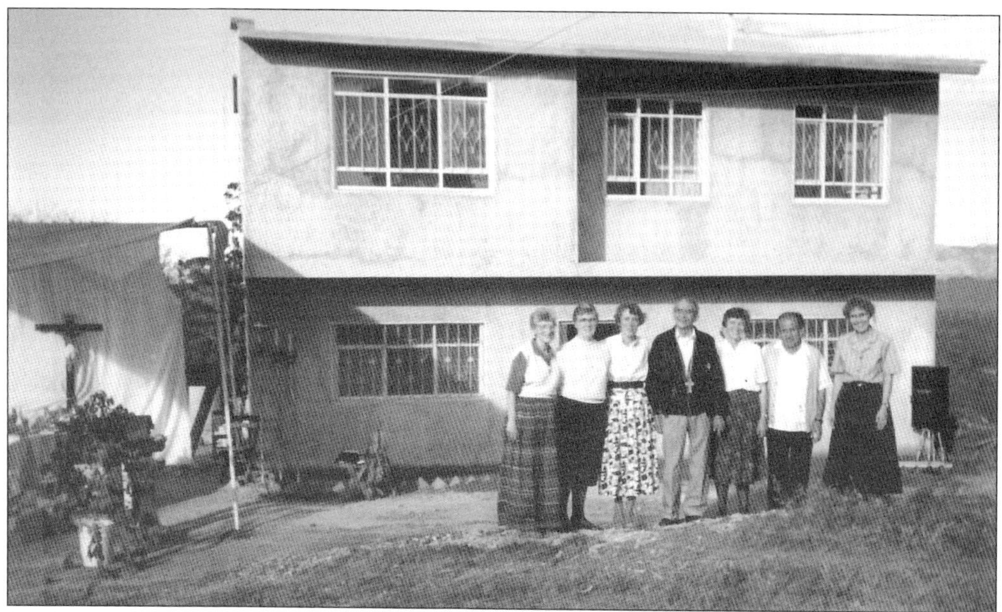

Srs. Beatrice Donnellon, Anne Finnerty, Rita Nealon, Bishop Robles Cota of Tepik, Sr. Marian Murray, Pastor Manuel Parada, and Sr. Loretta Armand stand in front of the building at Santa Maria del Oro on New Year's Eve in 1994. The clergy blessed this new house. On the left of the building is an outdoor altar to celebrate the Eucharist.

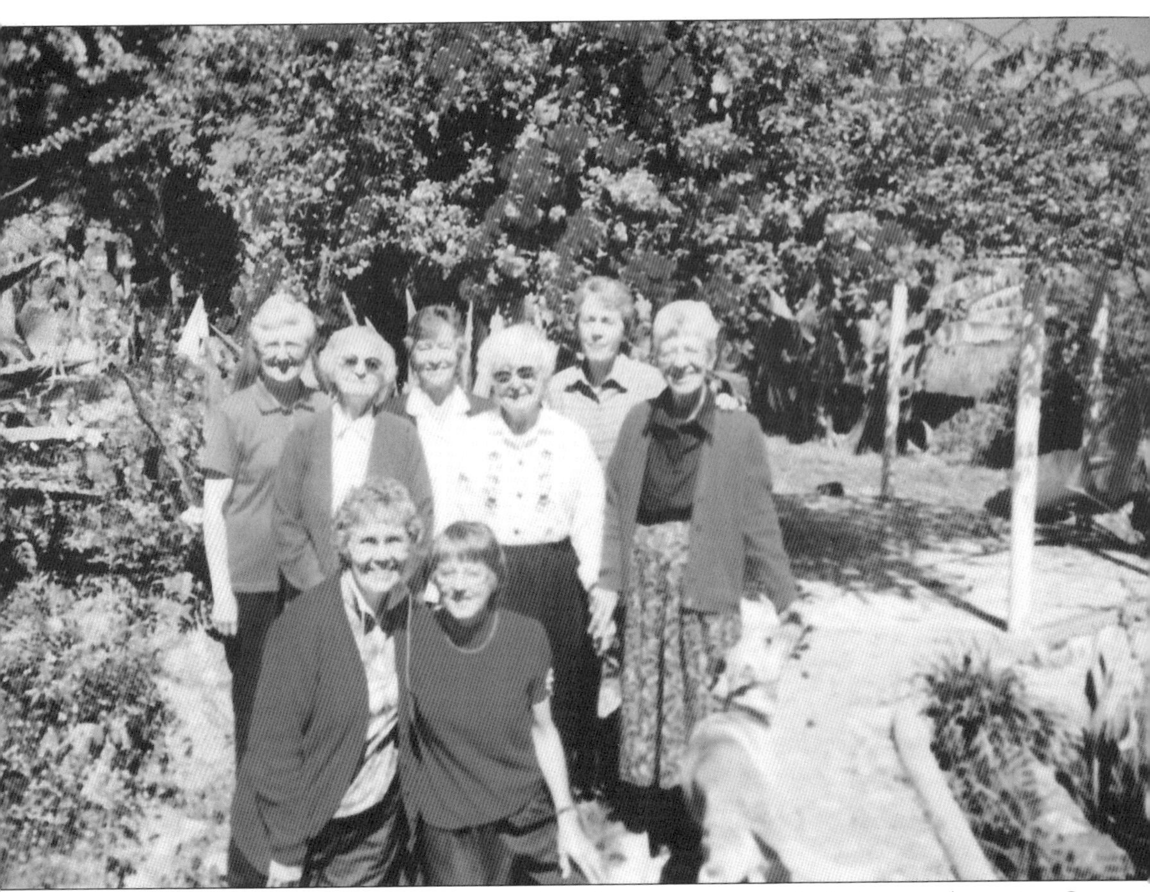

In March 2004, the Sisters of the Holy Spirit had a meeting with their general superior, Sr. Veronica Cahill in Santa Maria del Oro, Nayarit, Mexico. The sisters from Xoxocotlan, Oaxaca, Ixtlan del Rio, Nayarit, and Santa Maria del Oro, Nayarit, met in Santa Maria del Oro. The sisters posed for this photograph in the back of the Santa Maria del Oro house. From left to right are (first row, kneeling) Srs. Loretta Armand and Peggy O'Flaherty; (second row, standing) Srs. Therese Cunningham, Kathleen O'Connell, Marian Murray, Magdalen Kilbane, Rita Nealon, and Beatrice Donnellan. The dog's name is Paloma.

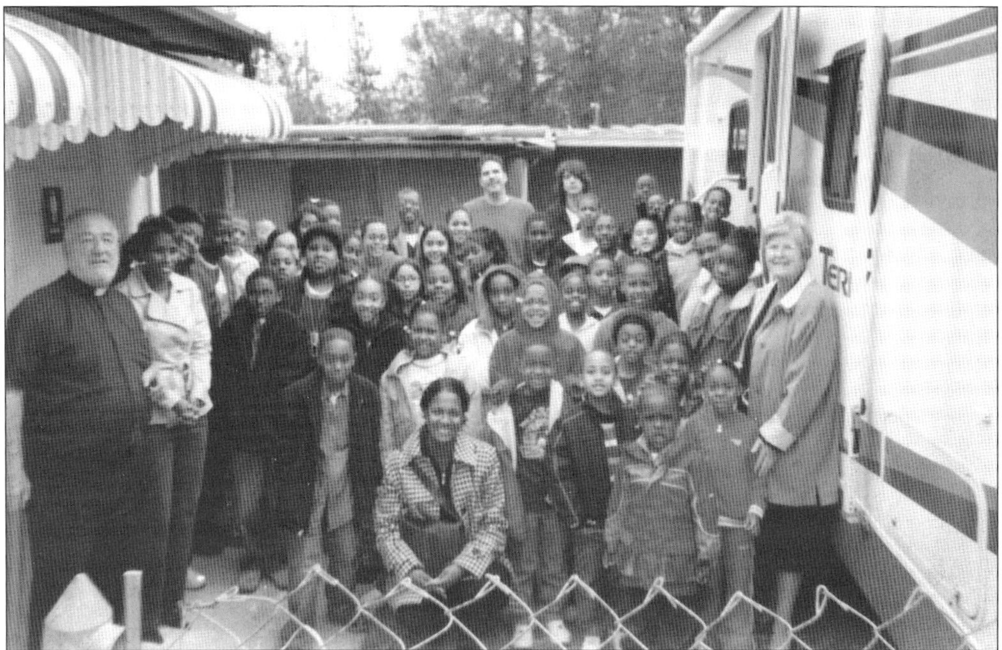
When Hurricane Katrina pummeled the United States in 2005, it swept away Sr. Carmelita Mulry's home. The category 5 storm left her homeless while she was working in two church parishes in Mississippi. The students from the CCC classes on Sunday and the staff from St. Therese's Church were treated to a tour of her new FEMA trailer, where she lived for two years.

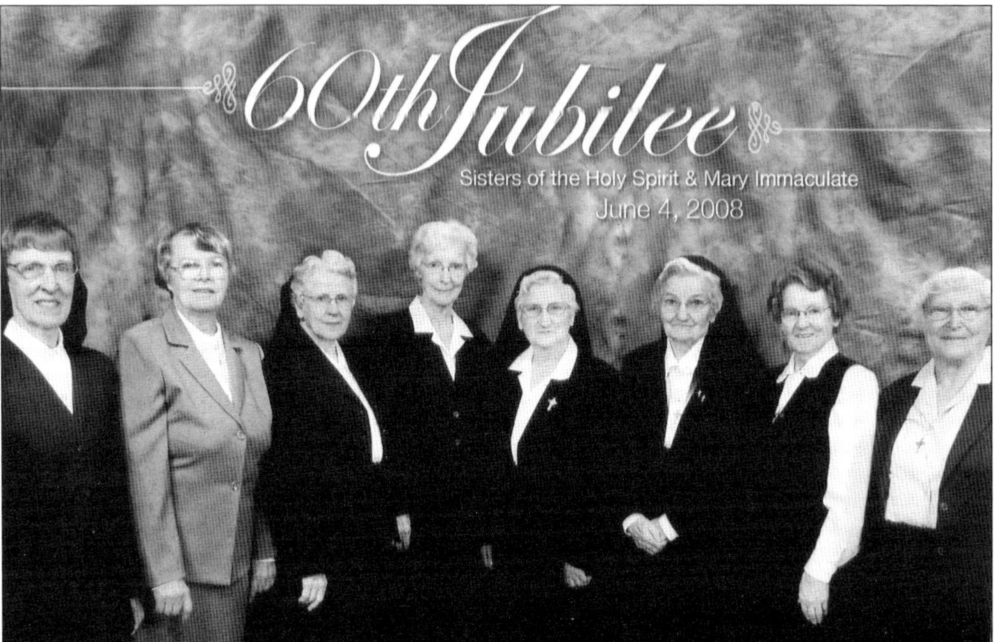

These eight sisters celebrated their 60th Jubilee on June 4, 2008. Celebrations such as this are always a means of renewing friendships and enjoying family, while acknowledging dedication, sacrifice, and work. From left to right are Srs. Patricia Walsh, Mary Martin Walsh, Gabriel Hession, Lucy Collins, Madeleine Cannon, Florita Burke, Bertha Dempsey, and Magdalen Kilbane.

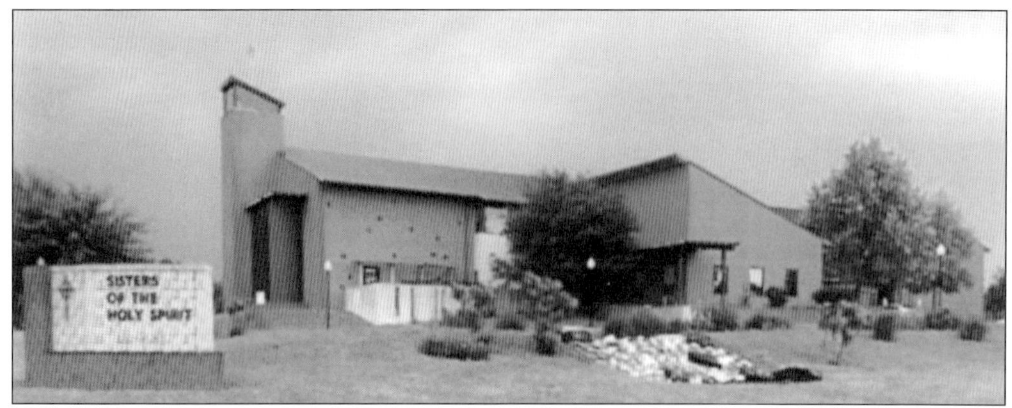

After much discussion, the Sisters of the Holy Spirit and Mary Immaculate decided to construct this convent to become their new motherhouse in 2009. This building faces the old motherhouse across the street, and the chapel contains huge windows that provide clear views of the old building.

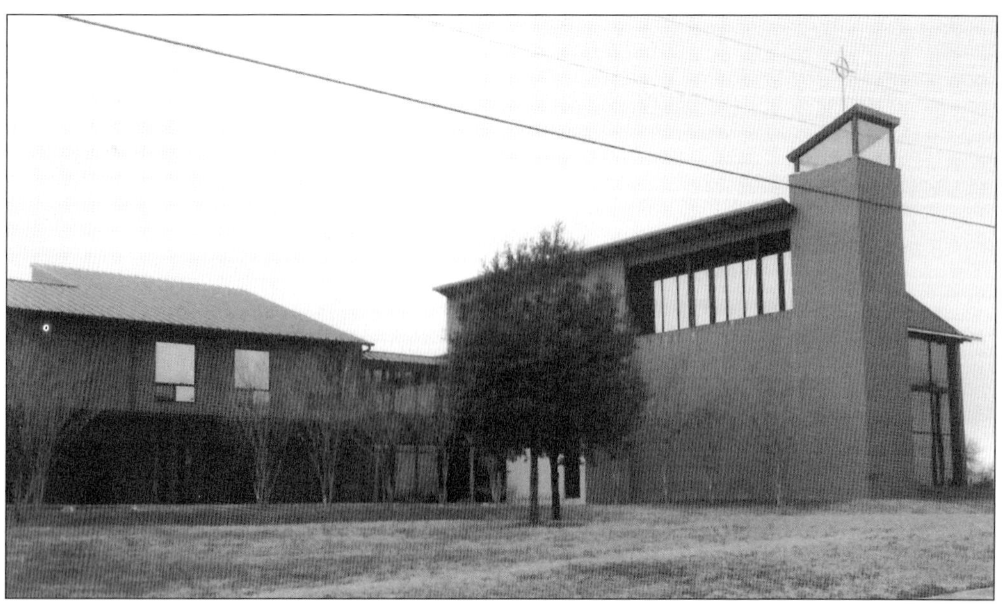

This is another view of the motherhouse for the Sisters of the Holy Spirit and Mary Immaculate. The building was constructed by Malitz Construction and the Roby architectural firm.

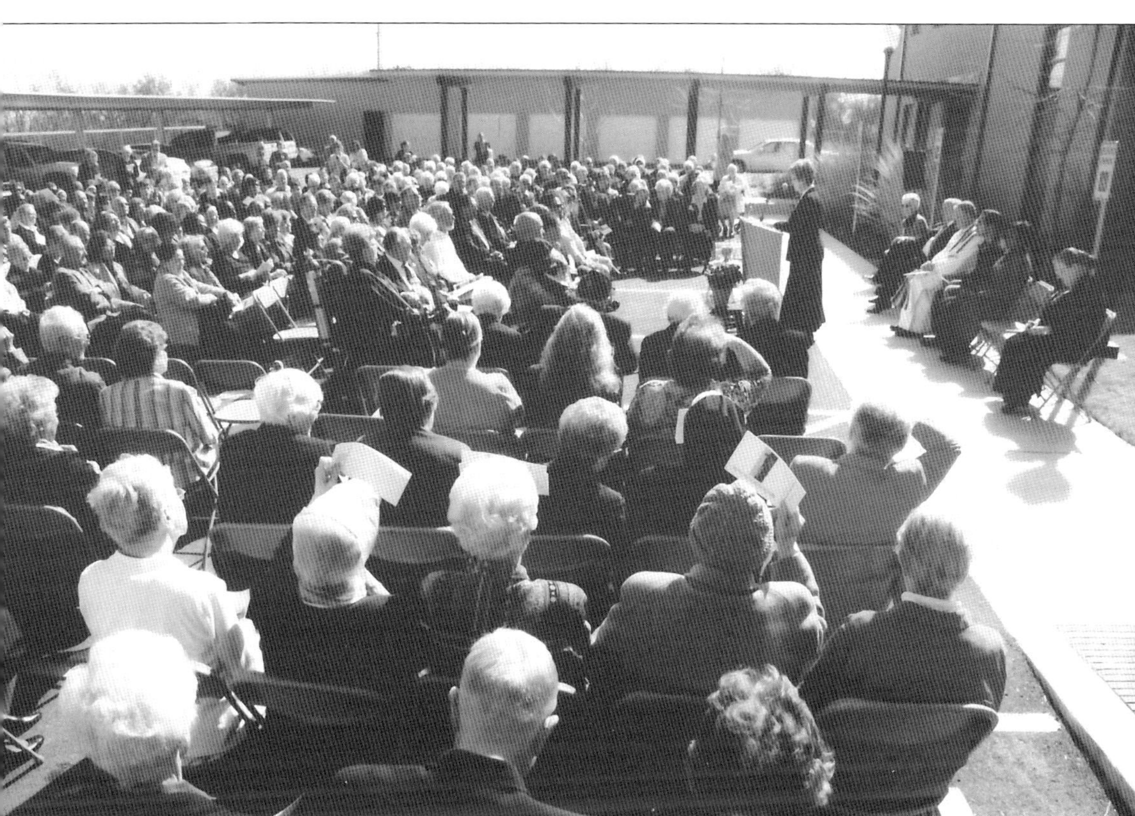

On February 3, 2010, the new convent received the blessings of the archbishop. The sisters entertained guests and dignitaries who helped rejoice in the completion of the new building. Guests learned the history of the sisters and celebrated their accomplishments with well wishes for a bright and blessed future.

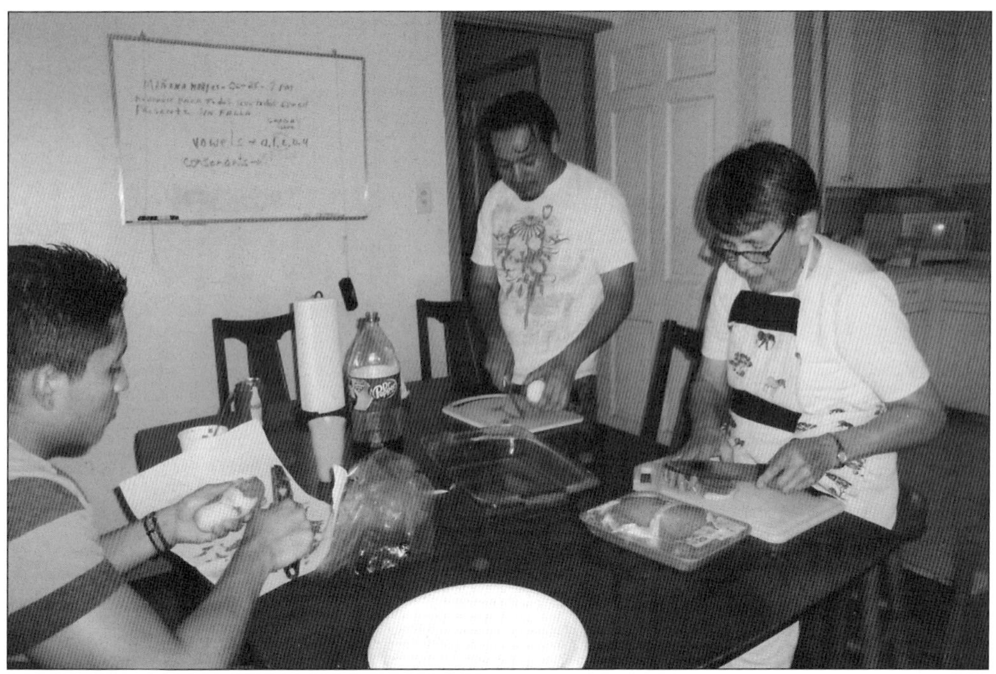

Sr. Irene Arrendondo is preparing a meal for the immigrants at Casa Guadalupe on the West Side of San Antonio.

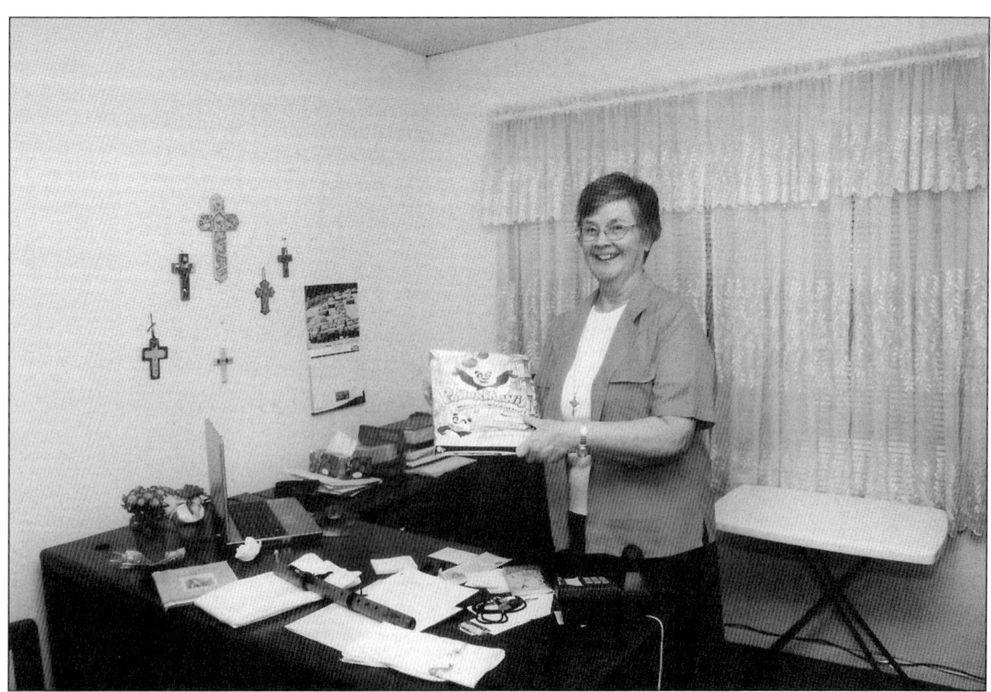

Sr. Dympna Clarke poses with a children's book. Sister Dympna worked with Parish Ministry for several parishes, aiding families with religious education.

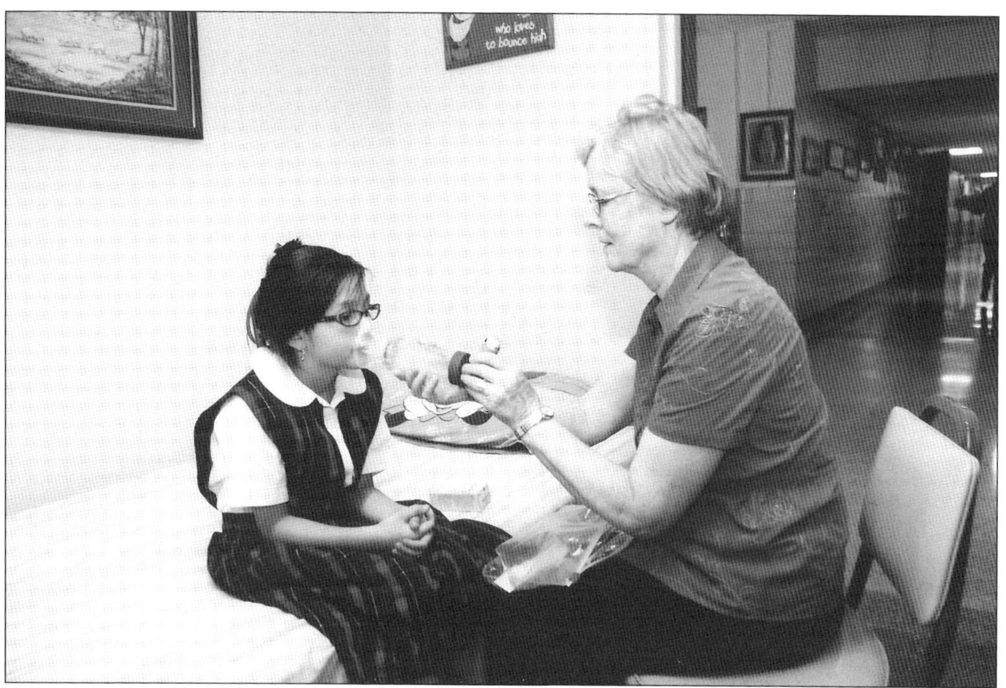

Sister Genevieve was the health coordinator with Little Flower School in San Antonio. She is shown providing a student with a breathing treatment.

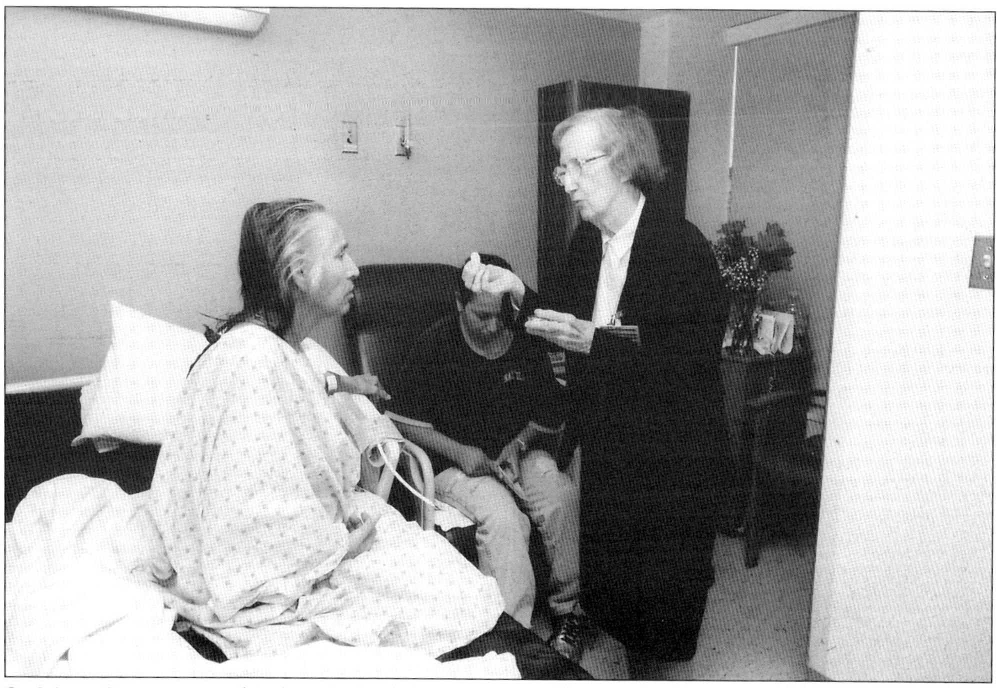

Sr. Mary Greene served in hospital ministry at several hospitals. She consoled the sick, provided spiritual guidance, and prayed with the families.

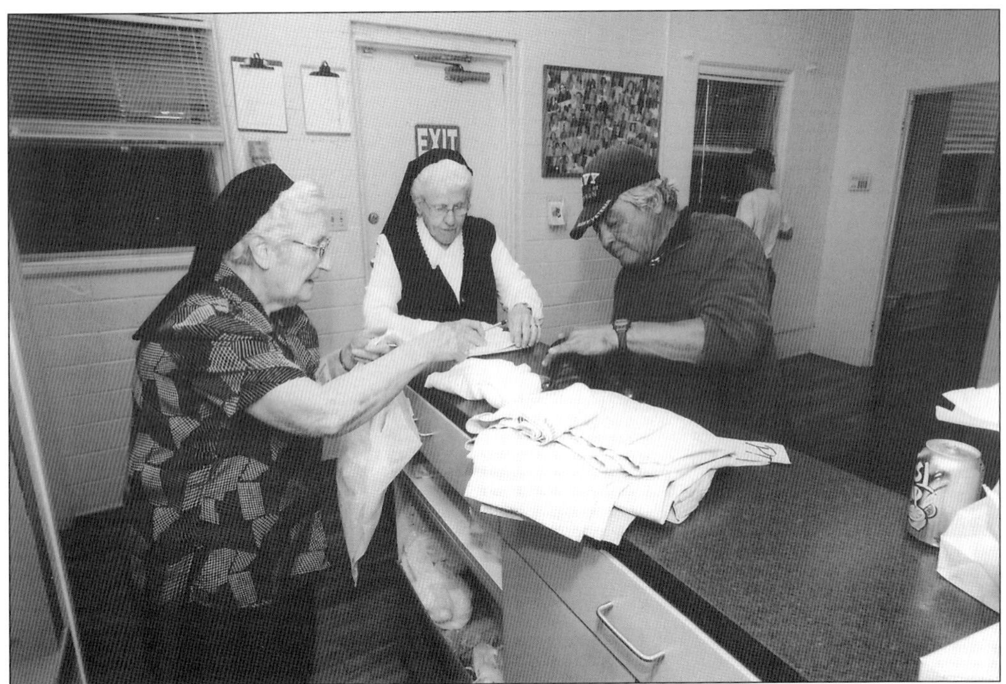

Sr. Madeleine Cannon and Sr. Gabriel Hession sort out paperwork at Christian Assistance Ministry (CAM) in San Antonio. They distribute clothing and other materials to the poor in the area.

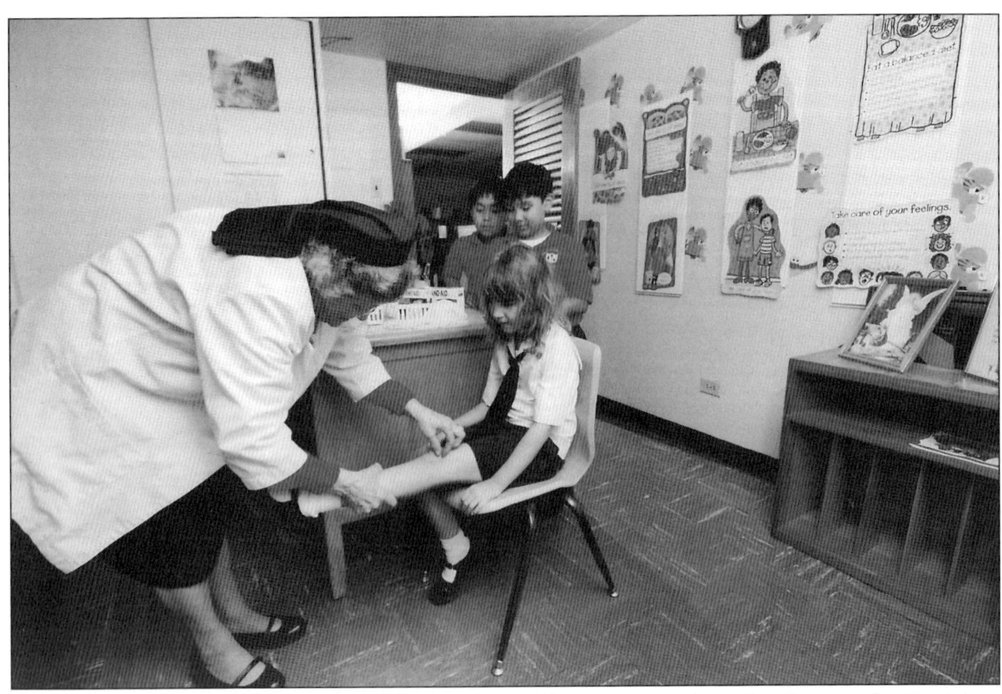

Sr. Veronica Mitchell doctors a child's leg. Sister Veronica was the school nurse for St. Mary Margaret's School in San Antonio.

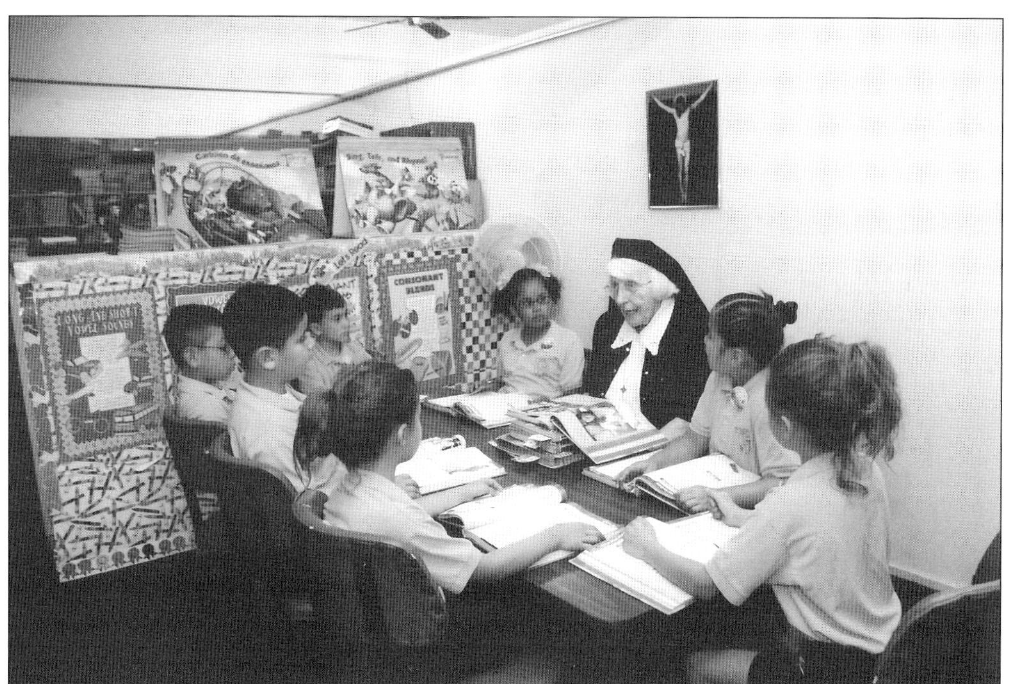

Sr. Doloretta Madigan engages her students at St. Cecilia's School in San Antonio. She helped the children improve their reading and led many lively discussion groups.

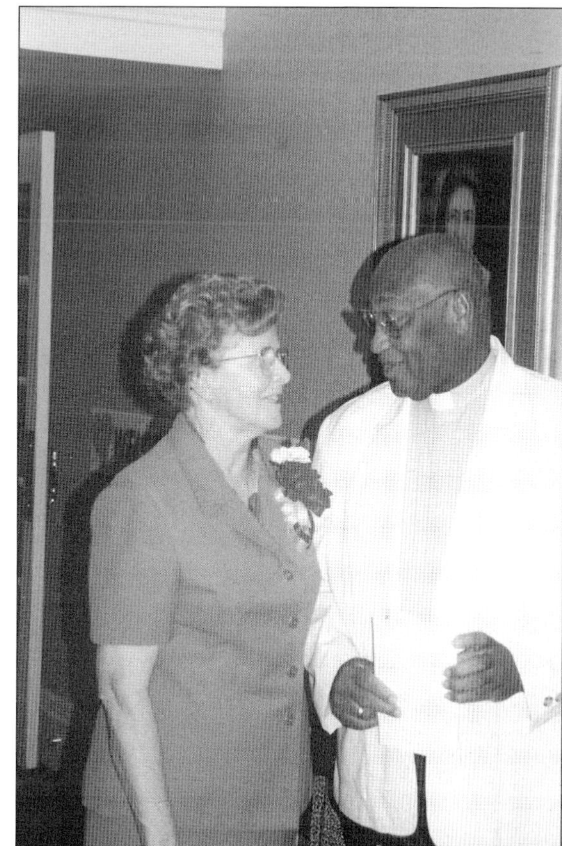

Sr. Carmelita Mulry experienced a joyful moment with Fr. Edwin Johnson. Father Johnson attended St. Peter Claver High School as a child and later returned to teach at the school for many years before being ordained a Marianist priest.

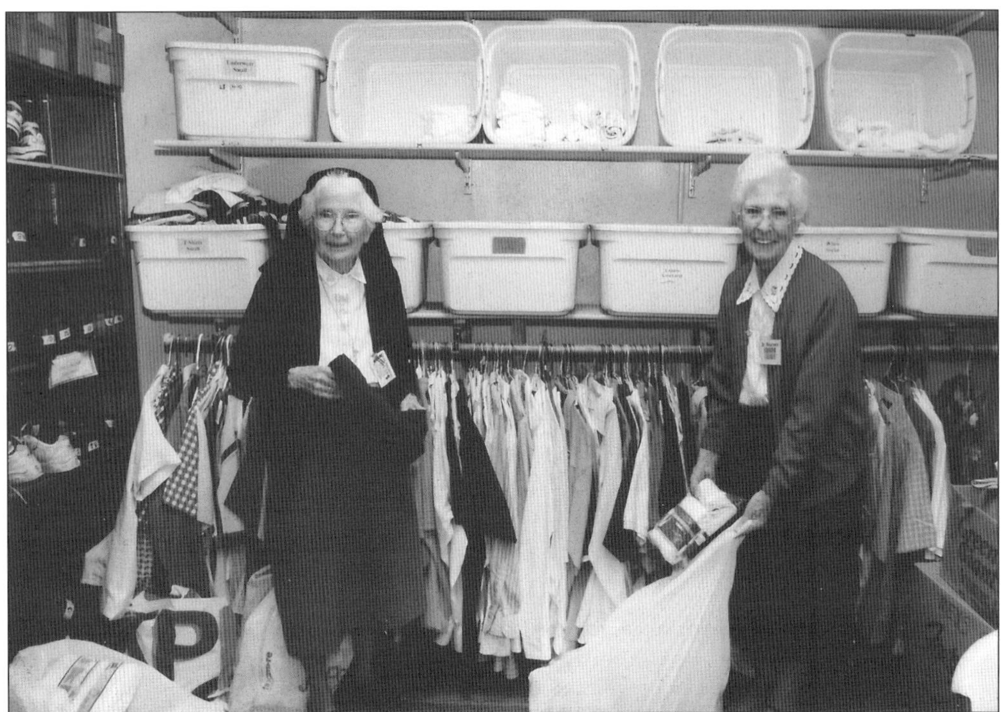

Sr. Ferdinand Connerney and Sr. Maureen Finnerty are sorting clothes for CAM. This organization started in 1977 and distributes food and clothes to residents of San Antonio.

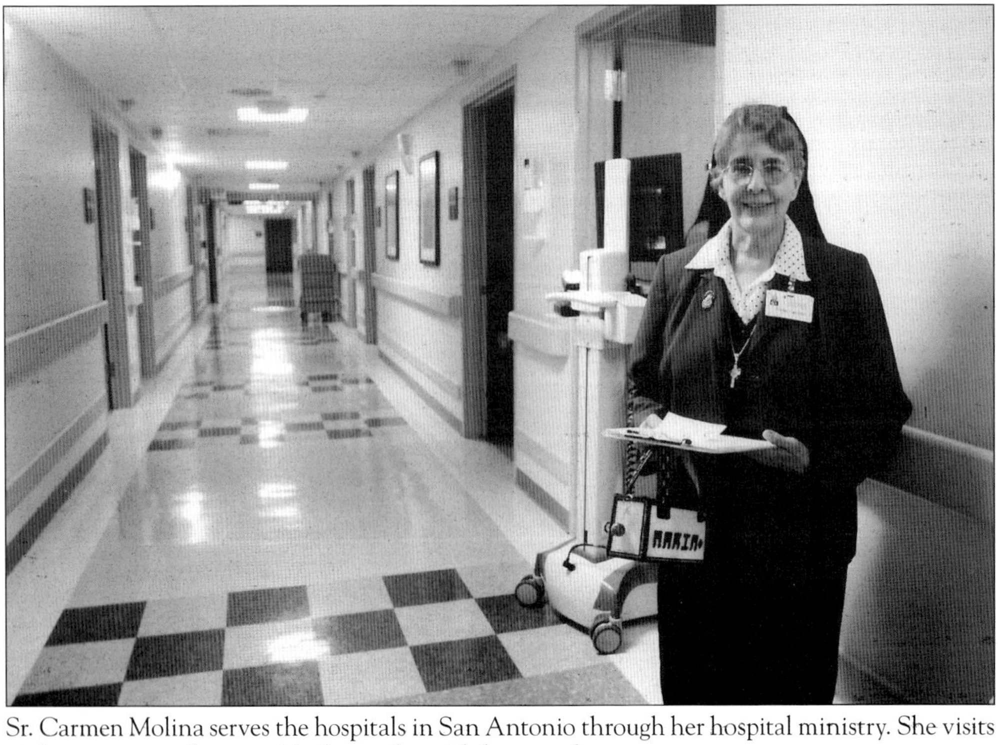

Sr. Carmen Molina serves the hospitals in San Antonio through her hospital ministry. She visits with everyone and prays with those who wish her comfort.

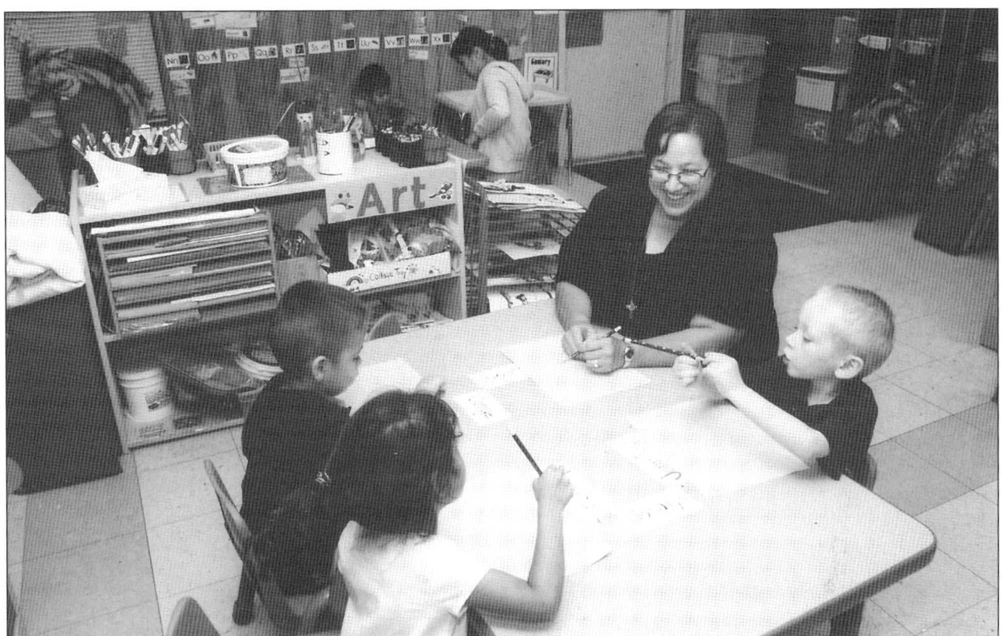

Sr. Kathleen Huguet works with the children at the Healy-Murphy Center in San Antonio, Texas. The Child Development Center provides students who attend Healy-Murphy High School a place to leave their children while they are in class.

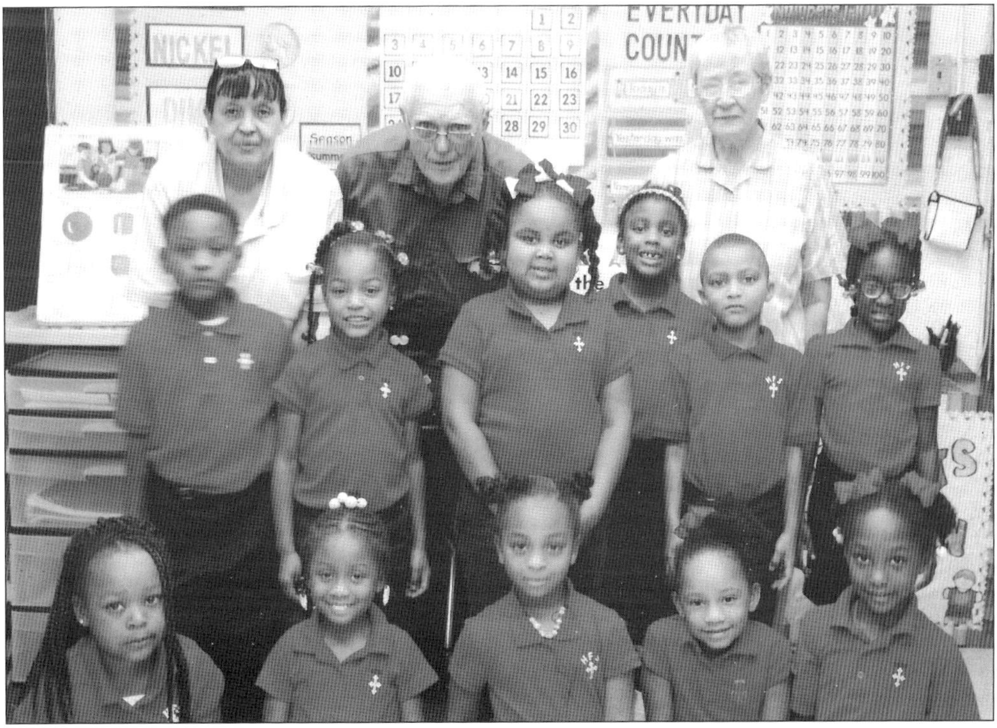

Pictured here are Faye Barnes, Father Fallon, and Sr. Louise McLoughlin and the kindergarten class of 2017 in Natchez, Mississippi. Sister Bernadette was the principal and development director for Holy Family School for almost 10 years.

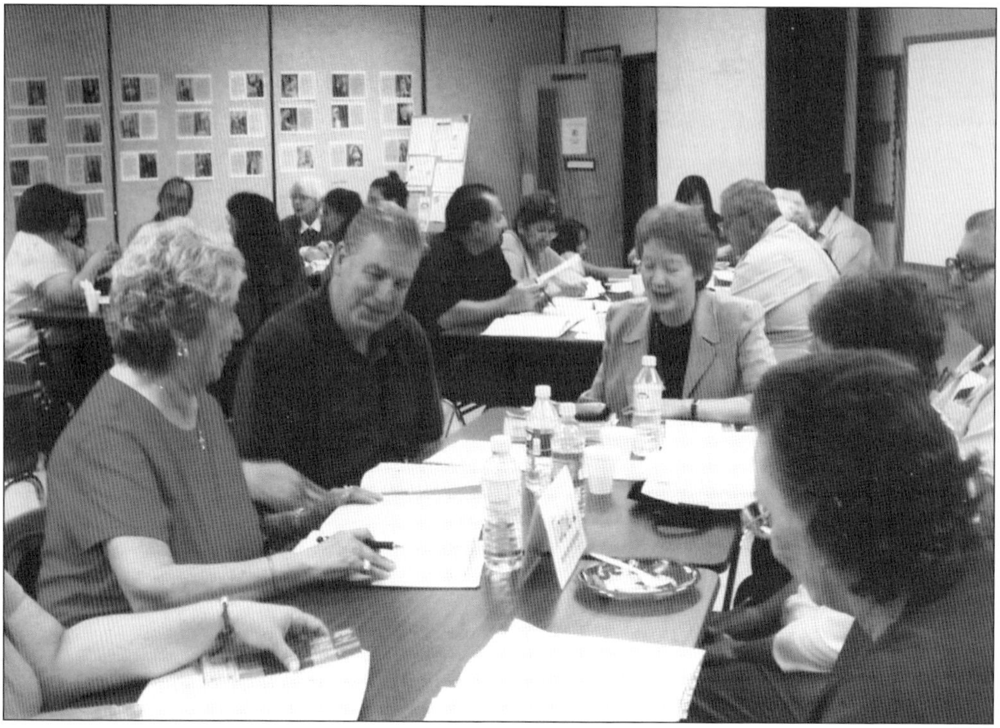

Sr. Katrina Ruane conducts an adult faith formation at Our Lady of Perpetual Help Parish in Selma, Texas. Sister Ruane taught for many years and was a principal before working in parish ministry.

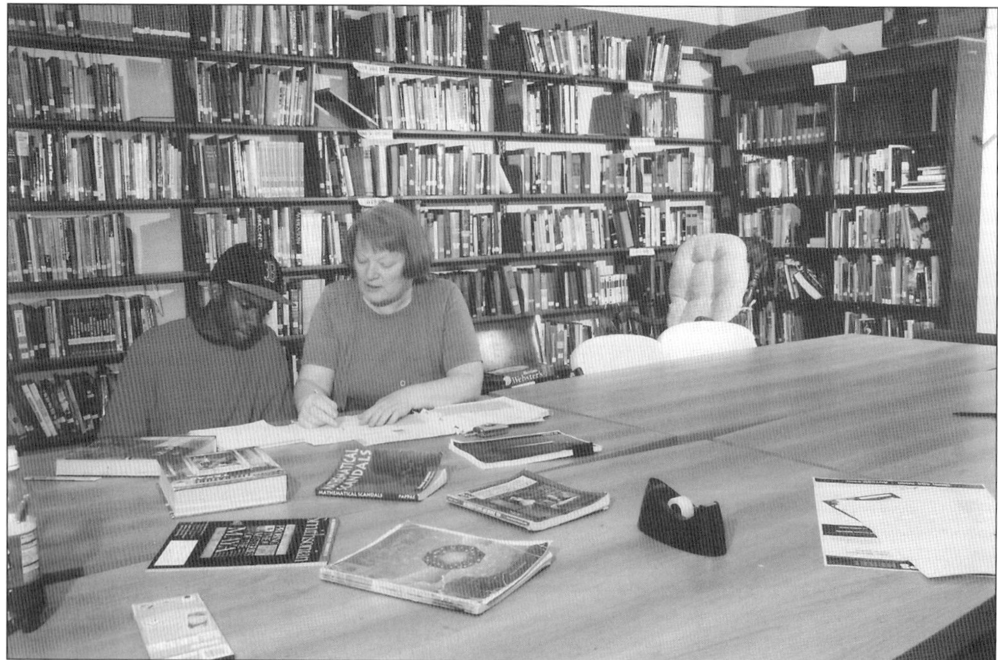

Sr. Veronica Cahill works with students at the Healy-Murphy Center in San Antonio. She is involved with the GED program.

Sr. Janet Nall is pictured administering to a patient in hospice care. A trained nurse, she provides hospice care in San Antonio and surrounding areas.

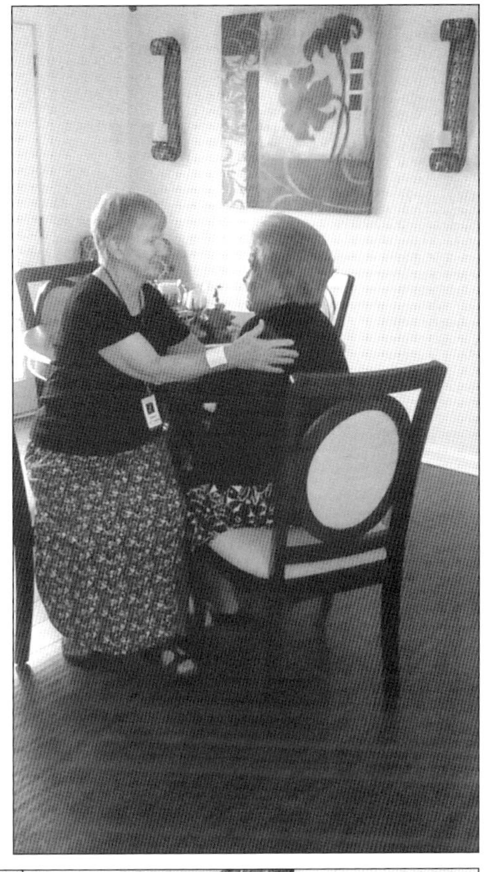

Sr. Nora Gavin reads to the young children at the Healy-Murphy Center.

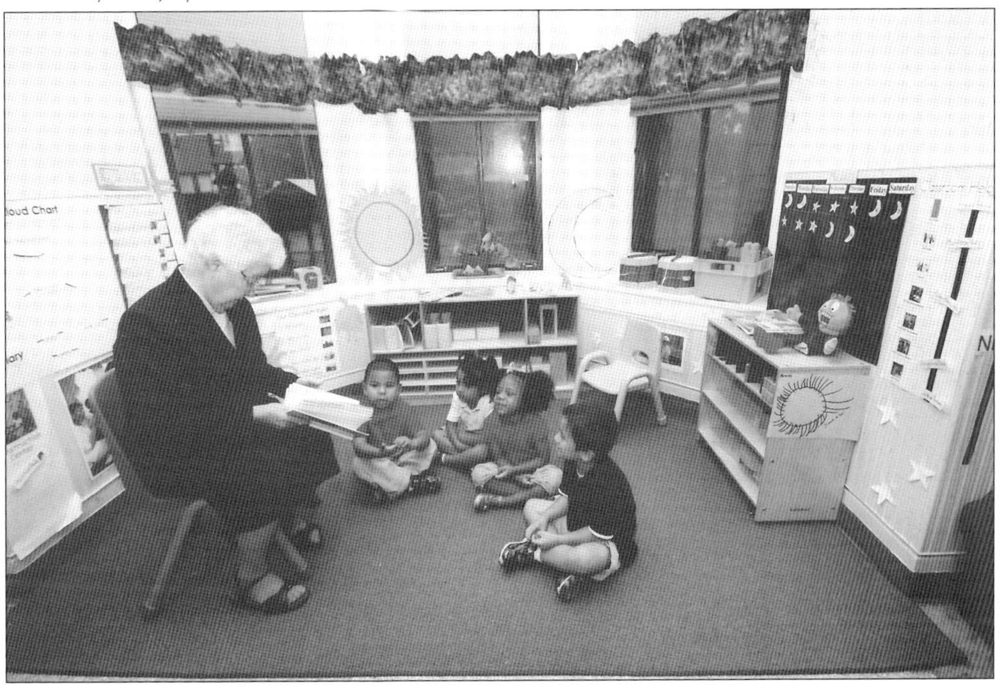

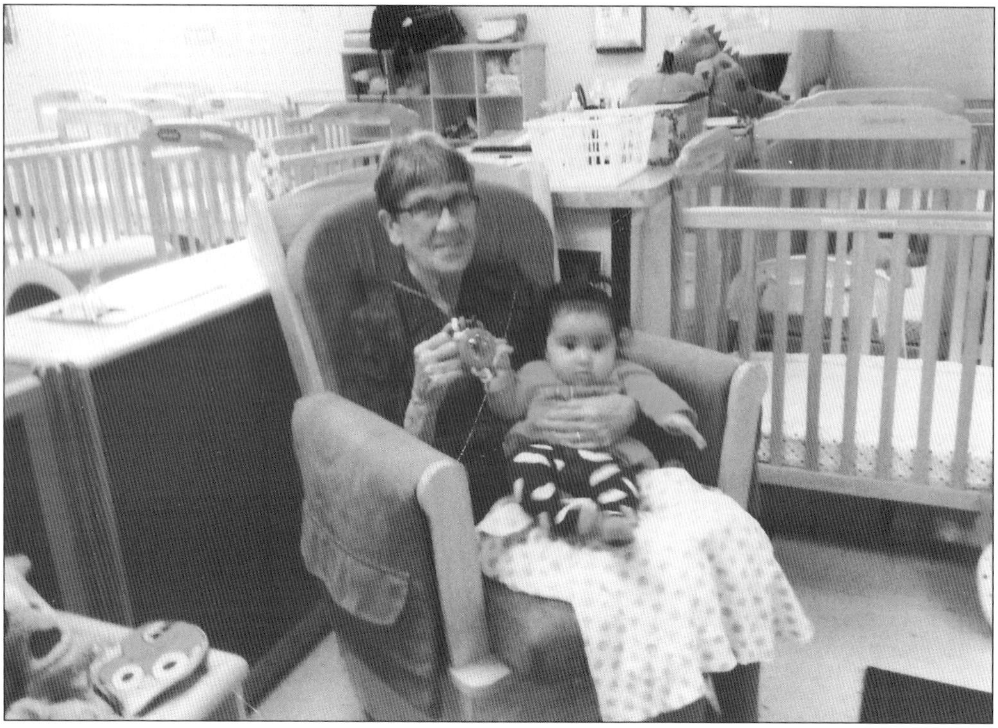

Sr. Kathleen Higgins volunteered at the Healy-Murphy Child Care Center after she retired from teaching.

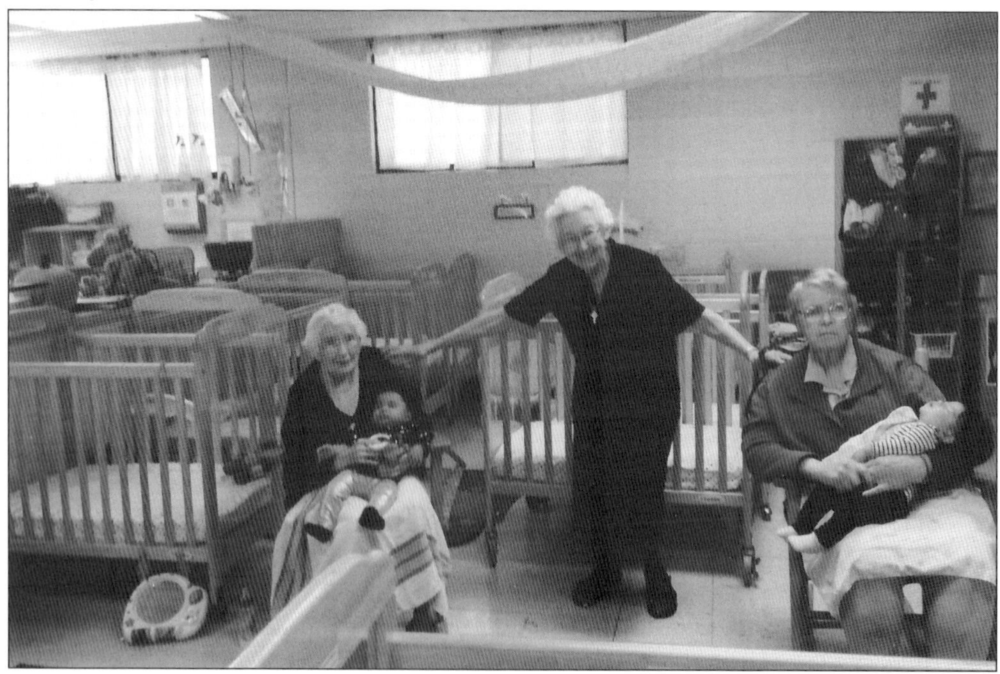

Srs. Ferdinand Connerney, Bernadette McNamara, and Mary Walsh also volunteer at the Healy Murphy Center. They comfort the babies until their parents return to pick them up after school.

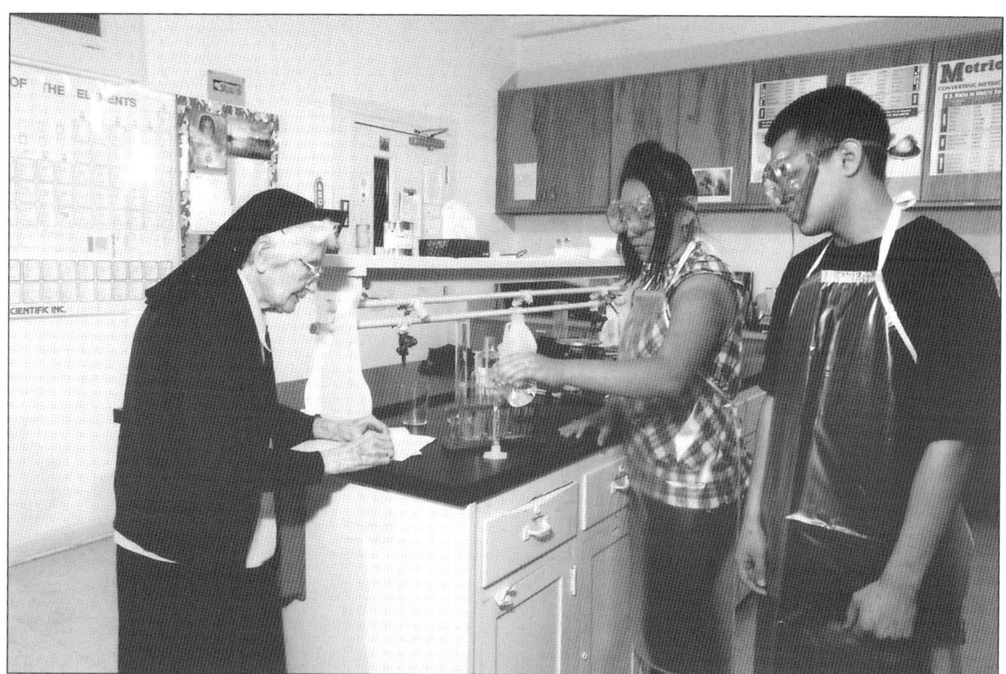

Sr. Ferdinand Connerney taught for many years in Louisiana and Texas for several schools. She is pictured here tutoring students in science at the Healy-Murphy Center.

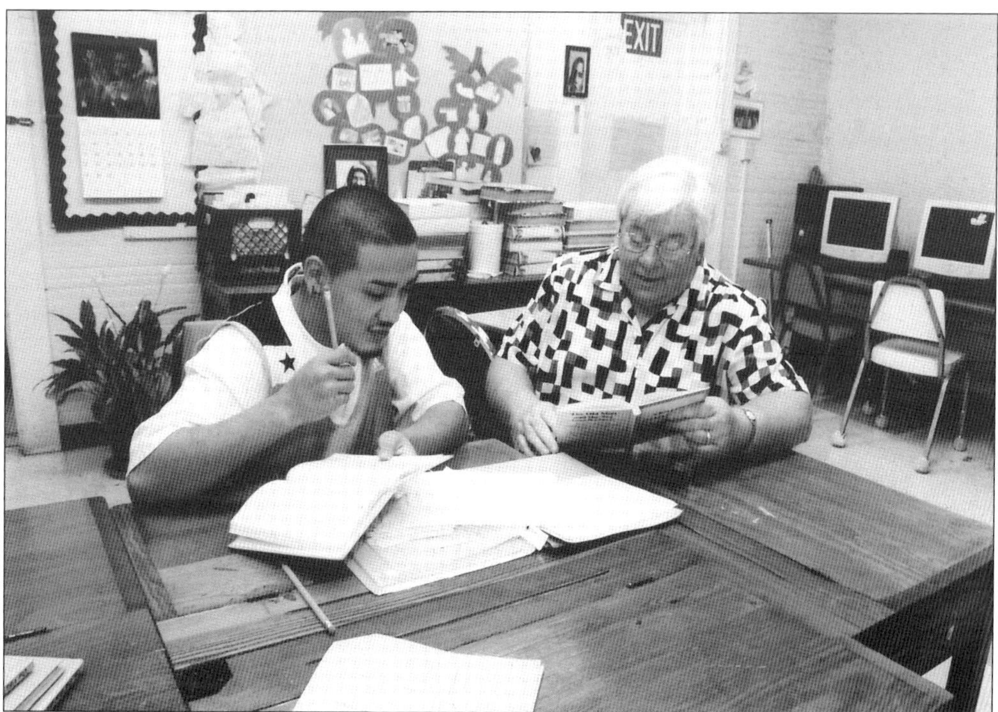

Sr. Mary Fagan is pictured helping a student with his English class. She has taught at the Healy-Murphy Center for several years.

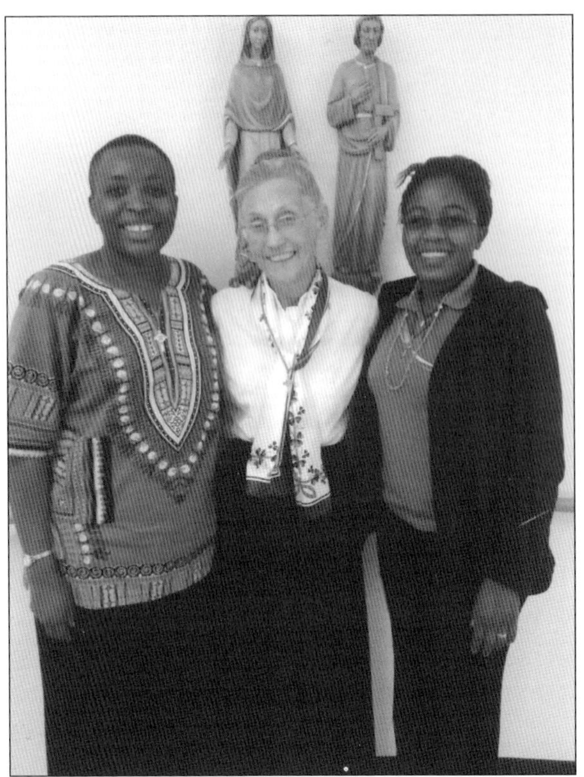

Srs. Maimbolwa Lutangu, Christina Mitchell, and Angela Kashela came from Africa to the motherhouse in San Antonio for a general assembly meeting in March 2017.

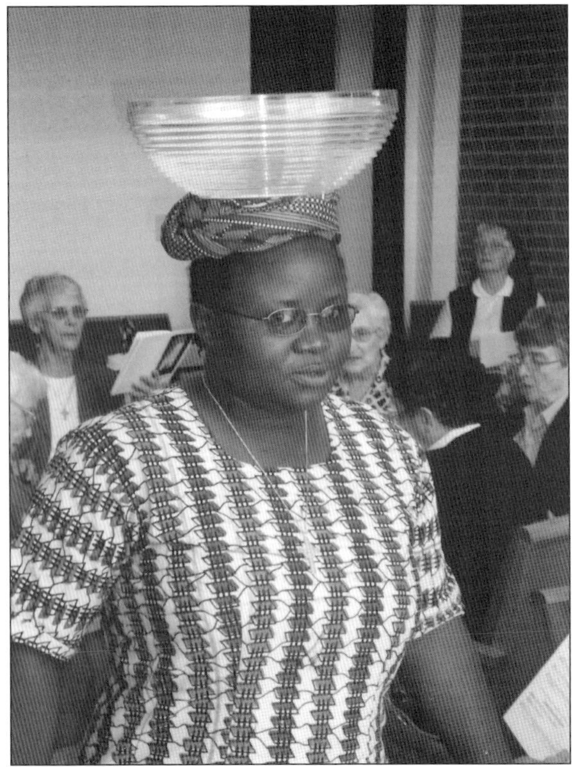

Sr. Matilda Chanda, attending a general chapter meeting at the motherhouse, carries water down the chapel aisle. Water symbolized one of the elements for the environment at the meeting.

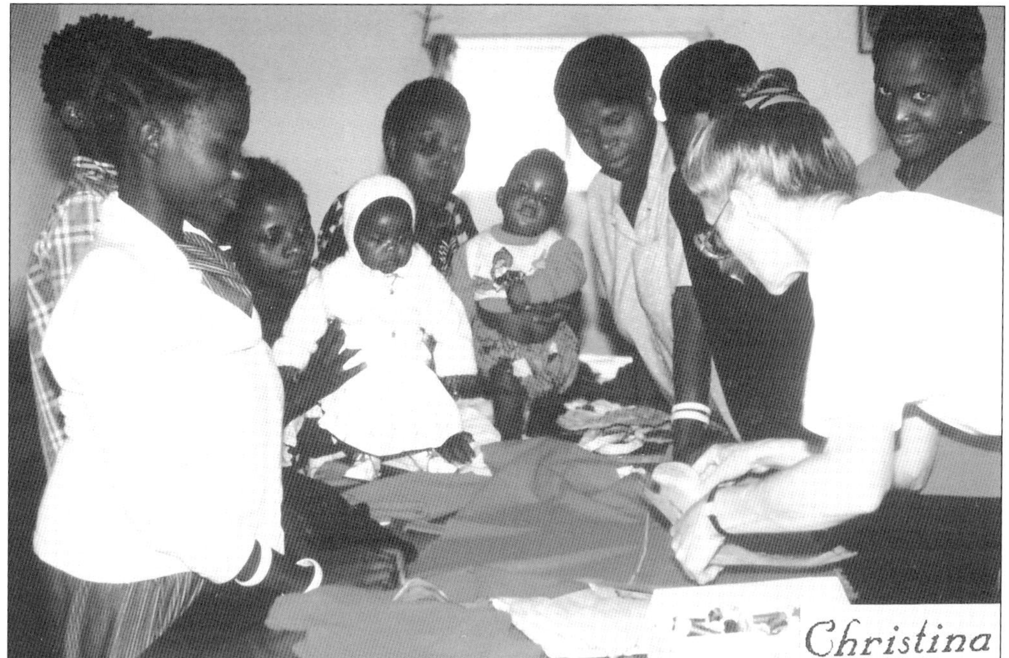

Sr. Christina Mitchell is pictured teaching mothers and young women to sew in Kalabo, Zambia. Sister Christina worked in Zambia for more than 20 years, teaching religious education and sharing her various skills with the local people.

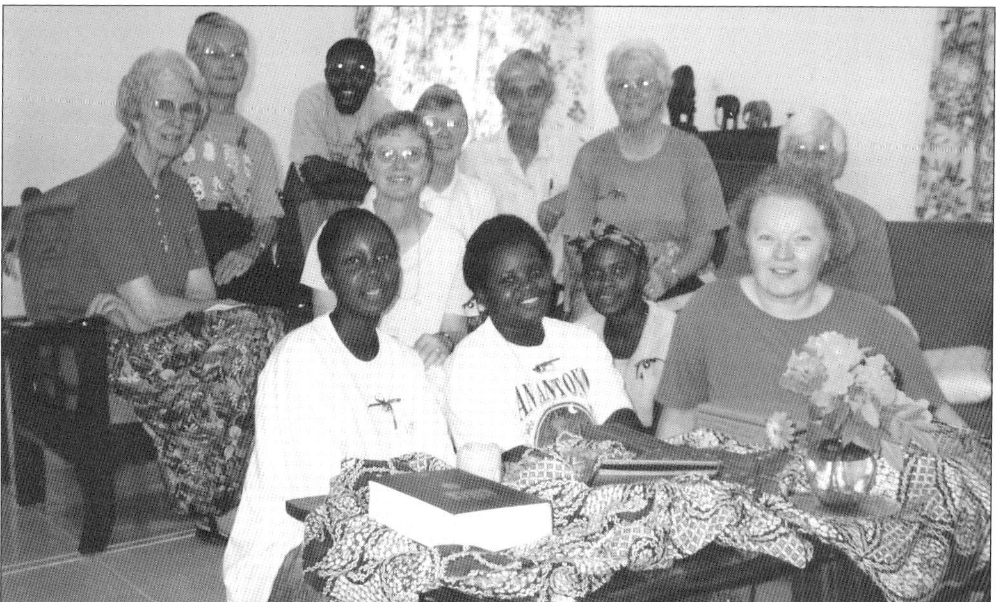

Sr. Veronica Cahill, general superior at the time of this 2005 photograph, traveled to Zambia and held a retreat on the lives of women saints. The items arranged on the table are used to prepare the environment for the retreat. From left to right are (first row, seated) unidentified, Sr. Matilda Chanda, unidentified, and Sr. Veronica Cahill; (second row) Srs. Mary Margaret O'Grady, Christina Mitchell, Maimbolwa Lutangu, Janet Nall, Anne Finnerty, Geraldine Klein, Rose McHugh, and Monica Carroll.

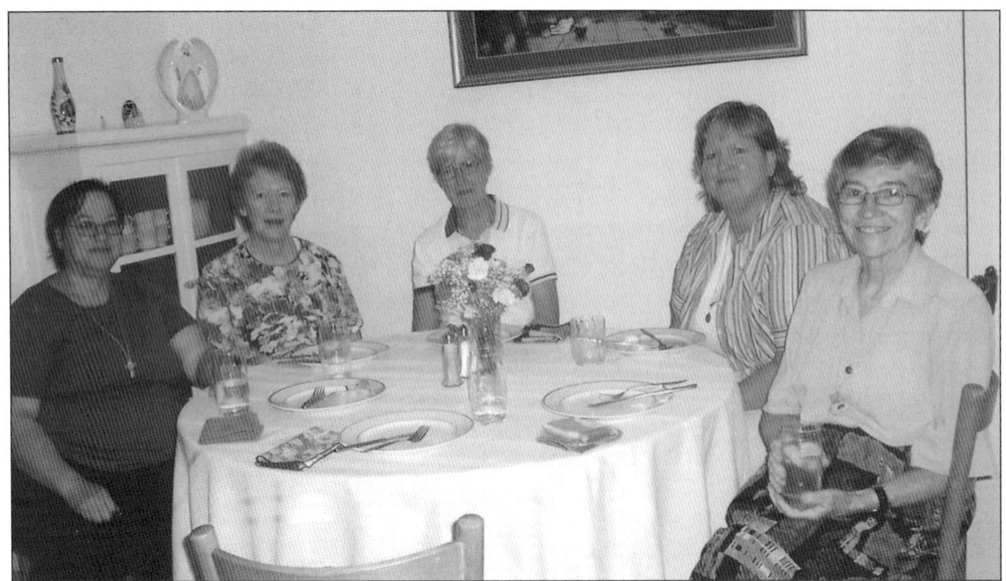

Sr. Kathleen Huguet, Sr. Katrina Ruane, Sr. Eileen Mannion, Alexis Aikens, and Sr. Marian Murray sit around the table at the formation house in July 2011.

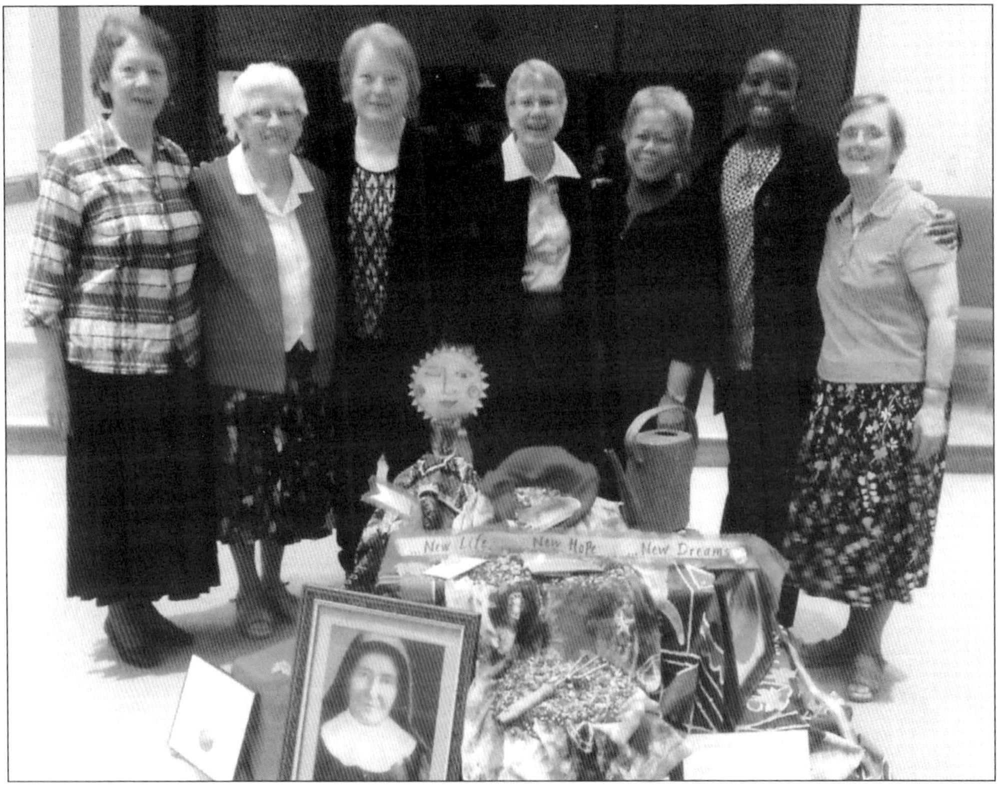

In preparation for the General Chapter 2006, the sisters were involved in a retreat process directed by Sr. Constance Phelps, SCL. Standing around the prayer altar are Sr. Katrina Ruane, Sr. Jo Murray, Sr. Veronica Cahill, Sr. Janet Nall, Sr. Constance Phelps, Maimbolwa Lutangu, and Bernie Barrett.

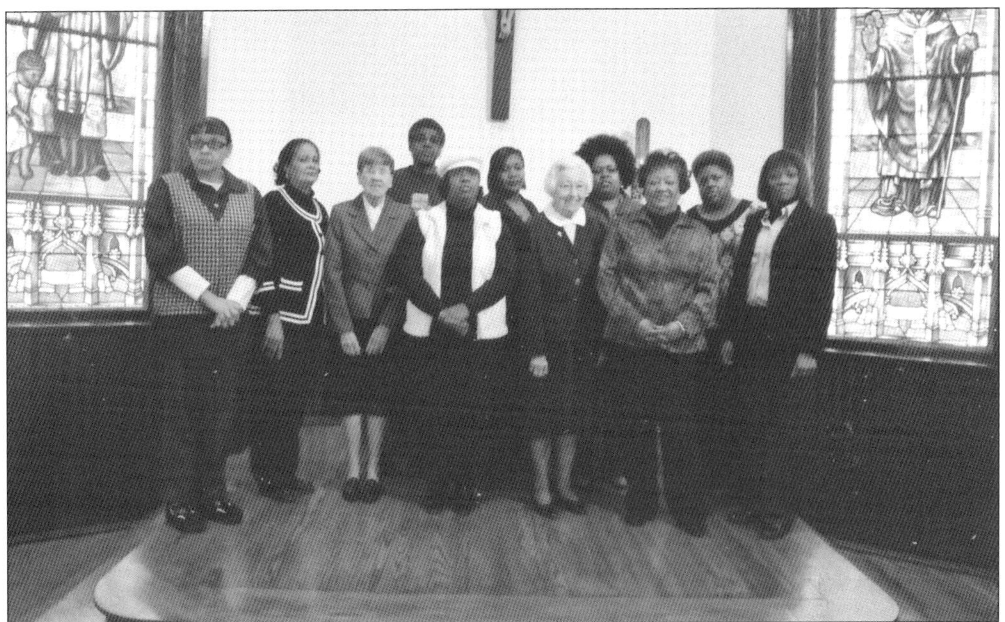

Pictured in Holy Family Church in Natchez, Mississippi, after a meeting are, from left to right, Faye Barnes, Joyce Carlston, Sr. Kathleen Higgins, Leroy Brown, Shirley Gains, Ira Young, Sr. Bernadette McNamara, Jennifer Prater, Mildred Ealey, Tiffany McKnight, and Deanne Johnson.

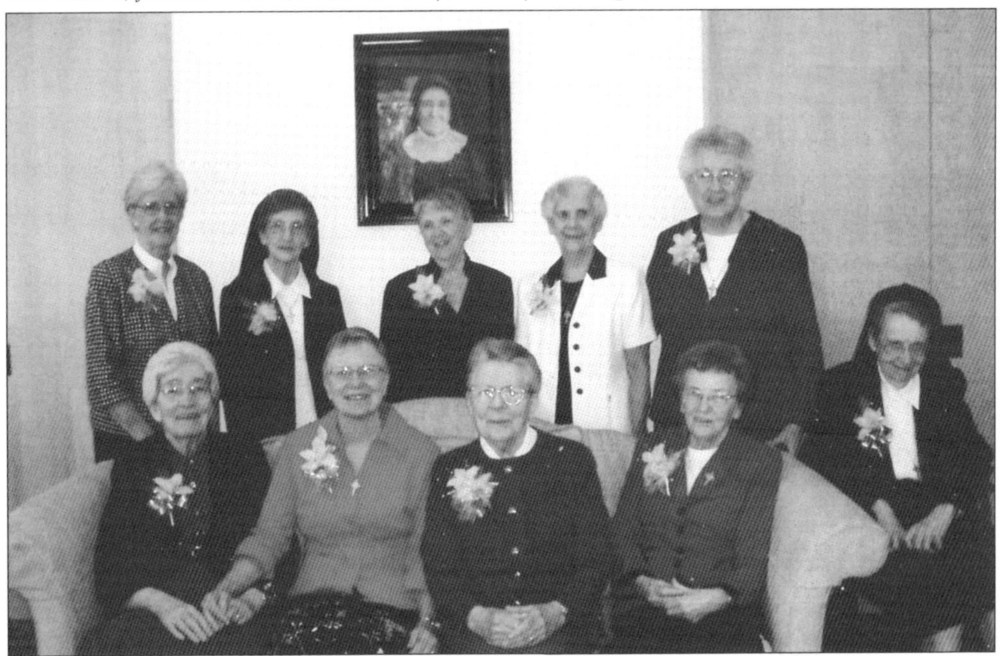

Jubilarians posed for this March 2011 photograph underneath an image of the foundress of the Sisters of the Holy Spirit and Mary Immaculate, Mother Margaret Mary Healy Murphy. From left to right are (first row) Srs. Laura Melody (70 years), Janet Nall (25 years), Mona Gavin (60 years), Marie Leonard (60 years), and Kathleen Mary Walsh (70 years); (second row) Srs. Eileen Mannion (60 years), Theresa Queally (60 years), Rosario O'Connell (60 years), Marguerite Connors (60 years), and Theresa O'Toole (60 years).

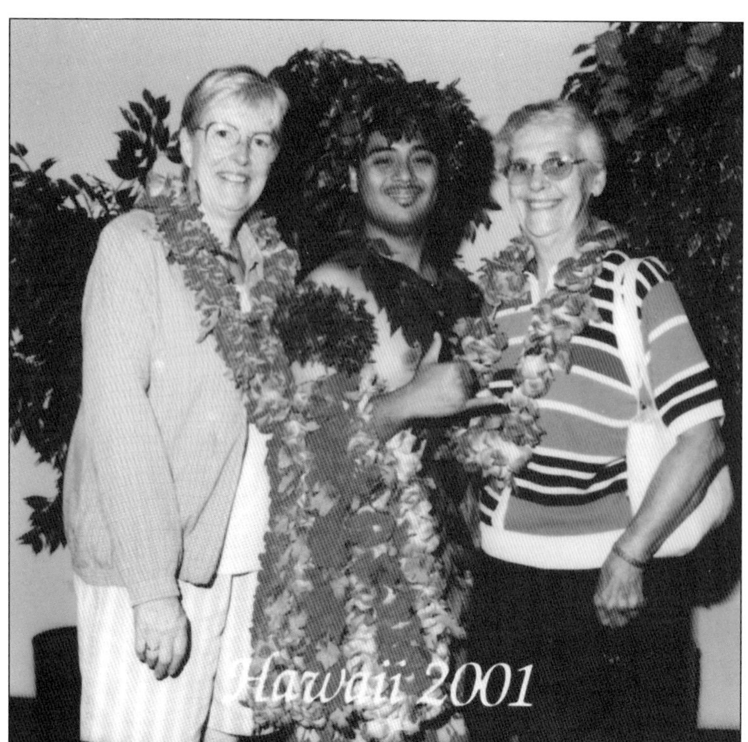

Srs. Eileen Mannion and Marguerite Connors celebrated their golden jubilee of profession in June 2001. They enjoyed a trip to Hawaii and visited three of the islands.

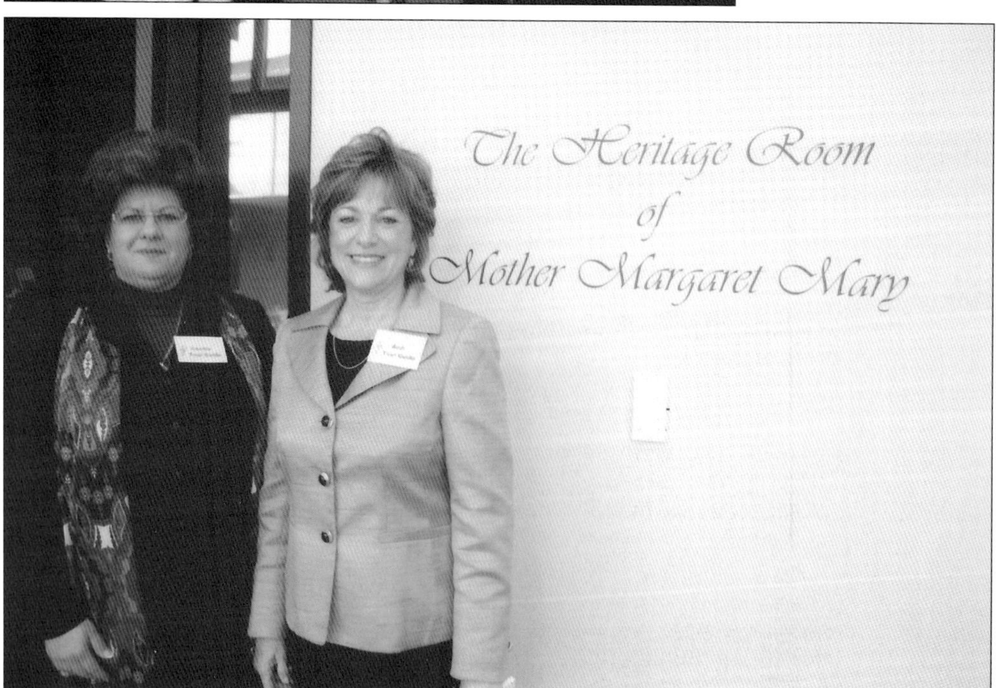

Cecilia Gutierrez Venable and Andrea Estes pose outside of the heritage room. The sisters' history room was established by the time of the blessing of the new convent at 300 Yucca Street in San Antonio in 2010. Venable and Estes worked on the signage and placement of artifacts in the display cases. They continue updating the room and researching the history of the sisters.

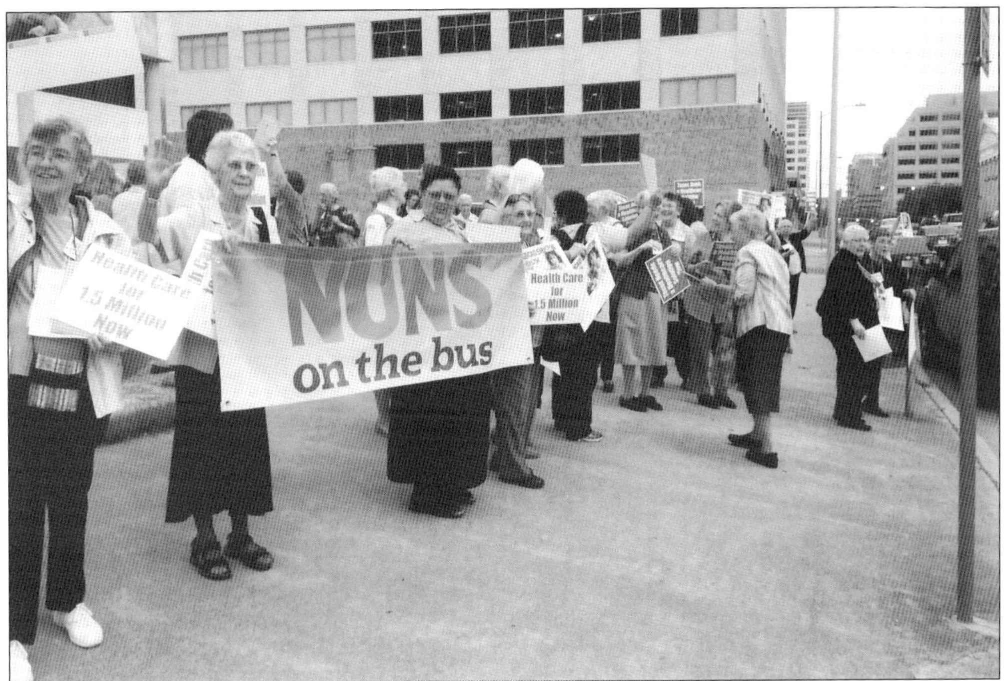

The Sisters of the Holy Spirit participated in Nuns on the Bus, the Catholic advocacy group that travels in buses promoting social justice issues. The organization, started by Sr. Simone Campbell, SSS, travels throughout the United States promoting various causes. Srs. Marian Murray, Marguerite Connors, and Gabriella Lohan carry signs in support of health care in Austin in 2013.

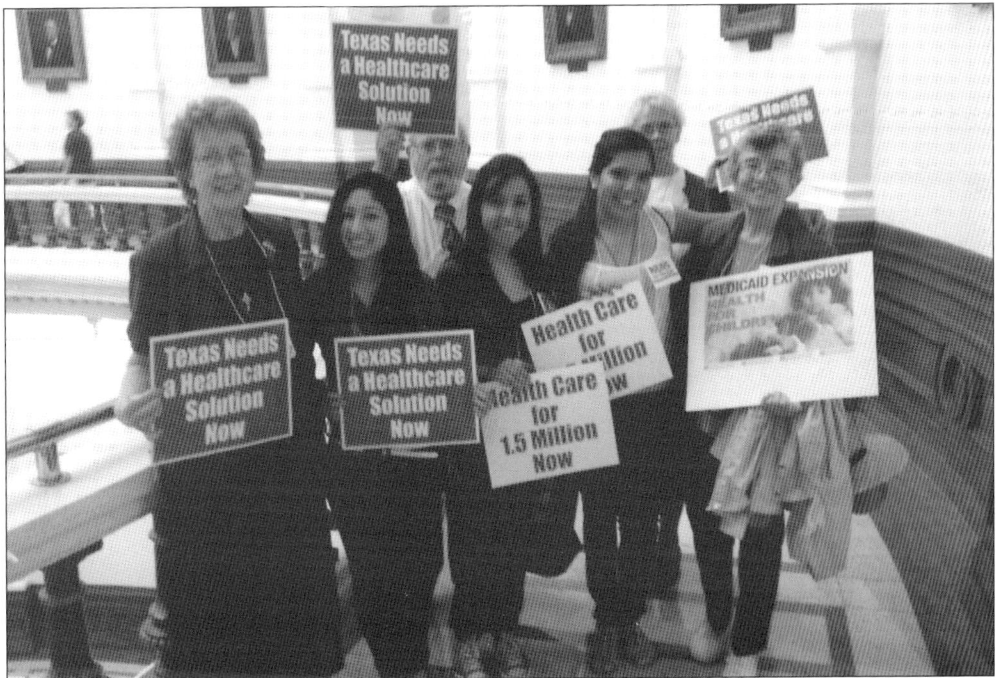

The sisters went to the state capitol to visit Texas state legislators concerning health care. Pictured are Srs. Miriam Mitchell, Marguerite Connors, and Marian Murray.

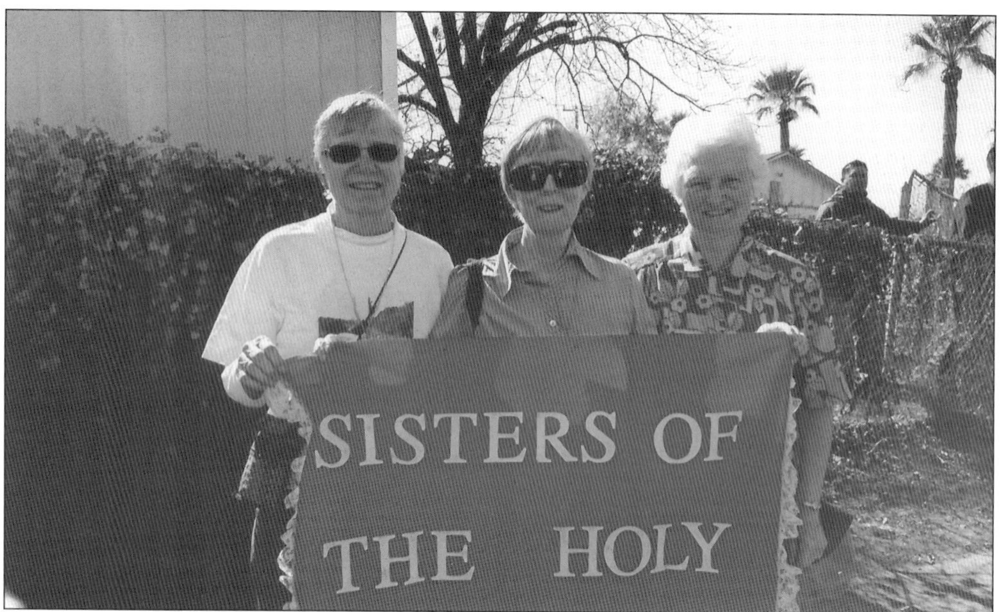

Srs. Janet Nall, Genevieve Cunningham, and Rosetta Leonard walk in the Martin Luther King March in 2016. The sisters regularly participate in MLK marches in the South.

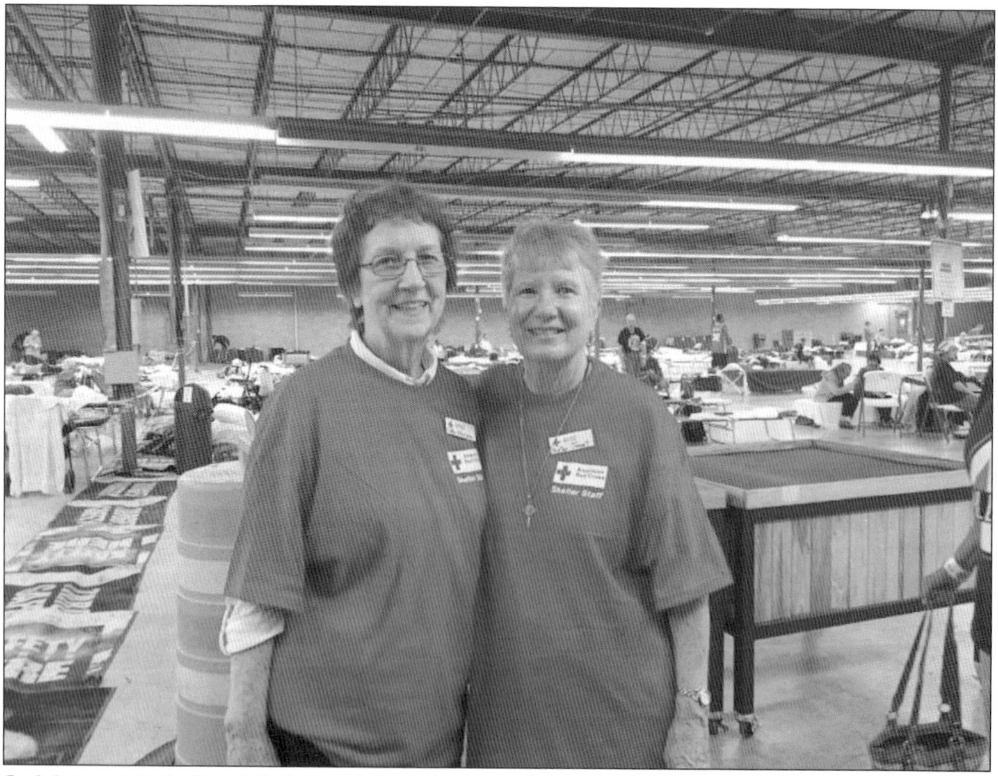

Sr. Miriam Mitchell and Sr. Janet Nall worked in a shelter for hurricane evacuees in San Antonio after Hurricane Harvey hit the Houston area in 2017. Over the years, several of the sisters have aided hurricane victims after storms slammed the Gulf Coast.

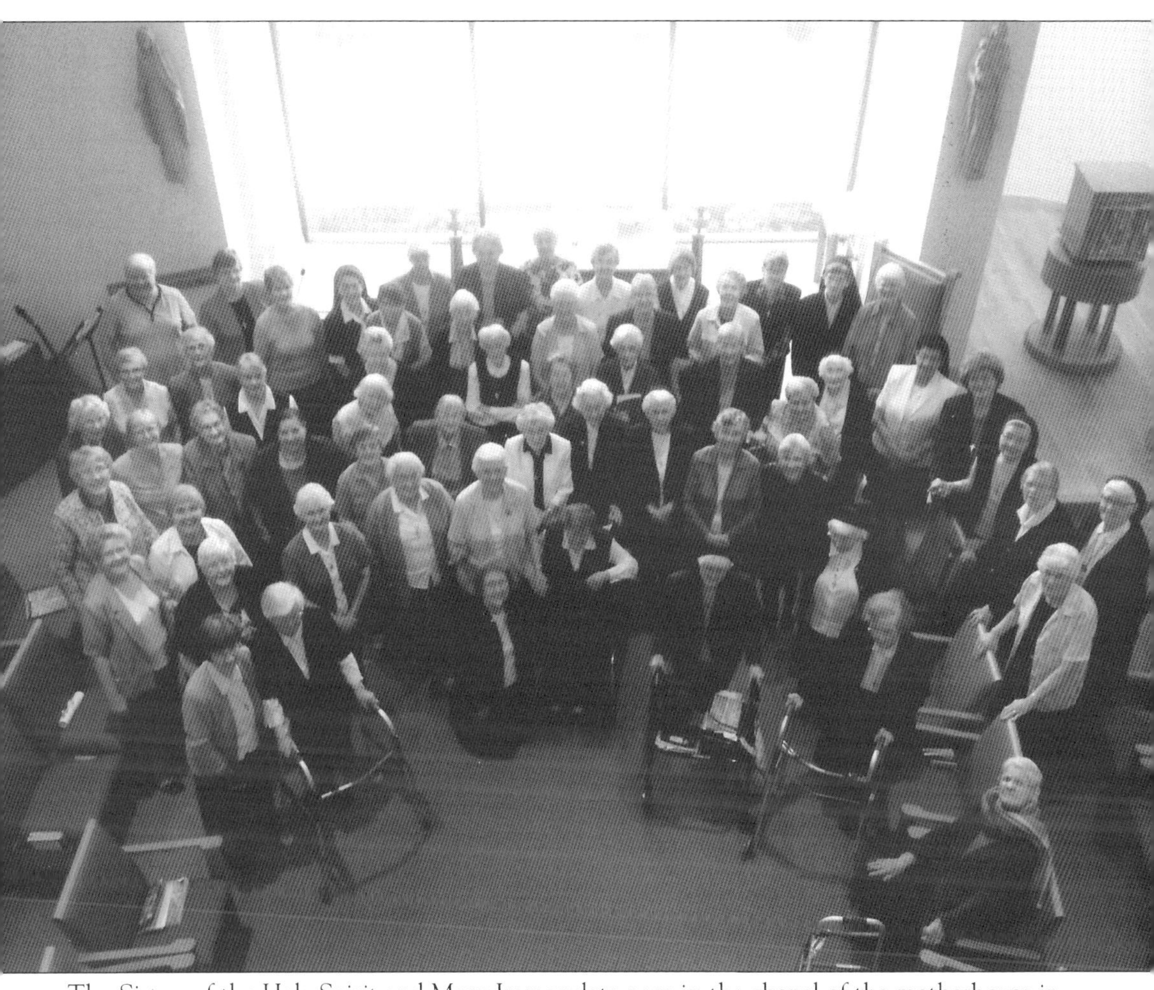

The Sisters of the Holy Spirit and Mary Immaculate pose in the chapel of the motherhouse in 2017 after a general assembly meeting.

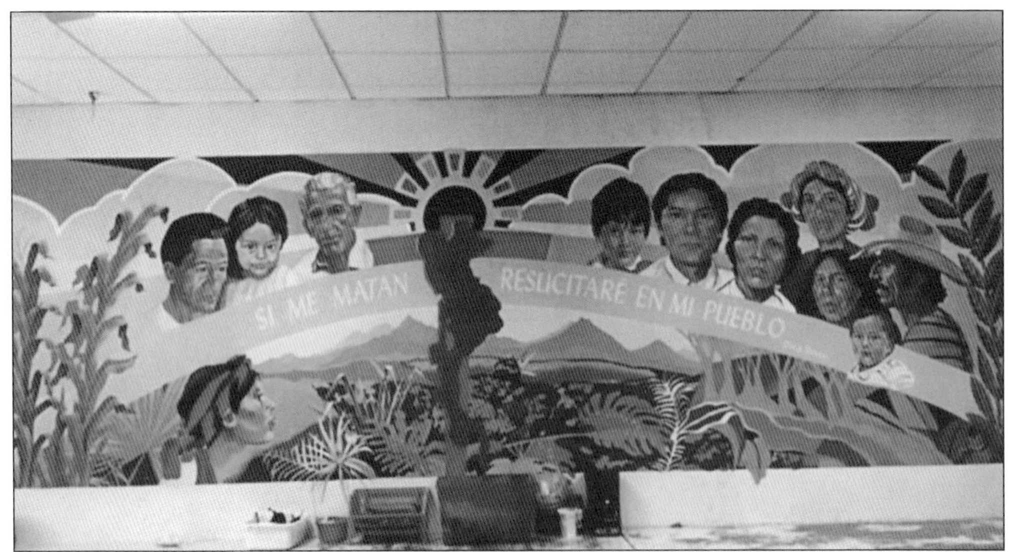

This mural covers the wall of Annunciation House in El Paso, Texas. The mural depicts a family murdered in San Salvador during the insurrection. The pillars in this building also bear the names of others who were killed. Sr. Beatrice Donnellan works with the immigrant community and the poor. This nonprofit provides meals and shelter for people having to come to the United States by law, or to be reunited with relatives.

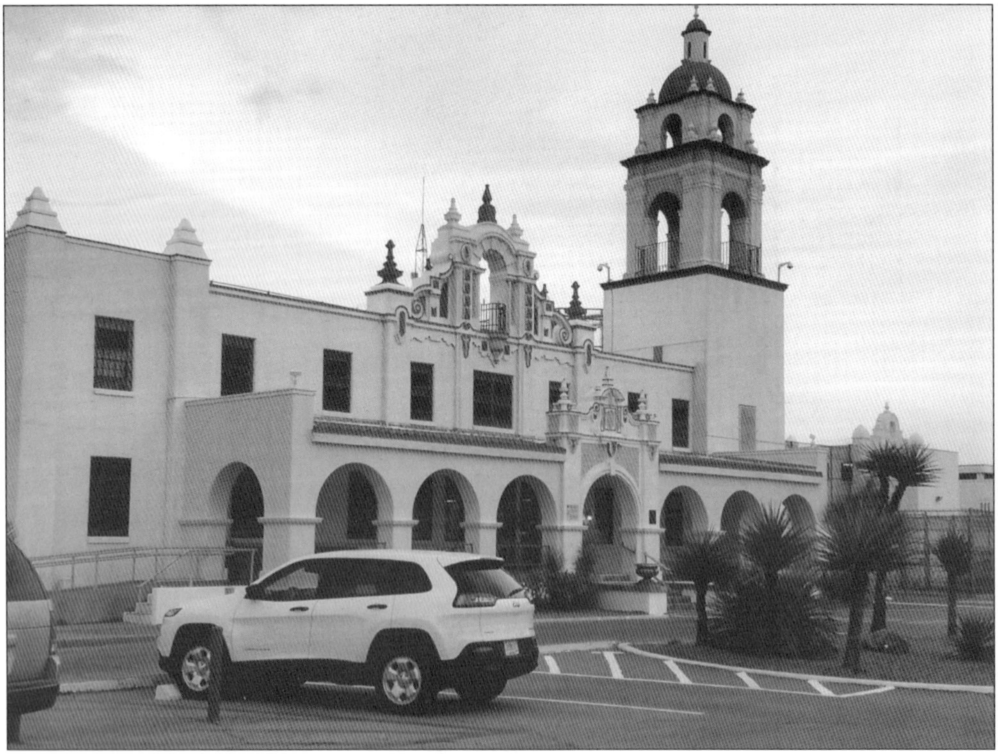

This historic federal correctional institution at La Tuna in El Paso County is a medium-security prison. As a jail, it opened in 1932 and held offenders from Texas, New Mexico, Arizona, Colorado, Wyoming, and southern Utah. Sr. Rita Nealon ministers to the inmates at this location.

The sisters are working on getting out the *Sisters' Journey* for mailing. This semiannual newsletter updates supporters and the community about what is happening within the congregation. The journal reveals the projects the sisters are undertaking, as well as community accomplishments and celebrations.

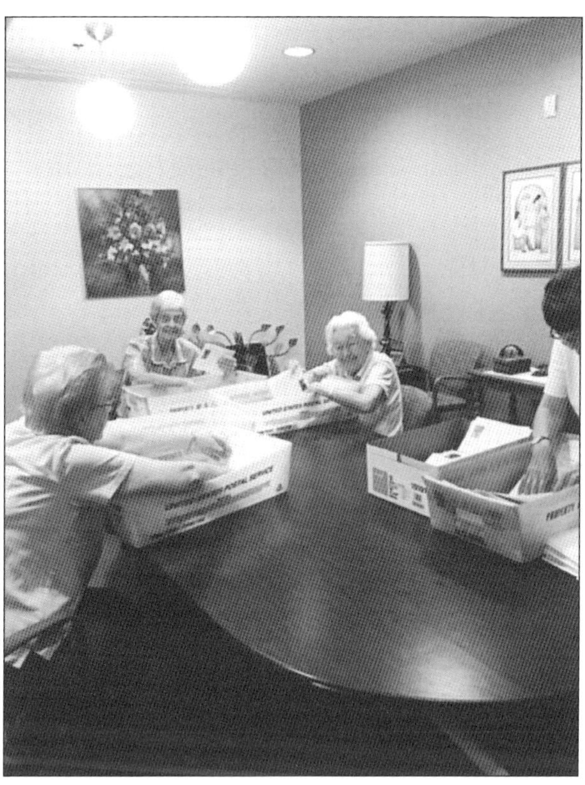

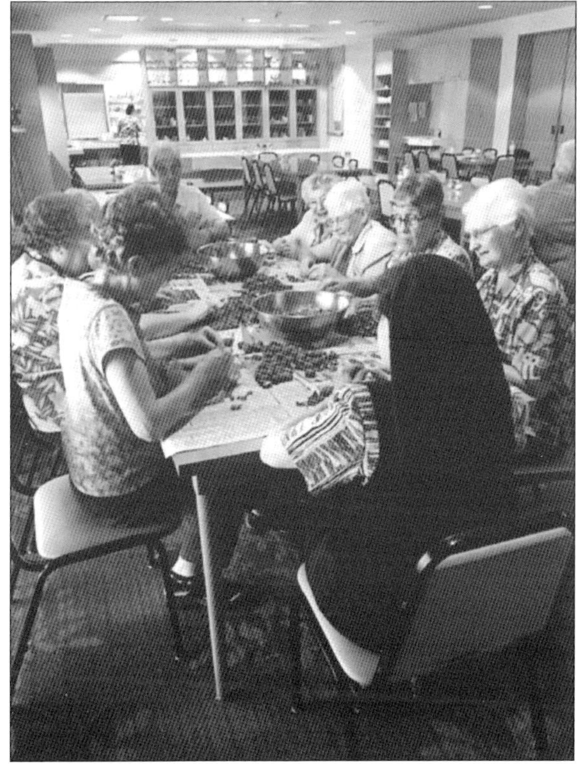

Some sisters gather around the table in the cafeteria shelling pecans to make pecan pies for Thanksgiving dinner.

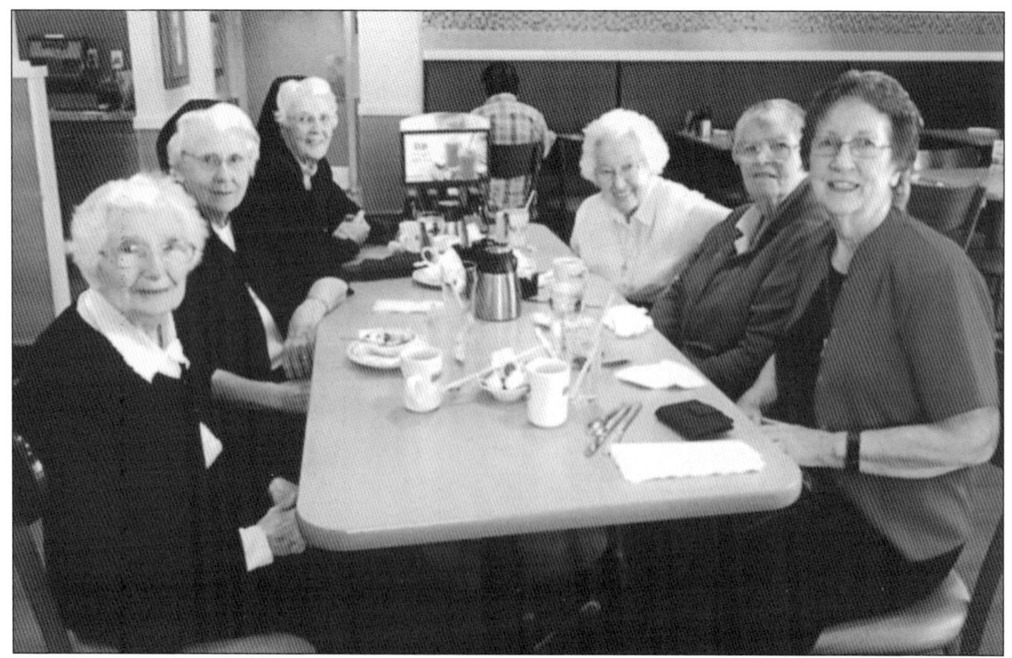

From left to right, Sr. Ferdinand Connerney celebrated her birthday at a restaurant with Srs. Garbriel Hession, Eugenus Gallagher, Miriam Mitchell, Mary Walsh, and Bernadette McNamara. Sister Ferdinand turned 96 in 2017 and was the oldest member of the Sisters of the Holy Spirit and Mary Immaculate. Her energy and wit were admired by the rest of the congregation.

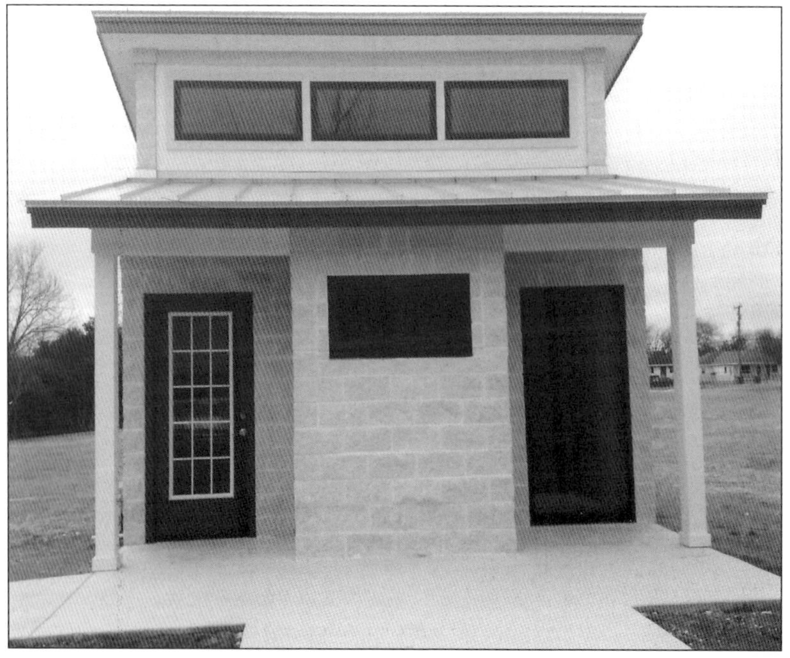

This shrine located in the back of the 300 Yucca Street motherhouse in San Antonio was completed in 2018. This monument was a place for reflection and prayer for the Sisters of the Holy Spirit and Mary Immaculate.

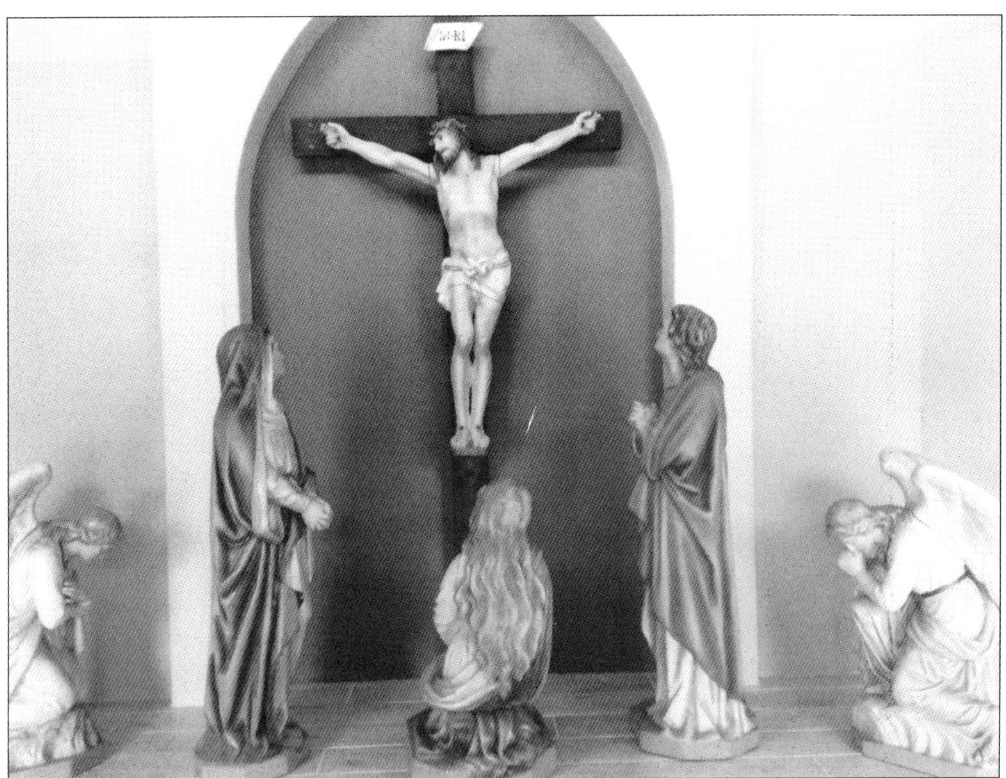

Inside the shrine at the motherhouse stood the statues Mother Margaret Healy Murphy erected in St. Peter Claver Church. The statues were returned to the Sisters of the Holy Spirit and Mary Immaculate by Rev. Edward Walsh, SSJ, pastor of St. Peter Claver Church. They were blessed at the old shrine at the rear of the 301 Yucca Street convent on February 11, 1958, and blessed again in this new building in 2018.

General Superiors of the
Sisters of the Holy Spirit and Mary Immaculate
And Dates Served

Sister Margaret Mary Healy Murphy 1893-1907
Sister Mary Aloysius McMullen 1907-1909
Sister Evangelist Jennings 1909-1923
Sister Francis Hughes 1923-1935
Sister Agatha Ryan 1935-1947
Sister Imelda Brannelly 1947-1959
Sister Ambrose Griffin 1959-1965
Sister Perpetua O'Laughlin 1965-1975
Sister Bridget Mary Quinn 1975-1983
Sister Monica Carroll 1983-1991
Sister Anne Finnerty 1991-1999
Sister Veronica Cahill 1999-2007
Sister Miriam Mitchell 2007-2015
Sister Geraldine Klein 2015-

This is a list of the general superiors who served the community of the Sisters of the Holy Spirit and Mary Immaculate and the dates they served. The dates of service varied through the years because the term length changed.

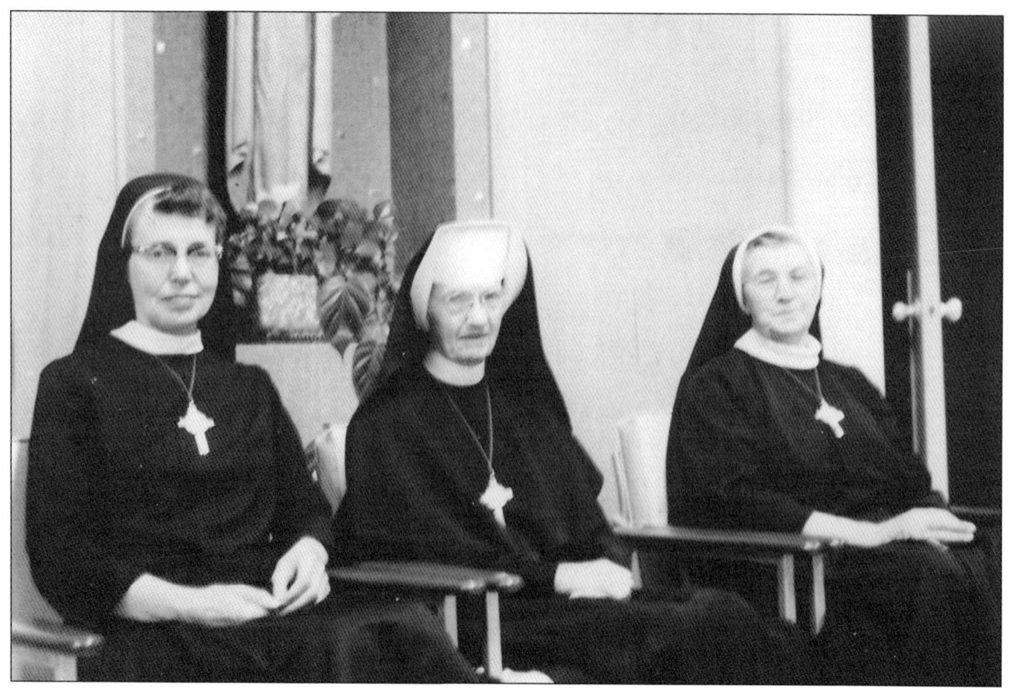

Three general superiors sit for this picture. From left to right are Sr. Perpetua O' Laughlin (1965–1975), Sr. Imelda Brannelly (1947–1959), and Sr. Ambrose Griffin (1959–1965).

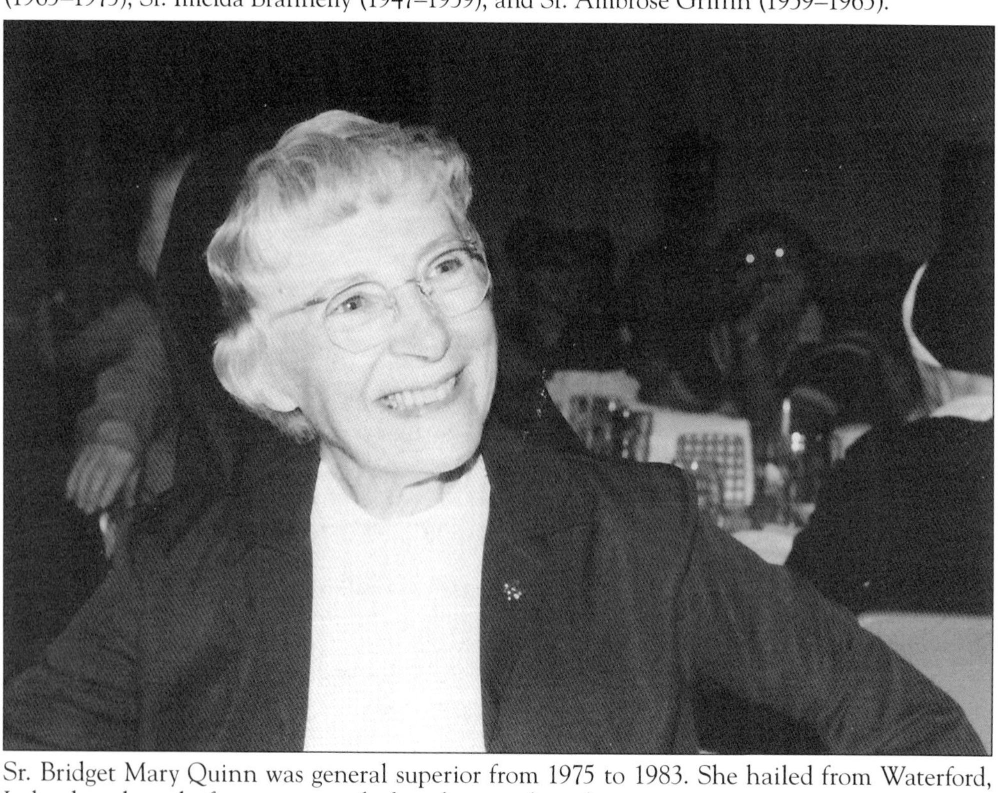

Sr. Bridget Mary Quinn was general superior from 1975 to 1983. She hailed from Waterford, Ireland, and taught for many years before she was elected.

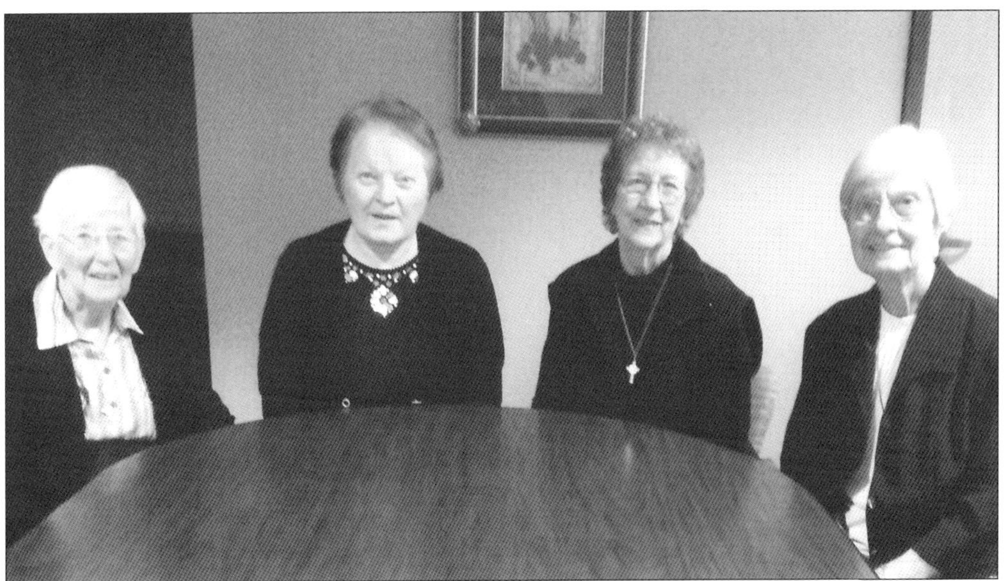

Four general superiors posed in the motherhouse for this photograph in 2017. From left to right are Sr. Monica Carroll (1983–1991), Sr. Veronica Cahill (1999–2007), Sr. Miriam Mitchell (2007–2015), and Sr. Geraldine Klein (2015–).

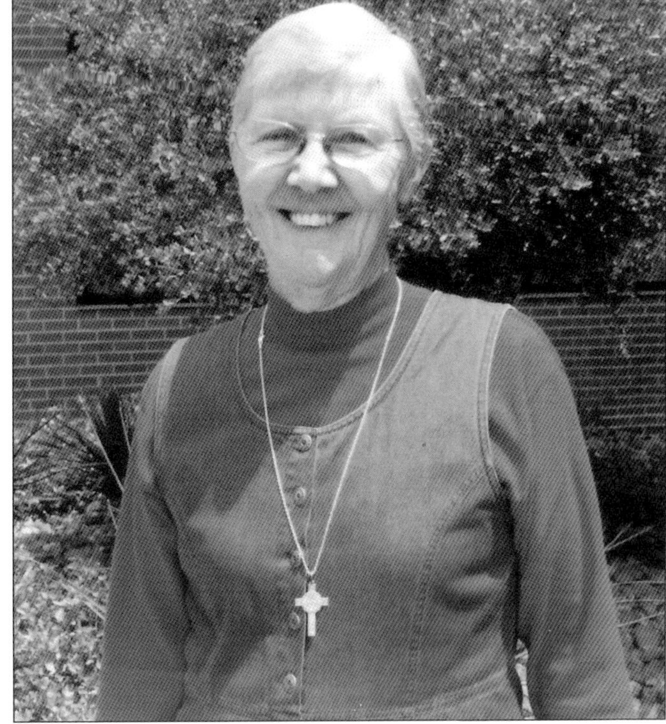

Sr. Anne Finnerty served as general superior from 1991 to 1999. She taught for 15 years in various schools in Texas, Missouri, and Louisiana. She worked in the diocesan office in Oklahoma and Texas before going to Zambia in 1999. Sister Finnerty worked with the bishop in Mongu and managed the orphans, infants, and elderly in Namashakende.

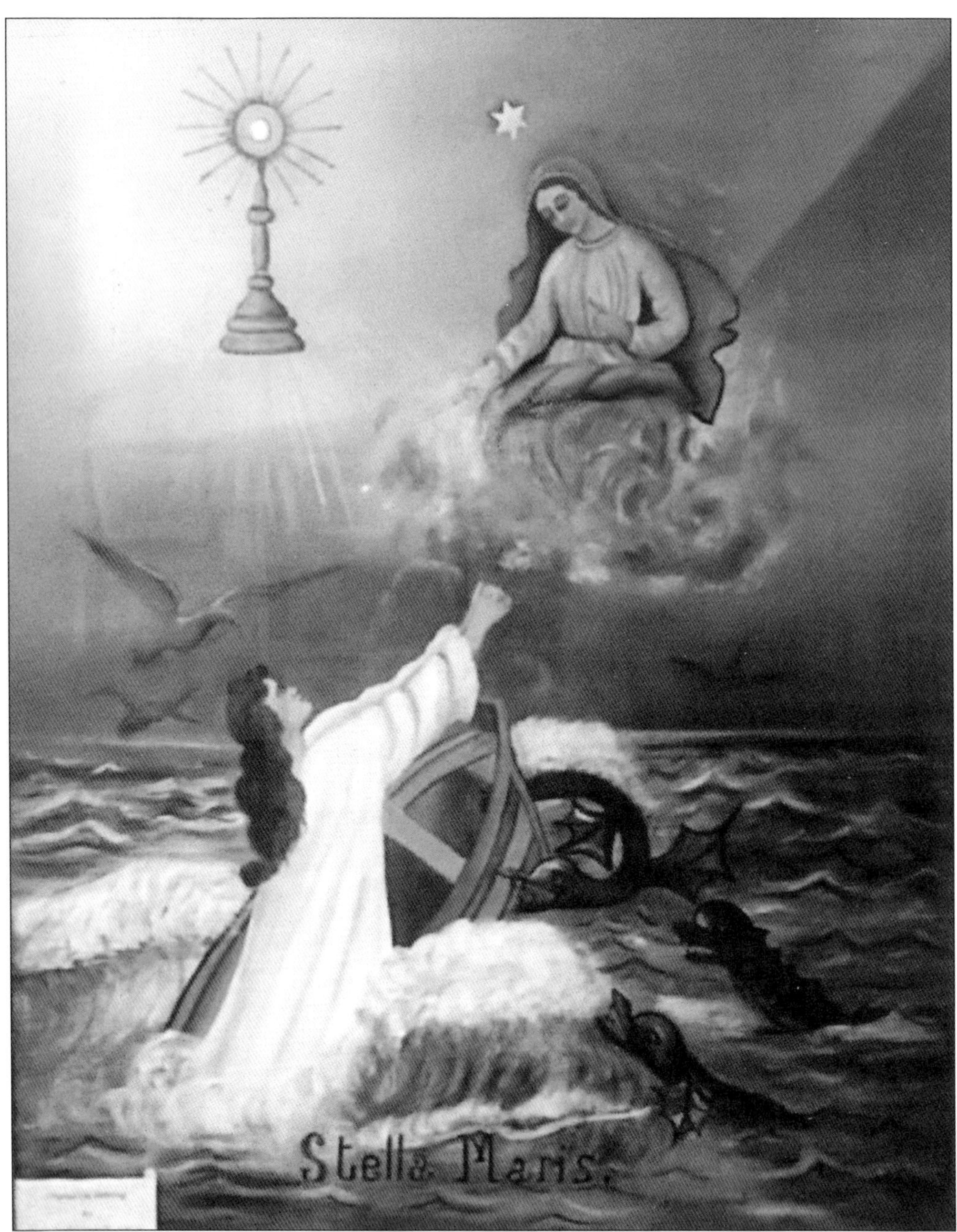

At St. Philip's Convent in Mount Bellew, Ireland, in 1939, seven women (Srs. Celine Martin, Eithne O'Dwyer, Eucharia Quinn, Laura Melody, Cletus Walsh, Ethelreda Glynn, and Pauline Hynes) left to join the Sisters of the Holy Spirit and Mary Immaculate in San Antonio. Sister Evangelist, however, sent a telegram to urge them to stay because of the extreme weather and the dangers of World War II. They had already set sail. The rough seas forced them to dock in Dover, England, for a week, then for another week in France, waiting for the seas to calm and for the ocean to be swept for land mines. They finally arrived safely, and Sister Cecilia promised to paint a picture acknowledging the Blessed Mother's care of the young postulants during their journey. She kept her promise with this picture.

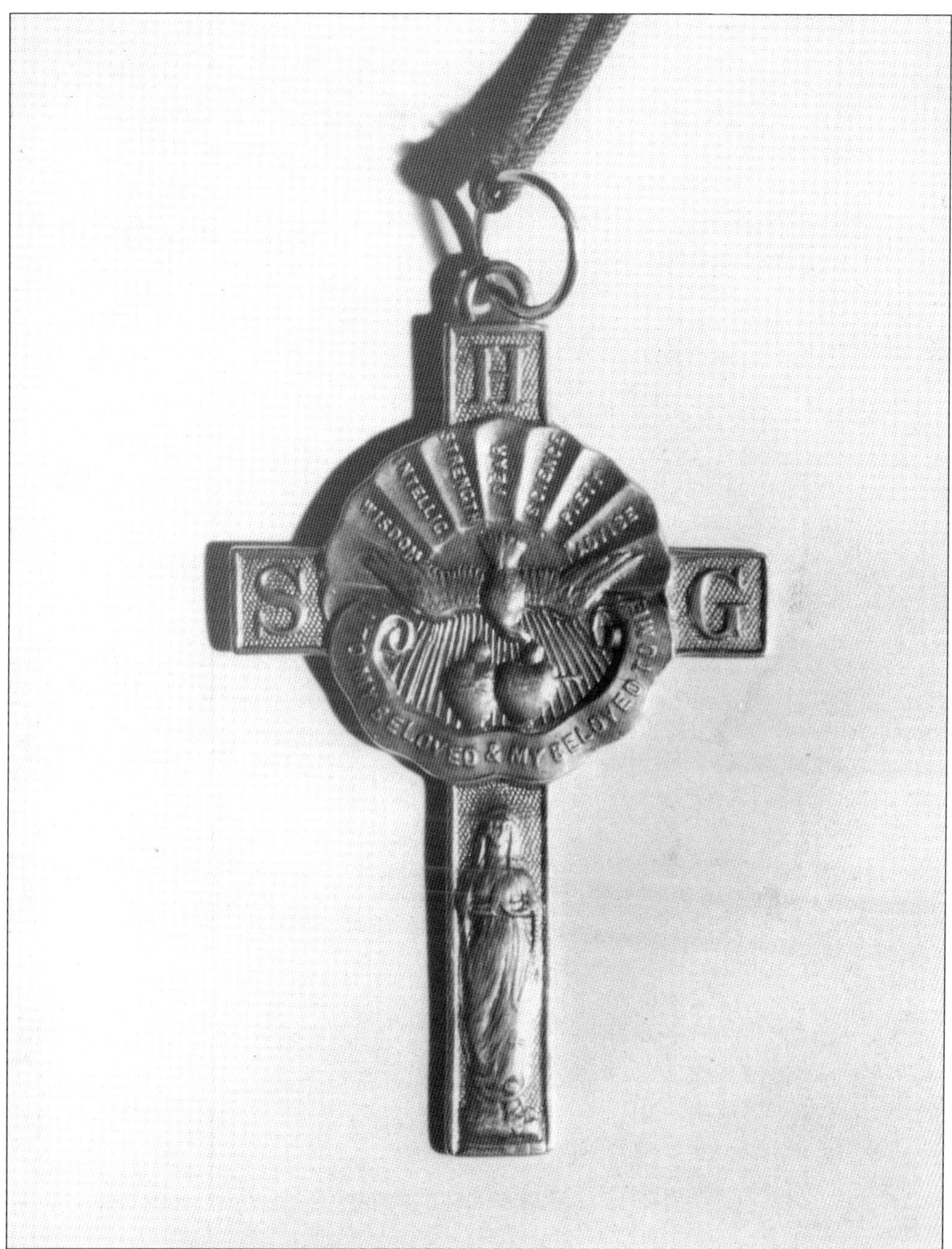

This cross is unique to the Sisters of the Holy Spirit and Mary Immaculate. The letters at the tip of the cross are the initials for the Sisters of the Holy Spirit. The center of the cross has the seven gifts of the Holy Spirit: Wisdom, Intelligence, Strength, Fear of the Lord, Science, Piety, and Advice. In the center of the cross is the dove, which represents the Holy Spirit. The rays symbolize the power and gifts of the Holy Spirit descending on the Heart of Christ united with our human hearts to bring his compassion to the world. The scroll reads, "I To My Beloved & My Beloved To Me." [Christ is our beloved, and we commit our lives to him.] Immaculate Mary stands at the bottom of the cross. She is the patroness of the Sisters of the Holy Spirit.

Sisters of the Holy Spirit and Mary Immaculate (2018)

Ambrose, Sister Jane F.
Armand, Sister Loretta
Arredondo, Sister Irene
Barrett, Sister Bernie
Cahill, Sister Veronica
Carey, Sister Dorothy
Carroll, Sister Monica
Chanda, Sister Matilda
Clarke, Sister Dympna
Connerney, Sister Ferdinand
Connors, Sister Marguerite
Crehan, Sister Pat
Cunningham, Sister Genevieve
Cunningham, Sister Therese
Dempsey, Sister Ellen
Donnellan, Sister Beatrice
Evelo, Sister Kay Jo
Fagan, Sister Mary
Finnerty, Sister Anne
Finnerty, Sister Maureen
Finnerty, Sister Teresa
Gallagher, Sister Eugenius
Gavin, Sister Mona
Gavin Sister Nora
Gordon, Sister Mildred
Greene, Sister Mary
Hession, Sister Gabriel
Higgins, Sister Kathleen
Huguet, Sister Kathleen
Kashela, Sister Angela
Kenny, Sister Peggy
Kilbane, Sister Angelina
Kilbane, Sister Magdalen
Klein, Sister Geraldine
Leonard, Sister Marie
Leonard, Sister Rosetta
Lohan, Sister Gabriella
Lutangu, Sister Maimbolwa
Madigan, Sister Doloretta
Mannion, Sister Eileen
McHugh, Sister Annette
McHugh, Sister Rose
McLoughlin, Sister Louise
McManus, Sister Patricia Ann
McNamara, Sister Benadette
Mitchell, Sister Christina
Mitchell, Sister Miriam
Mitchell, Sister Veronica
Molina, Sister Carmen
Moran, Sister Elizabeth Ann
Mulry, Sister Carmelita
Murray, Sister Josephine
Murray, Sister Marian
Nall, Sister Janet
Nasche, Sister Teresa
Nealon, Sister Rita
O'Flaherty, Sister Evelyn
O'Flaherty, Sister Peggy
Ohia, Sister Blessing Mary
O'Sullivan, Sister Shiela
O'Toole, Sister Theresa
Queally, Sister Theresa
Readore, Sister Martha
Renken, Sister Margaret
Ruane, Sister Katrina
Ruane, Sister Vera
Scarry, Sister Maura
Walsh, Sister Mary

Bibliography

Archdiocese of San Antonio 1874–1949. San Antonio, TX: Archdiocese of San Antonio: 1974.

Begnaud, Sister St. John, SSMN. *A Little Good: The Sisters of St. Mary in Texas.* Eugene, OR: Wipf & Stock, 2011.

Butler, Anne M. *Across God's Frontiers: Catholic Sisters in the American West, 1850–1920.* Chapel Hill, NC: University of North Carolina Press, 2012.

———. "Building Justice Mother Margaret Murphy, Race, and Texas." *Southwest Catholic. A Journal of History and Culture* 13 (2002): 13–36.

Davis, Cyprian. *The History of Black Catholics in the United States.* New York, NY: Crossroad Publishing Co., 1995.

Foley, Patrick. *Missionary Bishop: Jean Marie Odin in Galveston and New Orleans.* College Station, TX: Texas A&M University Press, 2013.

Hinfelaar, Hugo. *History of the Catholic Church in Zambia 1895–1995.* Lusaka, Zambia: Bookworld Publishers, 2004.

Mason, Kenneth. *African Americans and Race Relations in San Antonio, Texas, 1867–1937.* New York, NY: Garland Publishing Inc., 1998.

McNamara, Jo Ann Kay. *Sisters in Arms: Catholic Nuns through Two Millennia.* Cambridge, MA: Harvard University Press, 1996.

McQueen, Clyde. *Black Churches in Texas: A Guide to Historic Congregations.* College Station, TX: Texas A&M Press, 2000.

Monday, Jane Clements and Frances Brannen Vick. *Letters to Alice: Birth of the Kleberg-King Ranch Dynasty.* College Station, TX: Texas A&M University Press, 2012.

Moore, James Talmadge. *Through Fire and Flood: The Catholic Church in Frontier Texas, 1836–1900.* College Station, TX: Texas A&M University Press, 1992.

———. *Acts of Faith: The Catholic Church in Texas, 1900–1950.* College Station, TX: Texas A&M University Press, 2002.

Turley, Sister Mary Immaculata. *Mother Margaret Mary Healy-Murphy: A Biography.* San Antonio, TX: Naylor Company, 1969.

Venable, Cecilia Gutierrez. "From Corpus Christi's First Lady to Mother Margaret Mary Healy Murphy: Teaching at the Margins, a Transnational Story and Legacy." *East Texas Historical Journal*, vol. 54, Spring 2016.